BEYOND
VEILED
CLICHES

Also by Amal Awad

The Incidental Muslim
Courting Samira
Coming of Age: Growing up Muslim in Australia
This Is How You Get Better

AMAL AWAD

BEYOND VEILED CLICHES

VINTAGE BOOKS
Australia

A Vintage book
Published by Penguin Random House Australia Pty Ltd
Level 3, 100 Pacific Highway, North Sydney NSW 2060
www.penguin.com.au

Penguin
Random House
Australia

First published by Vintage in 2017

This book was supported by the Commonwealth through the Council for Australian–Arab
Relations, which is part of the Department of Foreign Affairs and Trade (the Department).
The views expressed in this book do not necessarily reflect the views of the Department,
or those of the Australian Government. The Commonwealth of Australia accepts no
responsibility for any loss, damage or injury resulting from reliance on any of the
information or views contained in this book.

Addresses for the Penguin Random House group of companies can be found at
global.penguinrandomhouse.com/offices.

National Library of Australia
Cataloguing-in-Publication entry

Awad, Amal, author
Beyond veiled clichés / Amal Awad

9780143782612 (paperback)

Muslim women – Public opinion
Muslim women – Islamic countries
Muslim women – Western countries
Women, Arab – Anecdotes

Cover image by Anna Poguliaeva / Shutterstock Images
Cover design by Christabella Designs
Typeset in 12/16 Sabon by Midland Typesetters, Australia
Printed in Australia by Griffin Press, an accredited ISO AS/NZS 14001:2004
Environmental Management System printer

Penguin Random House Australia uses papers that are natural, renewable and
recyclable products and made from wood grown in sustainable forests. The logging and
manufacturing processes are expected to conform to the environmental regulations of the
country of origin.

CONTENTS

For my parents, Samia and Mahmud Awad

For the seekers, change-makers and ground-shapers

PROLOGUE: A DANCE IN THE DESERT

I came to explore the wreck.
The words are purposes.
The words are maps.
I came to see the damage that was done
and the treasures that prevail.

– Adrienne Rich, 'Diving into the Wreck'

I was in the Dubai desert, traipsing across hard earth, below a night sky that was clear and bright. It was past dusk but the temperature hadn't dropped as much as I'd hoped it would. In a small desert 'camp', I navigated low tables and cushions that surrounded a large round stage; bar to the right, a shisha station tucked beneath a small tent to my left.

In the centre of it all, a man had taken to the stage to perform. He twirled sticks lit up with fire to a receptive crowd, their coos of approval splintering the quiet of the desert night. The people here had come for 'an authentic Bedouin experience', which was difficult to swallow given the camp is one of several, delivering the same substandard meals and glimpses into Arab culture to six hundred people a night, with nary an Arab to be seen. Even the belly dancer, an impressively curvaceous woman who could balance a sword across her bosoms while swivelling her hips, was not Arab. Of course not. While Arabs themselves have no qualms about propping up belly-dancing as a cultural delight, it's steeped in hypocrisy because Arab women would never be employed to tantalise foreign men in such a way. And that apart, belly-dancing is, in fact, historically a dance of fertility, only performed among women – not a dance of seduction. Yet it's used to get bums on cushions now, and, apparently, to seduce men over chicken skewers and garlic sauce.

The staff were composed of expats from India, Pakistan and Asia. One man sauntered among the customers, a falcon perched on his hand, inviting them in a soft voice to stroke its head, achingly polite. Outside the main arena, two camels squealed as tourist after tourist hopped on for a thirty-second march in the sand. A few people crowded the small tent where shisha was on offer. Others made for the bar to get alcohol before they dived into their authentic experience.

My group was seated on cushions – the way of the Bedouin – and getting to know each other. As well as my husband, Chris, and me, there were two other couples – a pair from Canada and a husband and wife from India, who had with them their infant son.

Chris watched me approach, with a sympathetic look. 'Any luck?'

'It won't dry,' I said. I was trying to keep my forearm level to stop the dark brown henna painted across its inside from dripping down and turning the swirls into a stain. In a normal setting, henna dries in twenty minutes and you scrape it off to reveal an elegant pattern of flowers. But here, in the heat of the desert, it was refusing to. I sat down. I didn't much like the idea of this place, but henna always seems like a good idea and I figured it would be a consolation prize. But I felt ill at ease, and I wasn't quite sure why.

Dubai is many things – interesting, enthralling, unusual – but it's not a genuine glimpse of the Arab world. That's not to say

I didn't like it. But it felt more like a business centre dropped into the middle of the desert than the Middle East I knew. It's a world designed to encourage and promote the growth of ideas and invention. And it's making great inroads in the representation of Emirati women in the workforce and in government. At the time of my visit, the UAE had eight female ministers in its thirty-member cabinet, and its ambitious 2020 Expo was being led by Reem Al Hashimy, another high-achieving woman. With its large expat community, many women are also active in the workplace. Laudy Lahdo, a Lebanese-Australian woman, is based out of Dubai as the general manager of Servcorp Middle East. She has found great success in her industry: in her first year working there, she won an award for manager of the year. So Dubai may have its critics, but arguably it is a place of dreams – easier to reach than the US if you're from the East; attractive to Westerners for its financial benefits and imitations of Western life.

But my authentic Bedouin experience was quickly turning sour.

I had longed to touch the desert sands, and after a month of intense interactions and travel in the region, I wanted to have some fun with Chris. So I'd registered us for this expedition of desert exploration. I had no idea at the time that trips like this in Dubai constituted an entire industry, so large in scale that the only variations between tourist providers was whether you paid more and got a bottle of booze thrown in.

It was a decision I was now questioning, despite the joy I had experienced earlier, feeling the coarse sand fall through my fingers, the rush of being in a wide space where sky and earth are all you can see. That is, if you could tune out the vehicles speeding past as they bashed into sand dunes.

'How many trucks come through every day?' I'd asked our driver when we pulled over for photos, feeling a rising sense of unease. Everywhere you looked, a cluster of white four-wheel drives did their worst against mountains of sand, the echo of passengers' excited yelps resounding in the humid air as the vehicles sprayed sand with every sharp turn.

'About a thousand,' he'd told me, without skipping a beat. His four-wheel drive was parked alongside two others, all of which had the hoods up to allow them to cool down.

I quickly started to regret my part in this tourist procession. I didn't want to think about the environmental impact, the discarded glass bottles littering the earth around me. One thousand four-wheel drives polluting the desert sands daily, and the trash their passengers leave behind, are going to leave a footprint.

'Did you hear that?' I said to Chris. 'It's not *One Thousand and One Nights*, it's one thousand and one jeeps.'

Now, back at the camp, we were both ready to leave.

I was quiet in the car as we drove back to Dubai, deep in thought, trying to decipher what truly irked me. Eventually it hit me, staring out of the window at the procession of those four-wheel drives heading back into the city: the tackiness of the so-called Bedouin camp appeals to tourists because it is, perhaps, the only way they can digest the Arab world.

One Thousand and One Nights. The legendary storyteller Scheherazade. The romance of the desert. Its intoxicating 'otherness'. Gertrude Bell, whom Arab men apparently named their 'queen of the desert', an Anglo woman more greatly esteemed among them than Arab women themselves.

It wasn't the myth or mysteries of the desert I was seeking that day. It was one step in a greater journey through the Arab world. I had hoped to fulfil a desire to connect to earth, to my heritage, transmuting an exoticised symbol into something more meaningful. In my mind, my ancestry trailed behind me, connected, unbreakable. I wanted to rebalance myself, and make peace with my culture, at once something I treasured but also found complex. I inherited this culture and my perspectives were influenced by many things, so I wanted to go back to a beginning. To create a new narrative.

Instead, here we were in a clichéd theme park version of the Arab world. Fire-eaters, belly dancers, camels, henna tattoos and shisha pipes. Like a choose-your-own-adventure for fifty dollars. It was overblown, simplistic and in no way genuinely engaging.

I have never felt that it's appropriation to experience another's culture. I do think it's appropriation to dress it up and present it as a gimmick. It might be more forgivable if it's done by people within the culture on display, but it's no less tacky.

I felt a bit sick as I thought about how inaccurate this cartoon-ish depiction of Arab life was – also, that it was so popular among tourists. Is this how people want to see us? In simple, romanticised terms?

There are so many stereotypes around Arabs, especially Arab women. In pop culture, numerous books sell repression with veiled clichés. Hollywood has pilloried Arabs for as long as it has made cinema, trading in limited categories – taxi drivers, convenience store owners, oppressed wives, belly dancers – rather than three-dimensional characters who are inciden-tally Arab. Thanks to these books and the treasure trove of 'Bad Arab' tropes in Hollywood, the Arab world has come to conjure in the mind of many the arresting image of a veiled woman, whose only visible features are her eyes; she is an exotic mystery – and a symbol of oppression.

This limiting motif says nothing of real life in a region as complex as any other, where women can be as looks-obsessed as anywhere else in the world, and, equally, as uncaring. On my trip I saw women spending upwards of ten minutes perfecting a selfie, one unforgettably perched on a seat in a café, lazily puffing away on a shisha pipe as she did so. The extent to which women dress and beautify themselves in the Middle East does, however, vary greatly depending on the location. In Dubai, veiled women were generally heavily made up; even women in niqab elaborately lined their eyes. At the airport in Amman, Jordan, we saw a woman with a face veil give her eye make-up a touch-up before taking a selfie.

We're either disparaged for not being 'advanced' enough, I thought to myself, for having a conservative nature or for going to war over religion, or we're admired for anything that can be considered beautiful. Kohl-lined eyes and hips that won't quit.

Evidently there is no shortage of accounts and analysis that try to unpack the experience of being an Arab woman, the major problem being that the women in these discourses are so often exoticised or minimised; or the complexity of life in a different country, which enjoys a rich and diverse culture, is buried under the assumption that the Western way is superior. Problems are seen as cultural, not human; the solutions as needing to come from the outside, not within. And in stories from the Arab world, we are not often portrayed as sensual, sensitive beings. In many of the stories about us, we're rendered mute or helpless. There's no denying the Arab conservatism that shapes our interactions, but the truth is we are feeling, vibrant women who experience love, longing and heartbreak like anyone else.

This was the reason I had come to the Arab world. I had just journeyed through five countries in the Middle East – UAE, Lebanon, Jordan, Palestine and Qatar – to meet with women of all stripes. I was in search of, and thought there would be great value in reading stories about, the lives of women *in* the region, rather than the many I have read by Western authors examining the lives of these women and assessing them according to their own standards, fascinated by their 'otherness'. Indeed, this strange portraiture came up often enough in my conversations, both in Australia and the Arab world. I didn't meet anger so much as frustration and puzzlement. 'You're complicated. We're complicated,' the secretary-general of the Jordanian National Commission for Women noted. '[Western perspectives are] very simplified. Very flat.'

The Middle East is in focus for troubling reasons much of the time – the war in Syria, the after-effects of the invasion in Iraq, the occupation in Palestine – and women have long been held under a collective gaze. At the heart of this curiosity is a desire to understand how we live, and my discussions with women of Arab heritage – both in Australia and the Middle East – were intended to unpack this.

The stories in this book by no means constitute an exhaustive examination, nor are they academic or even wholly instructive. Because we are shaped by our experiences, and we all view life through a unique set of lenses, my narrative necessarily has its limitations. But please don't just read this book. Listen to it. Connect to it. Get to know the women featured within. They sat with me and opened themselves up in trust, seeing only my face, not the faces of those who would come to read about them.

These accounts are treatments on life experiences, possibilities and difficulties. I hope they alter your understanding in some important way, as they have mine.

INNER PAIN AND OUTER TURMOIL

Out of suffering have emerged the strongest souls; the most
massive characters are seared with scars.

Kahlil Gibran

In the Middle East, I was always late. Not by a mere few minutes. I could leave someone waiting for up to half an hour. One evening in Beirut, having no conception of just how far my destination was from my hotel and the unforgiving amount of traffic I should expect, I was a whole hour late. The ride felt eternal. Not even the spectacle of the city's traffic could distract me: drivers smoking and texting, mothers cradling babies in the front seat, a mess of loud horns piercing the warm night air.

In my defence, nobody cared when I was late, because in Beirut time is a malleable concept.

It was early September 2016 when I arrived in the famed cosmopolitan city to humid weather and a solid dose of culture shock. I was settled there for several days in the suburb of Dekwaneh, about twenty minutes from the popular area of Hamra, where, as it turned out, most of my meetings took place. Beirut was the second stop on my ambitious month-long journey in the region to make connections, and share thoughts, ideas and experiences with Arab women from all backgrounds and walks of life.

When I was younger, the Middle East held enough mystery and charm for me that I fell for it every time I visited. There can be something hypnotic about vibrant disorder – traffic jams snaking up streets, horns being tooted even when there is nowhere to go, electricity cutting out without notice, people moving easily among the noise in a way that suggests order is not the only way. But really such things also remind you of what it means to be supremely aware of your surroundings, to be engulfed in feeling.

Its nightlife is impressive and not reliant on alcohol, though the countries I visited weren't short on bars and liquor stores. As a cousin in Jordan advised me, 'Everyone drinks now.' He didn't himself, inclined as he is to adhere to the Islamic ruling that alcohol is forbidden. But apparently it's overlooked nowadays. And if you don't drink, you do *shisha* or smoke, both of which are permitted in restaurants and cafés.

My previous visits to the region had been mainly to Jordan and the West Bank, both of which I thought would be adequate preparation for this trip. I'd been to Amman in Jordan enough times to recognise that Middle Eastern pace, the energy that pushes and pulls you and expects you to spring back into place. The West Bank, while not as modernised, offers its share of vibrancy. It reminds you that even when the once-fruitful scenery of your life fades, you can feel completely alive and, if you're not used to a visible military presence, in a constant state of unease.

But this was my first visit to Beirut, a city I had heard so much about but had no real conception of in terms of atmosphere. I wasn't sure what to expect, or how it would compare to my imaginings. I grew up with Lebanese friends, kids who had similar family lives, a better handle on the language, and a notable passion for being Lebanese. And Beirut, like Cairo, has a certain mystique attached to it. In the collective imagination, it is a place of mystery and romance, sophisticated and liberal despite its undercurrent of conservatism. To many in Lebanon itself, the country as a whole isn't even really Arab *per se* – a lot of its people see themselves as Phoenician, a form of Lebanese nationalism prompted by Lebanese Christians, the idea being that Lebanese people are descendants of the Phoenicians (also known as Canaanites), rather than Arabs.

It's not a position I encountered a lot, but it was there, a silent hum in the background of a chaotic city that seemed effortlessly to crash into itself but survive. It would be difficult to be in Beirut and not be alert to the intensity of the place: everywhere you go, there is hustle. In Hamra, a humming district well known for its shopping, cafés and nice apartments, as well as the American University of Beirut, traffic crawls along at a snail's pace. Stopping for even a moment delivers you a taxi driver who toots at you, seeking your business, or a beggar, requesting money.

And of course, if you read the commentaries on Beirut by Westerners, it's a haven for the daring, a place to dance on table-tops in bars and explore your sexuality. Its women are beautiful, cosmetically altered and focused on their looks.

I prefer journalist Robert Fisk's take on his adopted country: 'It's a Rolls-Royce with leather seats, flat-screen TV in the back, a cocktail cabinet – but square wheels. Beautiful, luxurious, coveted, it doesn't work. But thank God it's got the Lebanese people.'

For the most part, my interactions in Beirut were normal and pleasant, but the angry, frenetic tone of the city could cause me ripples of anxiety. Every day I got stares and interrogations about my life, about Chris, about my Arabness. Did Chris convert? Does he speak Arabic? No? I should teach him. It's not that I found it offensive, but the drilling for information never ended.

I also spent a lot of time on the road, quickly understanding that driving in Beirut is, in a word, mad. It shouldn't work, but it's like a language; either you speak it or you don't. One taxi driver was memorable because he took pains to differentiate himself from other drivers, asking me if I appreciated how calm he was. 'Do you see how I don't use my horn and just push in?' he said in Arabic, making eye contact through the rearview mirror. I assured him that I did appreciate his good driving, full of praise. He was a sweet man, opening up about his life, trying to convince us to pay him a visit so that we could meet his new wife and have lunch with them. At the end of the journey, he handed my husband a fake rose, his mouth widening in a shy smile as he glanced at me. Chris and I understood that the rose was intended for me, but that it would have been impolite for him to offer it to a woman.

For Chris, whose only understanding of Arab culture has come from his interactions with me and my family, as well as a handful of Arabic films, his introduction to the Middle East was a revelatory experience; he was so used to the comparative serenity and calm of Australia, but the energy of the place was infectious. The Middle East seeps into you that way. It isn't a region, overall, that makes solitude easy. Whether you like it or not, you're quickly embedded into the fabric of the city you're in, getting pulled this way and that. It may well be different for its residents, but I found it difficult to not feel *full* all the time.

In Beirut, there is something to take in anywhere you turn: gutted buildings that look abandoned or incomplete; street art that hints at the grievances of a fatigued but talented, and stoic, population; rubbish in the middle of a busy road that depicts the reality of life without effective government. Add to that electricity outages up to five times a day, so common that when they happen no one blinks and the chatter and activity continues. I hadn't realised this the first few times I experienced them. When I went down to the hotel reception to ask about the outages – we'd had about three in quick succession – the man behind the counter was polite but looked at me in mild amusement. 'This is just what happens in Lebanon,' he explained in Arabic. 'But we have two generators,' he added with confidence. Sheepishly, I returned to my room.

For all of the exotic parables about the Middle East, its greatest appeal is not in its ordered chaos, belly-dancing and shisha; it's in the people, as Fisk said, and the way they navigate complexity. This much was true for Beirut. The wistfulness I detected in the women I met with affected me; you could tell that Beirut had lost some of its charm, an emptied husk following years of turmoil.

But the women there also blew me away with their passion for art, theatre and telling the truth. The feminist undercurrents were strong in some, while others exhibited a passion for living, their worries not defined by their womanhood. They were warm, tended towards wry humour, and were deeply fervent, no matter the activity or discussion.

LEARNED HELPLESSNESS

When I arrived at Myra Saad's art therapy studio, I was, as usual, late. The din of Hamra faded as I entered the building, a tired-looking medium-rise with an old-fashioned elevator, which delivered me to her floor. I wanted to interview Myra after following the work of toy photographer Brian McCarty. Brian, whom I now consider a friend, is a clever chap who makes a living out of his passion. When he's not taking photos of toys for big names like Disney and Nickelodeon in the US, he trots off to war-torn areas to work with art therapists in order to document children's experiences of war. On his most recent visit to Lebanon he'd worked with Myra, and when he heard about my writing plans he suggested I reach out to her.

I entered flustered and ashamed that, once again, the city had got the better of me. Thankfully, Myra met me with warmth and understanding. She was young, well presented and offered an apology, a smile lighting up her face. 'I should have given you my little blurb that I give to all new visitors. Kind of a primer for what to expect,' she said.

I blurted out a jumble of observations: that I was happy to be there but felt exhausted, bewildered and weary after just a week. 'It's like this country is fighting itself,' I said.

Myra smiled. 'That's a great observation.' She looked thoughtful. 'Actually, it's reflected in everything, everywhere. We lived war trauma for thirty years and it was never dealt with. And we always have this attitude of "just live day-by-day and you'll survive and whatever" – that was functional during the war. But it's not anymore. Now it's almost self-destructive, and self-mutilation. And people don't realise it.'

She went on to tell me about a psychotherapist she knew who'd studied psychology in the early nineties, right after the civil war in Lebanon had ended. The war didn't get a mention in this woman's studies, nor did the consequent trauma. No one wants to talk about the trauma of war, even if they can't stop talking about the war itself.

In Myra's sun-lit studio, a place of refuge from the outside noise, she told me about her journey, and more about the Lebanese mentality. There was no denying the collective scar left on the country's people. The war might have ended in 1990, but that end came after thirty years of horrific turmoil that produced stories even the hardest hearts would struggle to digest. And its effects continued to manifest in people's actions and beliefs. This had become quickly apparent in the interviews I'd carried out with other women in Beirut. I didn't need to ask about the civil war – it always came up. There was playwright Aliya, who was kidnapped then freed in a single night when the perpetrators realised she wasn't of value; Sabine, who works as a professional clown – she moved thirteen times in her childhood and relied on imaginary friends to get her through; Aida, an actress whose young artistic pursuits had started and stopped to the soundtrack of war. Their revelations ran deeper than their misfortunes, but what was evident was how these experiences had shaped them and their relationships – dealing with family still feeling trauma; or the loss of career opportunities because of the country's economic state. Sabine offered a fascinating observation on her own experiences: studying clowning requires discovery of your own clown, and she was surprised by what she encountered. 'My clown was this paranoid, army-like clown who's like ...' She pretended to machine-gun everything around her. 'And here I am, I thought I was the sweetest person. Ah, no.'

I asked Myra what people were fighting now. Were they in denial?

'Usually healing has to go through many stages,' Myra began. 'A big part of it is reconciliations and confessions and forgiveness and recognition of what has been done. None of this has happened. Instead, they just agreed, "Okay, let's stop fighting and each one get a part," and *khalas*, that's it. But there was no forgiveness, no reconciliation, none of this.'

Of the women I'd interviewed, some had explained their civil war experience in terms of survival. Their stoicism is a very Arab trait. Some survive trauma, rather than deal with it. But many women I interviewed – Sabine, Aliya, Aida, for example – used it, often creatively. I suggested that an obstacle to dealing with trauma is not a lack of courage; it's the vulnerability it requires. It asks for you to deep-dive into yourself. Inner work, in a sense, which is not a very 'Arab' thing to do.

'That's true,' said Myra. This is the culture, she said. 'And along the same lines, I can't tell you how many times I've had people come here for therapy ... for something not related to war, but very soon – it takes not more than two to three sessions – war and trauma and everything, all the changes that happened to them, come up.'

Myra, a Christian, is a graphic design graduate in her early thirties. After school she studied in the States, at Boston University, where she was dealt a profound culture shock. 'It was overwhelming for me, and I had to question everything, from my beliefs to the way I think, to what's right, to what's wrong, to what I want to do with my life, to everything that we suffered – was it worth it during the war?'

I asked Myra how this 'culture shock' in the US influenced and shaped her.

'The fact that I had to challenge all of my belief systems eventually got me to a place where I had to form my own ideas. And ... it's very liberating. And with this liberation comes tons of other liberations: of how to be, how to live your life, how to see yourself, how to use your body, how to accept it, how to embrace it. Even ideas, I can't tell you how many times in the groups here we talk about motherhood and womanhood and expectations. And the biggest liberation is in the idea of you can also choose what you want to do and how you want to be.'

'You can choose what your life looks like.'

'Yeah. Which is not common here. Because the expectations are very limiting, it's almost like you don't have a choice.'

Also shocking to her was hearing about events that had happened in her country, but which she'd never been told about. 'I started to hear things about the genocides that happened in Lebanon when I was in the US. For example, like Sabra and Shatila [refugee camps that experienced civilian massacres in Lebanon in 1982].'

It was a symptom of Lebanese culture; either you were knee-deep in the war, even to the extent of being in militias, or you plugged your eyes and ears. 'Distancing yourself' is how Myra explained it.

The outcome of war is a physically corrupted country, splintered into religious divides. 'People never had problems with religion before the so-called civil war, which wasn't actually really just civil war – it was regional war on Lebanese soil. So I think this is how you can control people ... make them fear each other and to divide them by religion ... And now it's more problematic because, again, the trauma was never healed, so we act as if we don't care, but actually people do care.'

This observation struck a nerve. In Australia, religion and race have exploded into major sources of conflict. They take up newspaper column inches almost daily. If you're active on social media, identity politics can fill your feed. New generations are finding their voices as they try to make sense of their place in a society that compels them to question or leave it.

I suggested to Myra that this division is what people do in other societies, on a daily basis, on a much smaller scale than war trauma. I thought of all the ordeals of childhood that haunt people as they grow older in body and mind, but not necessarily in spirit, stuck as so many of us are in the past. There's a reason why self-help and self-care are billion-dollar businesses, after all.

Myra agreed, and told me, 'I went through this whole kind of self-search, and decided that I wanted to do art therapy.' I already knew the answer when I asked her if being an art therapist is common in Lebanon. She laughed – it's not, she said.

'Do you find that people are receptive to what you do? Or is there still resistance?' I asked her.

'In general, when people come, at some point they are ready, because they chose to come here. For me, it's more guiding them and offering them the environment where they can go [as far] as they want, or [as far] as they are ready to go. But in general, if I talk about society, society's not ready.'

I wondered if, in hindsight, Myra felt she was drawn to the practice because she had her own experiences to unpack.

'I think there are maaaaany reasons,' she laughed. 'I feel very privileged to have lived during the war. I was born during the war and I stayed here throughout the war, and I feel very privileged to have never lost a loved one who's very close to me. And I feel very privileged for not losing any limbs, for example. Or not losing my health, or ...' She paused, thoughtful. 'Or seeing someone pass away in front of my eyes. So I've been privileged in so many ways. And I think my parents did a lot to protect us during this time. So you do feel – I don't want to say "survivor guilt", I don't like the word "guilt" – but more this responsibility, that by being privileged, you also have responsibility, and you have the awareness. So there's this part of you, you want to give back. And then of course it's rewarding ... it can be very draining, but at the same time it's very rewarding.'

There was another essential reason, Myra added. 'Do you know in psychology the concept of "learned helplessness"?'

Learned helplessness posits the argument that no matter what you do, you can't control the outcome, or your outside environment.

'I'm a big believer that people here have learned helplessness,' said Myra. 'Because no matter how much you try, no matter how much you build, tomorrow your house may be bombed and everything may go away. No matter who you vote for, nothing's going to change. That's why you hear so many people going around saying, "Well, what can I do? There's nothing I can do. It's not in my hands." What exhausts me here is the sense of helplessness. That's the biggest thing. And what I'm doing now, consciously ...' she said, with a laugh, 'is countering that.'

So Myra's response was not to criticise but to offer a new way of dealing with life and the trauma it sometimes hands us. It's easy to point to a problem; coming in with a solution is a greater challenge.

'Someone told me that if you want to go back to Lebanon, you need to pick your battles,' said Myra. 'This learned help-lessness is a battle I picked on my own, through my work,' she said. 'But it's one where you need to get to the core of a person and make them believe in themselves and make them believe in the potential they have. And this is basically the process of therapy.'

In the West, New Age and alternative healing and therapy modalities are gaining wider acceptance, but they are also frequently ridiculed. I can only imagine the difficulty associated with selling therapy in countries where mental health is not easily discussed, or treated adequately.

'Thank you for bringing that up,' said Myra. 'One is the pure psychotherapy and mental health. And I'm a big fighter of trying to put art therapy, as in the US, as a mental health profession. I wouldn't consider it really New Age or trance. And I'll tell you why I'm saying this: psychotherapy in general is a long process. It's not a quick fix. And same thing goes for art therapy. Art therapy is a long process, it's not a quick fix. When we talk about mental health and psychotherapy, it's still a big taboo.

'And, second, not just in Lebanon but all over the world, art therapy is trying to prove itself as a scientific method. So there is a battle to fight even in the scientific world of mental health and psychiatry and psychotherapy. And there is the battle to fight that psychotherapy *is* okay and mental health *is* okay and getting away from "insane" and all these taboos.'

Herein lies the confusion for Myra and the people she wants to reach. How to promote her work while dealing with mental health taboos? People, she said, have warned her against using mental health to advertise because of these taboos. In addition, she's competing with those offering what she considers quick fixes – coaching and positivity offerings. I didn't get the impression that Myra was disparaging positive thinking or life coaching, but as she went on to explain, 'Lebanon loves trends, and unfortunately art therapy is becoming a trend. But they're not doing it the real mental health professional way. You'll probably find twenty people who claim they're art therapists, but out of those twenty, there's probably three with actual education.'

Quick fix or not, life coaching has tangible benefits and is gaining traction, even among Arab women – in Australia. In

Brisbane, I met with a life coach named Hanan, of Palestinian heritage who spent the first sixteen years of her life in Saudi Arabia before moving to Jordan. A marriage to an Arab man subsequently led her to Australia, where she now resides. Hanan became a coach when its benefits grew apparent: this sort of guidance had helped her repair after her divorce from the man with whom she had come to Australia, which left her a single mother and unable to return to Jordan for fear she would lose her child.

'I think I started life coaching just to save myself, really,' Hanan told me.

Like Myra, Hanan said it wasn't common for Arabs to enlist services like life coaching, though she acknowledges that most of her clients are women, and among them are Arabs. When it 'saved' her, Hanan recognised the gap in these options both in Australia and overseas. Jordan, for example, has no such thing, she said.

'It's either you go to a psychologist or psychiatrist, who give you a bunch of pills to take so that you feel better ... and there's something wrong with you. There is no professional life coaching where we don't need medication, [where] we just need some guidance and mentoring and somebody to walk along the way with us.'

Part of the reluctance to embrace such an option could be tied in to learned helplessness. Myra made the point that that way of thinking means people don't invest in fixing something because they don't know what tomorrow will bring. Add to this society's hostility to therapy, and who wants to commit to something in the long term?

'How does this play out more specifically among women?' I asked Myra. 'Do you find that there is a different level of trauma, or additional heaviness or issues for women because we have so many responsibilities?'

'Very much so. Because with everything that's happened, and with everything that we already talked about, add to it gender roles and expectations that come with it.' Things familiar to any woman around the world: marriage by a certain age; having children; appearance and looks; skills and education.

'In Lebanon there are a lot of subcultures, and this gender role is huge,' she continued. 'I see that a lot, often with the women who come here.'

Something extremely interesting emerged out of this dissection of women's challenges in Lebanon – the tendency to focus on shallow, external elements that we can pick on to avoid dealing with the darkest parts of our lives and ourselves. A perfect allegory is the way in which Beirut, once esteemed as the 'Paris of the East', is now a jumble of contradictions. The chaos of the old uncomfortably juxtaposed beside the Western-style new. Myra called it 'layering'.

'In Beirut we have lots of ruins, lots of Phoenician ruins and Byzantine ruins, and even from the Bronze Age, and layers and layers and layers and layers of cultures and heritage, but we do nothing with it. Instead we just build a new modern downtown that looks like anywhere in the world.'

The same problem plays out with women undertaking, for example, cosmetic surgery.

'Just walk out on the street and you'll see that, and it's the same thing: someone would be torn inside, they feel they have no control inside of them, no self-confidence, no sense of identity, what they can do, what they can't do. The only thing they can control, and the only thing that's expected of them is to look good, so we fix the outside and the inside is ignored. Just like the layers of the city.'

Looks hold great value in the Middle East. The paler the skin, the more brightly coloured the eyes, the better. And any Lebanese person will tell you that there is a huge focus on appearance in Lebanon, perhaps even more than in other parts of the Middle East. That said, the women I met with tended not to be dressy or heavily made up. Still, plastic surgery is popular in Beirut, and its love affair with cosmetic upgrades are well documented. The *Washington Times* reported in 2010 that 20–40 per cent of plastic surgery patients are 'cosmetic tourists': it's significantly cheaper to alter your appearance in Lebanon than in Europe. For many, including the Lebanese themselves, pressure to look good – particularly in this social-media-led world – is high. In general, dressing up, even if you're in hijab, is important in Arab societies. In Beirut, hijab was by no means absent but it wasn't as common a sight as it was in other parts of the Middle East.

This may seem surprising to people who have come to see the region as a big veiled jungle of inequality; one book about the Middle East – by an Australian – is literally called *The Veiled Lands*. In the film *Sex and the City 2*, admittedly a critical flop, the main characters sit at a table in luxurious surrounds in Abu Dhabi (filmed in Morocco), and watch, jaws dropped, as a woman navigates a bowl of French fries while wearing a niqab (a veil that covers a woman's face apart from the eyes). It's a spectacle for Carrie, who can't take her eyes off the woman; it's also a spectacle for the viewers. The film is one veil short of telling its loyal audience, 'Aren't you glad this isn't your life?'

This brings me to perhaps what are the most common errone-ous beliefs about Arabs – that everyone is Muslim, or that only Muslim women dress conservatively. The Middle East is religiously diverse – beyond the three Abrahamic faiths, there are people who identify as Druze, Bahai'i, Yazidi and Zoroastrian, to name just a few. And within Christianity and Islam, sects abound – from Christianity's Maronites, Greek Orthodox and Coptics, to Islam's Sunnis, Shi'ites, Alawis and Sufis. The Middle East is anything but 'one size fits all'.

Myra's insights into Beirut's inner pain and outer turmoil, and how they affected women, were specifically about Lebanon, but her observations could just as easily be applied to other parts of the Arab world. There are clear differences in lifestyle in each country, based on class and wealth, but conservativism abounds all over. As one woman in Jordan pointed out to me, she might well be Christian but she lives in a Muslim society, which shapes her life in many ways.

Humans are naturally tribal, and within those tribes we're born into we will eventually gravitate towards the people who are most like us, or by whom we will feel accepted. After all, we generally want to belong. As Myra said, 'We're not an individualistic society. So you always have to think about the family and, almost, if you don't do what the family pressures you to do, you don't belong to them.'

In Australia in particular, a sense of belonging is even more valuable for women who feel torn between a society struggling to accept them and a culture that binds them to ideas not always easy to adopt in a foreign land. It seems fair to say that older Arab immigrants might engage in denial, even if a sense of helplessness wasn't at play when they moved to Australia, no doubt guided by a vision of a 'better life'.

While for many immigrants, war and occupation are an unforgettable history, the tendency towards denial and helplessness felt heavier in the Middle East. At the core of these behaviours were war and its debilitating effects. In Australia, the more ferocious antagonist is identity, the persistent and pervasive aimlessness of not belonging anywhere in particular, all the while being asked to declare fealty both to the country you live in and the one you might have been raised in. One foot here, the other in a land you might barely know.

HOPE SHIFTING

In Lebanon, denial was not limited to war trauma. A few days earlier I had met with Dr Hibah Osman, a palliative care physician. Hibah established the NGO Balsam – the Lebanese Centre for Palliative Care – a few years back. It provides palliative care to people with cancer and other advanced illnesses at home, and is the first of its kind in Lebanon.

When I asked Hibnah what her biggest challenges are, she said 'truth-telling'. 'There's still a major tendency here not to tell people when they have cancer.

'I think the whole "not well" thing to the family relates to the whole idea of success and failure, and doctors have a hard time telling families and patients that the patient is not well because they feel that they have failed them. So the doctor really wants the patients to do well,' Hibah explained.

Protecting patients from their diagnosis is common everywhere, she added, but she believes it's less common in other parts of the world because the rights of patients are more respected.

I knew she wasn't exaggerating: at least one relative of mine who had cancer was never given the diagnosis, only her family were told (though I heard from someone close to her that she had figured it out herself).

'The idea is if you tell somebody they have cancer then they're just going to fall apart. And you hear this all the time – *bifliq*,' Hibah continued, switching to Arabic. They'll split in two.

For Arabs, telling family members about someone's death is a prolonged process where the truth is stretched to its limits. First, you acknowledge that the person is unwell. Then they get 'worse'. Their condition continues to worsen, until finally they pass on. I have seen this play out to an extreme where there is distance involved and it's not possible for a person to get to their dying relative in time. So someone in Australia asks after a relative in the Middle East, and finds out the truth days after the person has passed on and been buried. In an effort to reduce the shock of the loss and soften the grief that can occur with sudden death, the news is delivered slowly.

Hibah said patients already know they're ill or dying, but have to pretend they don't for the sake of their family. 'And in my clinical experience, I've found that in many families people do know or want to know, and the family prevents you or blocks you from telling them. And as soon as you convince the family to tell the patient, the patient does better.'

Hibah also suggested that the multi-confessional system makes it more difficult to offer palliative care in Lebanon.

'People are very attached to their religious backgrounds and sectarian backgrounds, and that plays a big role in navigating that. So comparing it to the US, where I've done most of my training, you have chaplains, and you can have a Catholic man advising a patient who is Buddhist on the spiritual dimension of their care, and that's completely accepted, and here that's a challenge.

'But a lot of people from this area will tell you, "Oh, we're traditional, oh, the family structure, oh, our acceptance of life and death is different." But really it's not.'

Hibah told me about a palliative care concept called 'hope shifting'. 'You and I have our life story that we've kind of planned in our minds. You're married, you want to have kids, and then you want to put them through school, then you have hopes for your career … and then when you get sick, that story's interrupted. A big part of what we do in palliative care is help you piece that story back together or find new hope.'

It's a concept that resonated strongly for me given the interviews I had undertaken so far; seeing the brutal long-term effects of war on people and land, interruptions to normality that linger as Syria erupts nearby. Years after the Arab Spring, historical periods of transition that indicate a shift in the collective psyche but which don't deliver improvements, how important is it to have hope and shift your perspective? Remembering, meanwhile, that the challenges of ordinary human life do not slow down or disappear, like illness and ageing. Listening to Hibah, the significance of Myra's battle to tackle the learned helplessness that can come bundled with the difficulties of daily life was amplified for me.

At a time when ageism is increasingly on Australia's radar, and given respect is a cornerstone to interaction with Arabs – for elders, traditions, systems and even monarchies – I wondered if the issues facing older generations in the West were also felt in Lebanon. Things like not being heard, or not being prioritised in hospitals.

'We do have this sense of community that allows people who are getting older to play a different role, and a very valued role within the family, and that helps.'

But Hibah pointed to a bigger issue, perhaps: that many families are fractured due to people seeking work opportunities in other countries. 'You do have the elders alone in a way that didn't happen in the past, and that's created a social problem,' she said. She believes that the issue is a general one. Women, while often the care-takers, don't generally suffer more. 'The mother is loved and valued, and the father is loved and valued.'

It wasn't surprising to hear Hibah speak of family values. At the heart of all of my discussions with women were their families – the code they were raised under, and how they are bringing up their own children. That collective belonging of Arab society operates at a micro level within the family home – you always think of others in relation to your own actions, as Myra pointed out.

But amid the turmoil of displacement, civil war and regional instability, to use a well-worn phrase, 'life goes on'. The important thing is to maintain hope.

THE TRAUMA OF IDENTITY

Here a margin advances
There a centre recedes
East is not all East
Nor West is all West
Identity is open to diversity
It isn't a citadel or a trench

Mahmoud Darwish

The Middle East has every reason to be in a state of grief, so wide reaching and deeply felt is the upheaval across the region. Yet despite the many challenges it faces and a foreboding sense of political doom, people get on with things. Nor is there the pervasive sense of fear that afflicts Australians – the what-ifs of terrorism, which light up our minds and collective conscience in a way that only brews greater fear and resistance in a 'diverse' society. This is the case even when we haven't experienced anywhere near the amount of trouble other countries have, and continue to face, daily.

People living in the countries I visited are right next door to the strife in the region – Jordan and Lebanon both neighbour Syria – and this proximity could easily be frightening for people, but instead I found a sense of acceptance – perhaps the result of that learned helplessness Myra talked about; or, in some cases, simple indifference. More worrying for people was the stream of refugees coming into their countries, fleeing Syria and Iraq. Jordan and Turkey are taking in massive numbers despite not having the infrastructure or economic resources to accommodate them.

In spite of what to us would look like enormous social problems and intractable national concerns, the common narrative in these countries isn't one punctuated by collective sorrow. For women, the battles are specific: feminism, freedom of speech, sexual freedom; more broadly, women's basic and essential rights.

So what identity badge do you prioritise with all of these factors at play? Your Arabness isn't likely to be the focus. This is in stark contrast to the dilemma of the Arab woman in the West, who is far more likely to prioritise her identity.

MY PARENTS' DAUGHTER

I grew up in a quiet cul-de-sac in the eastern suburbs of Sydney, the daughter of Palestinian migrants. Our house was close to a series of cliffs that broke off into expansive, rough ocean, and if I closed my eyes I could hear the whoosh of the waves as they beat against the cliff faces and dream myself far away, romantically transported to . . . adulthood.

I believe my hunger to be an adult was fairly normal, but possibly more intense given I was brought up on a strict diet of rules, and gradually handed beliefs that I had no ability to unpack for myself. Even at a young age, I sensed that, as an adult, I would finally be able to decide how I saw the world.

I loved being near the water, and while we were hardly in the bush in the suburbs, we had a large park close by, and an easy pathway to the famous Gap at Watsons Bay. As kids, my brothers and I would walk up to the park and slide down its low hills on makeshift cardboard mats made out of vegetable boxes. Rickety old fences divided us from the cliff edges, but we would find the gaps and poke through them. My mother once had to pull me back when I audaciously tried to climb all the way onto the cliff with a friend.

Such explorations were the most fun we had on weekends that eventually came to include Islamic Saturday school lessons to teach us how to recite verses of the Quran. A bored teacher from Lebanon tried in vain to maintain our attention, but we were united in our discontent at being forced to give up precious leisure hours to further learning. Secretly, though, I didn't mind *so* much: I loved going out with my brothers and feeling like I was a part of things, especially as the youngest.

There were a few Saturday school incarnations. What began as a weekly visit to a western suburbs school eventually led to a coalition of Arab families located in the eastern and south-west suburbs of Sydney gathering their children for Arabic and Quran lessons. The class got so big that separate grades were created. I was in the beginners' class.

At home, Mum kept the household running. Most days after school she would iron clothes and I would plant myself on a nearby couch to watch *The Greatest American Hero* and *CHiPS*. I was a product of the Western world early on, but it gradually became clear that I wasn't represented anywhere in its culture. Of course, identity patches mean you'll latch on to the next closest thing, like the nerd or fat kid. As Lindy West humorously recalls in her book *Shrill*, this could pose a problem if you were the latter. 'There simply were no young, funny, capable, strong, good fat girls,' West wrote.

And where I lived, there were no hyphen-identity kids who inhabited duelling cultures, a life full of restriction and Saturday school. Later, I also became a fat kid, which meant I was really screwed. I looked for a version of myself in Judy Blume books, *The Babysitters Club* (did Claudia, the token Asian kid, count?), and even *Sweet Valley High.* I would have settled for a temporary character, a new Muslim student who gets caught liking – not even dating, just *liking* – a non-Muslim guy and be saved by Elizabeth. It never happened.

Eventually you forget that you're not represented and just look for the occasional nod to your existence. It's a slow burn, this exclusion. Life wasn't handed to me in one big ball of confusion. It was learned over time.

But I wasn't alone. My mother was the one constant, as well as my brothers. And I always admired my mother – even as a kid I could see she was strong, courageous and smart, special. My father was largely absent because he worked day and night, navigating more than one business at a time. He worked so hard. He would leave in the morning, come home for some dinner then head out again. So it was left to Mum to manage us. At night, she would sew while watching Arabic films, and occasionally I would position myself beside her.

One time, I was with my brothers who were watching a horror film, and a scene in which a man gets his head chopped off shaved years off my life. Terrified, I ran upstairs to my mother, who calmed me down. I remember lying on the couch while she worked on a cross-stitch of a dancing gypsy woman, a glimpse of romantic times past, the sounds of an old Arabic film filling the air. Despite the trauma of the evening, I was at peace.

Because I grew up in an Arab Muslim family of boys, it would be easy to draw the conclusion that my life was more difficult than theirs. My three older brothers could do things I couldn't, like swim at the beach and go out with their friends more often, but my parents' conservative and strict rules were doled out fairly evenly among us. In my favour was that I was the youngest (until my brother Anwar arrived in 1989, when I was eleven), but this did nothing to stifle the confusion that crept up on me as I grew older and started to hear the word 'no' more. The innocence and relative ease of being a kid morphed into something far more complex and challenging for a girl who was full of imagination.

It wasn't merely 'no' I had to deal with; it was an energy, and a few variations on the word. These included:

Ayb (inappropriate).

Haram (forbidden).

Inti binit (you're a girl).

These were all a big fat 'no' and a wider suggestion that, to be a good girl, you have to observe certain traditions and ideas. It's not that guys don't get pressured to behave well. They just get away with it when they don't. And no one – from what I have seen, at least – holds it against a guy when he screws up. Boys are almost expected to be screw-ups. Girls are expected to be good.

In the West, girls are rewarded and praised for being confident but not overbearing; active but not overly so; and sweet. Show too much personality and you're hard work. For an Arab girl, 'good' means many more things: quietly spoken; observant and faithful of your religion; modestly dressed; a virgin until you're married.

Which brings me to the other major thing Arab girls the world over are told when they're young: 'When you're married.' Arguably this phrase, as innocuous as it seems, is the worst one to be handed when you've asked permission for something. It could be anything, from going to the shopping centre to a weekend away with girlfriends. But this one answer is a double-zinger: not only is it a rejection of your request, it's also making your desires subject to an external event that may or may not happen. And of course, it says: you'll always need a man to be able to do this.

Mum and Dad handed me the 'when you're married' line too many times to remember. It was frustrating because I wanted to get married eventually – and had no qualms sharing this with people. But while there were a lot of things that I figured would be fun with a husband, I didn't want my life to revolve around a guy, and I certainly didn't want to view him as an authority figure.

In recent years, I have wondered how things might have been if (a) my parents had not peppered my childhood, adolescence and early womanhood with those defining words and phrases – if they had brought me up to think for myself, without deferring constantly to outside perceptions and a husband I hadn't yet met; and (b) if I had learned to block it out, to rewrite the language of my life.

I think things might have been very different.

It's easy to simplify your childhood into one of two things: a mess of memories you'd like to forget, or a sweet time of innocence you wish you'd appreciated more at the time. But I find myself forging an uneasy alliance between the two as an adult. It's not the fault of anyone in particular; I think I'm just uneasy about it because my childhood never felt like it belonged to me. From the time you're a baby and hear your first words, you are being taught what others believe and think, and you are instructed, or at best encouraged, to obey.

One day, when you're in a position to make up your mind for yourself, you don't even trust what you feel, because you were handed 'yes' or 'no' your whole life, not instructions on how to figure things out for yourself. Still, I don't think we realise how tied we are to communal expectation until we're challenged by something 'different', which catches our attention and refuses to go away.

This crystallised for me when I got engaged to Chris. Inevitably, my parents struggled to come to terms with the idea of me marrying a non-Arab. It would be easy to paint their reaction to my choice of partner as a typical, closed-minded response, yet it was anything but. The turmoil they experienced plunged far deeper than simply not wanting me to be with a white guy. It was fear, protectiveness and concern that any shred of Arab identity I had would be lost forever. Chris could convert to Islam, but he could never be Arab – and probably never connect to the culture in a way that is meaningful. How to explain to them that the identity they think defines me is only a part of me?

As a child of migrants, it's easy to get caught up in your own woes growing up inside the well-populated sphere of your cultural and/or religious community. It's also common to forget that your parents will also, eventually, experience the same sort of sacrifice you did. This was brought home to me when an ex-colleague, upon hearing about my engagement to Chris, said, 'Your parents deserve a bloody medal! You can tell them I said that.'

I understood why she was paying them the compliment: as difficult as it was for me to move out of home, and bring a non-Muslim, Anglo man to my parents, they eventually accepted all of these things.

It's not that I feel I should be grateful for being able to do what I want; it's that at the end of each of these major life shifts, my parents were still there, still loving me, accepting things even when they didn't like them. I think that would have been harder for them than my childhood of restriction was for me. Eventually

I could make my own mistakes and create the life I wanted. But they didn't get a similar choice when it came to their kids.

Ask any ethnic kid, and there is a high chance they will tell you that there's an extra layer of repression in your upbringing when your parents are migrants. You don't just download a religion or a set of cosmetic cultural practices; you divide yourself between two lands, two competing life spirits – in simplistic terms, a focus on yourself versus what other people think. You must navigate a Homeland, and The Place You Live.

It's harder than you think.

GO BACK TO WHERE YOU CAME FROM

When we're younger, children of migrants in the West tend to adopt a splintered identity that encompasses many ideas of who we feel we should be. We have to consider and navigate more than one culture, sometimes three if our parents hail from different countries, which can create 'minority within a minority' issues. Imagine the cultural confusion and complexities if your mother was, for example, Sudanese, and your father Iranian?

Identity confusion can be traumatic. One day, you wake up and understand that you're not sure *who* you are, not necessarily in an existential way, but in the most basic sense. As adults, many of us have found ways to laugh at these separations. The differences that once caused us grief now mean something else: we had a unique childhood; we have tribes in religion and culture; we have culture.

Still, the unease of not belonging to one 'side' sits in you like a stone throughout your youth, where you are constantly being asked to pick a side. This isn't necessarily explicit. It's in the things that separate you from others – explaining why you can't go to school camp, why you're wearing tracksuit pants under your netball skirt, and why you're fasting and need to take a minute during P.E.

The immediate effects are negligible; as a kid you either follow the rules, break them or try to find some sort of coalition. And while ethnic families may seem to rebuff the Australian/Western lifestyle, it's not always an explicit rejection; it's most often an attachment to the conservatism they carried with them when migrating, which is firmly at odds with a more liberal, self-focused society.

I was an eighties kid, but I don't think I'm alone in these feelings; for migrants kids who grow up in the West, identity crisis manifests when you have to make proper adult decisions about your life. Mentally you may tell yourself that you are not wedded to tradition, but the layer of guilt that weighed on your childhood and adolescence remains. The result is a deep questioning of all that you have been taught, and immeasurable guilt and shame for being a disappointment to your family.

Joumanah El Matrah, a Melbourne woman of Lebanese–Syrian descent, came to Australia during the civil war in Lebanon. She is the CEO of the Australian Muslim Women's Centre for Human Rights in Melbourne.

'People think girls stay in their [Arab] families because they're frightened and there's violence. That's complete nonsense. Most of the time young women stay in their families because they love their parents and they don't want to hurt them. And the idea of personal freedom at somebody else's cost, particularly your parent who you love very much, is an incredible burden to carry.'

This isn't adequately considered when talking about identity confusion. Children from ethnic minorities will reflect on the hard parts of being a 'wog' kid growing up in the West, but they are also fiercely passionate about and defensive of their cultures. We harbour guilt because we inherit the sacrifices our parents have made, experiences they have shared with us numerous times, which leave an imprint.

For my part, I embraced my identities. At various times in my youth, I was devoutly Muslim. I was fiercely Palestinian. I used to carry a keyring for my locker key at school with the flag of Palestine. On the weekends, I wore a gold necklace with a pendant of an olive tree and the word 'Palestine' written in Arabic (*Falasteen*).

Palestine. I had no precise conception of what it meant to me, except that it influenced what I ate, the smells of our kitchen, the unusual spices and sage that occupied the kitchen cupboard at home, the language my parents spoke. And that resounding stamp of 'No, you're a girl,' which always hurt so much.

I learned to deal with it by, at times, becoming stricter on myself than my parents. This began in high school and continued on into my twenties. Despite the rigidity my culture represented, I loved having Arab heritage. I enjoyed our visits to the West Bank every few years, marvelling at the differences in how Palestinians lived. Israeli soldiers were everywhere. They made me strip down to my underwear in a curtained-off room to scan for threats – I was six. Checkpoints were normal; donkeys were a common sight. My grandfather's neighbours would invite us over and offer us fresh goat's milk. (I never liked it, but etiquette demanded I try it.) To a kid from Sydney, this was exciting stuff, and it exposed me to a way of life beyond that of the more evenly paced, undramatic Sydney. It certainly planted a seed of affection of loyalty to the place I increasingly understood was my 'homeland'. I didn't just come to see myself as descended from Palestine, I felt connected to it.

While I never hid my identity patches, fading though they were at the time, in adulthood they took on greater significance.

Other people were always sure to remind me of my differences. By far, I experienced some of the greatest challenges to my cultural and religious heritage in the workplace. There was the manager who joked about my virginity in front of the entire team, using lewd language. There was the CEO who, upon me questioning a decision he'd made for me without any consultation or warning, asked me if I had issues with men due to my upbringing. And beneath all this was an insidious implication that I was somehow fortunate to be there; that I was succeeding in spite of my background.

As I got older, I became more comfortable with myself. I still didn't hide my identity, but I no longer felt defined by it. My identity, always a part of me, didn't amount to the whole of me. The discrimination that punctuated my life became 'normal'. I claimed the privilege of being composed of more than my inherited culture. I was just me.

But 9/11 fractured that newfound ease and stability. Everything changed and I had to start all over again.

If growing up Arab and Muslim has always had its challenges in a nation still trying to find its collective identity (a questionable goal), the post-9/11 world transformed the way children of migrants experienced and communicated their confusion, shifting the dynamic in many societies that were only tolerating Muslims, Arabs, Chinese, Greeks, and a whole bunch of other ethnic minorities. Not helping matters was the Australian government's resounding claims that refugees fleeing to Australia by boat were 'queue jumpers', a label that tainted them as illegal immigrants who posed a threat to our civilised society.

When the tragedy of September 11 shook the world in 2001, I was training to become a lawyer at a small general practice in

Sydney's CBD. I sat with my parents watching the coverage and I remember literally trembling. My body was cold and, shivering, I took a phone call from a friend who was concerned about me going out in a hijab. Until then I had never felt afraid to leave my house, but I was terrified of what awaited me in the morning and I was quite willing to admit it.

The next day I was met with many stares, some aggressive. On the street and on public transport, I felt exposed. On a bus, the driver loudly proclaimed to a nearby passenger that Australia would have to be careful now – they won't be letting in Arabs anymore. He glanced at his rearview mirror to meet my gaze, his expression smug. I showed nothing.

I felt emptied of emotion, stripped of the ability to care about what had happened in the US. I wasn't allowed to feel sadness because, in the collective Western mind, I was part of the problem. Moreover, I was somehow meant to explain it to people, or change myself to not represent a religion that, it was clear, would become more and more universally disliked.

It's not merely religious or racial discrimination that troubles so many Australians. It's how it ruptures all aspects of identity. For people like me, children of immigrants who balance or battle competing identities our whole lives, the constant need to defend our commitments to a country that seems to reject us is tiring, to say the least.

Joumanah El Matrah made a salient point about the lack of complexity when it comes to racism about Arabs. 'Racism gets very complicated, except when it comes to Arabs. You see very strange things happening around Indigenous people, where you feel like there's all this manoeuvering by people who want to do something about how Aboriginal and Indigenous peoples are treated, and take an interest in their life outcomes. But at the same time, the racism against them and their ongoing marginalisation and dispossession is unrelenting. And so you see a very complex picture of what racism looks like,' she explained.

'My experience after all these years is that actually racism against Arabs is very uncomplicated. It is just hatred. And I've come to that view more and more as I've aged and seen how racism plays out.'

I thought of my personal experiences of racism, the embarrassment you feel as someone hurls abuse at you as you pass by. How it can happen as you leave for work, or on public transport. In the workplace. Even migrants who themselves have experienced discrimination may not express solidarity with you, a rejection I've personally experienced: a bus driver with a thick accent kicking me off the bus; a taxi driver who was a migrant like my parents talking about crazy Muslims.

It's understandable that many of us feel frustrated at the treatment of non-Anglo cultures. We have long been unapologetically exoticised; racism is 'normal'. Perceptions that are insulting or even harmful abound. And we're expected to counter them.

Nowhere is this more apparent than with the treatment of Australia's Muslim population. For women in hijab, so visibly Muslim, discrimination is racial and religious – you don't have to be an Arab Muslim woman to experience it. But Arab Muslim women sure do.

WHERE DO YOU COME FROM?

'I wish there was a country that was called Islam and that had the perfect Islamic principles,' said Ebby, who, so tired of being asked where she was from, once told a customer at work, 'From the cradle of civilisation.' She's of Iraqi–Kurdish heritage.

I met Ebby in the Brisbane home of a Lebanese social worker named Salam, an environmentally conscious vegetarian who plied us with cheese, crackers and fruit. Ebby's lament pointed to the effects of the deeply entrenched 'us vs them' mentality that has settled in Australia since 9/11, endorsed in recent years by a man once charged with the responsibility of governing the nation. Former Prime Minister Tony Abbott's challenge to the population to commit to 'Team Australia' was widely viewed as a flimsy disguise for what was an attack on Australia's Muslims; a dictate to Muslims around the country to show loyalty to a government spooked by the possibility of so-called 'home-grown terrorism'.

'What I realised is that it doesn't matter. I didn't choose to be half-Iraqi, half-Kurdish ... so why should I feel bad, or why should other people try to make me feel bad for where I come from? You say Iraq – automatically you think of bombs, suicide bombers, distress and fourth-world countries. But Iraq was once a prosperous nation; it was the West that made it like that.'

Abbott's call for 'unity' was a similar refrain to those uttered during the 2016 presidential campaign in the US. Donald Trump and his desire to 'ban all Muslims' sat uncomfortably beside Hillary Clinton's wobbly declaration that American Muslims are at the frontline of the war against terror. It's not enough to suggest Muslims are as American as anyone; Clinton enacted a similar decree to that of Abbott's – tasking ordinary citizens with the responsibility of protecting the nation from their bad apples. Trump took the distrust of Muslims in a different direction: separation. Upon taking the presidency, he wasted no time enacting a ban against immigration from several Muslim countries, a move that was loudly rejected by many Americans and condemned globally. The ban was quickly overturned by the courts, but it signalled a major departure in how we talk about Muslims. This was serious; a US president, the so-called leader of the free world, was trying to normalise discrimination.

Muslims, it seems, must exist not only under the collective gaze of the world but also in relation to other Muslims, the assumption being that the baseline of the faith is an affinity for terrorism. Why else must we go to pains to categorise ourselves as moderate or secular?

A lack of acceptance by the broad base of Australian society, especially after 9/11 and the war in Iraq and all they unleashed, came up a lot in my conversations. When Ebby wished for an identity aligned with religion rather than nationality, she displayed the confusion of identity that plagues so many Arab Muslims at one point or another, and the frustration we feel in being asked to be the culture we were born into, rather than being allowed to figure out how to reconcile our heritage with Australian culture.

Take Lujayn, in her late teens, whose family is Muslim. She was born in Saudi Arabia to Palestinian parents and arrived in Australia at the age of one. She described her household as 'very Arab'. 'We're not even allowed to talk English at home,' she said.

Lujayn is passionate about Palestine, something reflected in her choice of studies: Islam–West relations and journalism. However, rather than fiercely identifying as all of these things, she admitted that she had difficulty identifying as a Muslim or an Arab. 'I sort of tell people that my parents are Arab, my parents are from the Middle East. I never tell them that I am.'

This was the first time I'd encountered resistance to identifying as Arab. Many people over-identified – like I said, I was so fiercely Palestinian at one point that it defined me.

Was Lujayn's rejection of identifying as Arab to avoid judgement?

'Yeah, I've been criticised a bit for saying I'm Palestinian. People give me a weird look. Australians. I actually never refer to myself as Australian ... Every time I try to do that, people will be like, "No, you're not. Tell us where you're really from, you don't look Australian."'

She continued, 'A lot of people also tell me I have an accent, which is annoying.'

Her accent is clearly an Australian one.

Lujayn expressed frustration with the current racial climate in Australia, saying she doesn't feel welcome and would consider moving to the Middle East. One day, she hopes to work for Al Jazeera.

Lujayn was brought up by her parents to not question religion or God, but, she said, studying Islam at university exposed her to another way of thinking about her religion; she understood that her parents' version of the faith was not absolute, which allowed her to question everything, to think critically. 'My faith started changing. I started taking my own path. Because I grew up being told you have to pray, you have to fast, otherwise you're going to go to hell.'

But her shift in identity didn't come solely through religion so much as a lifestyle overhaul. Remarkably, Lujayn found a sense of freedom in a vegan diet, a shift she said changed her life. In a culture that freely consumes animal products, Lujayn said she had always questioned eating meat, but she did it because she felt she had to. Then she investigated veganism, writing a research paper on it for her Islamic Studies course. 'I looked into the science factors and the religious factors, and how Islam advocates for equality between all creatures, and advocates for caring for the environment ... That is something that really connected me with my religion. And I felt like I found my identity through that.'

Lujayn said the transition hasn't been easy; her father objected to her decision. 'I would get into trouble at every breakfast and lunch and dinner. We would just get into a huge argument. He felt like [veganism] was Western.'

Her father worried she was losing her way and going down an incorrect path. It's somewhat humorous: here were these heavy issues to unpack about identity and belonging, and it was a vegan diet that became the biggest source of conflict in her home. It's understandable that her father would align veganism with Western ideas: Arabs are known for their cuisine, and while historically meat and chicken haven't always been easy to procure (they can be costly), Arabic dishes are usually packed with animal protein. Being vegetarian or vegan is not the norm.

However, Lujayn isn't alone in her environmentally aware identity. Other Muslim women I met with talked about being environmentally conscious, similarly linking it to religious teachings. Hana Assafiri, a Melbourne woman, told me, 'I find empowerment as a woman in Islam, and I find environmental empowerment in Islam. Economic empowerment. For me, Islam is a philosophy that, when interpreted in the intended spirit of the meaning, it's a philosophy unparalleled.'

Another was Salam, the social worker with whom I met Ebby. Salam not only works with victims of domestic violence, she is also studying to become an art therapist and has a very conscious connection to the earth. She adheres to a vegetarian diet, advocates organic eating, and thinks meat is over-produced. She talked extensively about Prophetic traditions and how they shouldn't be overlooked in today's world of mass production, citing a *hadith* (a tale of the Prophet Muhammad) in which the Prophet warned against over-consumption of meat. Deliberately vocal about organic eating, she said conversations with family and friends will see discussions raised about how the Prophet Muhammad lived. 'We ask each other, how did the Prophet do it? The Prophet really ate meat when he needed to, not whenever it's provided ... you don't just slaughter the animal whenever you want. It's not a need anymore, it's a want and it *has* to be on our tables, but Islamically it doesn't really need to be on our tables.'

While Lujayn seemed to reject any cultural identity based on religion or nationality, others have wrestled with this over the years. Youth worker Lamisse is in her late twenties, the daughter of a Muslim Egyptian father and Anglo Australian mother. She said that she spent a lot of her early twenties 'trying to be really Australian'.

'I didn't want to be Arab or Muslim anymore, I just wanted to be like everybody else. And then when I felt that emptiness and I really faced up to the fact that I was denying such a significant part of who I am, I ended up going to Egypt. I was like, "I'm going to try and live here now; I'm going to go reconnect and try and understand," and that was a huge turning point.'

Lamisse's time in Egypt amounted to six months before the 2013 coup led by General Abdel Fattah al-Sisi interrupted her journey; her father, afraid for her safety, told her to return to Australia.

'I enjoyed my life in Cairo. I was a bit of a party girl back then ... Every trip I'd had to Egypt up until that point was a very sanitised family affair, and going to Egypt on my own and being like, "Wow, there's this whole entire sub-culture of disaffected youth, agnostics and atheists, political activists." It's so beautifully intricate and complicated and this idea of a homogenous

Muslim world is such a farce. Everybody is struggling with their identity, and everybody is struggling with their issues, and everybody is struggling with their faith,' Lamisse said.

'I can't imagine what I would have been like if I'd grown up in Egypt, where Islam is a state-sanctioned thing, where people have a sense of being able to have ownership over your life just because you're a Muslim woman, this public morality. How would that have shaped my character? I grew up instead in a post-9/11 environment in the West. And that's what shaped my identity and how I've interacted with life. Seeing the possibilities of the contrast and that complexity of everybody's lived life and their experiences – that really brought me into being proud to be an Arab, proud to be an Egyptian, proud to be a Muslim. And just seeing that it's okay to be complicated because life is complicated, it's not easy. Everybody's got their struggles.'

Lamisse also had to unpack her 'own internalised racism' towards herself as an Arab of mixed race. 'Realising that I'm never going to be entirely Egyptian because I can't deny the fact that I've got an Australian mum and I've grown up in Australia, and that's okay. And I'm never going to be entirely Australian because I've got an Egyptian father, and that's okay. And I'm so tired of people trying to split my identity and tell me to pick a side.'

This was a universal grievance for the women I spoke to. The discourses of East versus West, of Islam versus the West – both here and overseas, though more persistently in Australia, tries to force a choice between ideas, rather than allow the development of a combination. So in my conversations with women in Australia the same identity issues popped up: religion, Arab culture, Western ideals, pressure to conform, as well as those other unexpected elements, like Lujayn's veganism and Salam's environmental awareness. That these women find connection in other things shouldn't be so surprising. It is, however, quite unique, because Arab culture is community-based and it can be challenging to stray from the herd.

In some cases, it can be a pleasant surprise to discover a source of connection is something gentler or more joyous than a severe cultural practice. Haleema* is a Lebanese woman who grew up in Australia but is currently settled in Jordan to study religion in a particular tradition of Sufism. Her idea of 'Arabness' has completely changed over the years. She says she had little interest in Arab culture growing up. 'Anything that was Arabic was sort of boring, a parents' thing, an older thing,' she said, adding that Arabic music and films held no appeal for her. '[But at] university I met a group of women who had come from different Arab lands [to study], and I found this really great connection with them and it was based on comedy,' she told me with enthusiasm. 'And I found that there was a level of comedy that you can only reach in Arabic ... with Arabic into-nation, with Arabic hand gestures. That really got me loving it. It was just banter ... I can't even tell you what it was, there was something about the back-and-forth, the quickness of it.'

Living in Jordan has only strengthened this connection, including her command of the Arabic language.

There were also women who had a desire to explore alter-native pathways and derive more personal meaning from life, among them passionate advocates of social justice. Hana Assafiri owns and runs the Moroccan Soup Bar, a deli in Brunswick in Melbourne.

'Everybody finds meaning in life through whatever it is that makes them tick,' she said. 'And for me it's always been social

* Some women's names have been changed.

justice and advocacy. It's not something I do nine to five, it's a way of life for me. And wherever I see injustice, no matter where, I can't just sit on my hands ... I feel compelled to say something or do something.'

For starters, Hana employs women, including those who have experienced violence, with the goal of helping them to achieve economic empowerment.

Another of those 'somethings' is an event she holds every fortnight, called 'Speed-date a Muslim'. On these Sunday afternoons Hana gathers Muslim women at her restaurant and brings out pastries and tea. She explains to members of the public attending that they can ask these women anything, so long as it's respectful. And, she says, the conversations that unfold are inevitably involved, personal and often profound.

One of Hana's primary concerns revolves around the rising discrimination facing Muslims in Australia, and the responses from our leadership – incendiary or absent. Australia's tense racial climate is a huge reason to run the event. The event is, Hana said, grounded in a belief in human decency, that we are misguided by misconceptions, and our fears are being manipulated – 'Division and hate are not innate human traits, they are grounded in fear, and we are trying to do away with some of that fear by having experiences and engaging Muslims and non-Muslims, where we all go on a journey beyond the simplistic narrative that's been on offer. You know, let's rescue Muslim women, or let's fear them. And we're trying to say there's a whole other reality in between. And there's an appetite for [the events] the more we run them.' When we met in 2016, she had been holding them for a year.

Hana also runs another regular event called the Conversation Salon, where she hosts inspirational, spirited speakers.

'We don't shy away from complex social issues. And the occasion is to genuinely contest ideas.'

A recent discussion was 'Islam and Feminism: Beyond belly-dancing, Bombs and Burkas'. 'It's a respectful contestation of ideas in the hope that we *can* walk away with a better version of ourselves, feeling more inspired.'

'Do you think that happens?'

'Yeah, absolutely.'

Hana mentioned a letter she wrote to the prime minister, Malcolm Turnbull. 'The more we don't have a leadership that can condemn this sort of nonsense, the more individuals feel [they have] a right to abuse and threaten and intimidate and bully others. And we've given them licence; as a society we're now saying – and this is what saddens me – "Oh, it's freedom of expression, it's our opinion, let's talk about the elephant in the room, let's talk about Muslim migration." No, let's not!'

In her letter, which she posted on the Facebook page of her Moroccan Soup Deli, Hana wrote: 'A visionary is what is needed at a time of global unrest, to navigate through our darkest hours and not repeat our most awful history of division and hate.'

As I read it, I couldn't help think she was such a person.

SNOW IN THE DESERT

So many Australian–Arab women are like snow in the desert. Growing up, at least, we're almost completely at odds with our environment, expected to exist and thrive under antagonistic circumstances. In some ways it isn't a challenge, especially if you are surrounded by people in the same situation. But at other times, differences matter. A realisation began to brew in my mind a while ago: that although being a woman in the Arab world has major challenges, including religious practice, cultural identity is not one of them. The Arab women I met were simply of Arab heritage, not entrenched in labels. Arguably, Arabs don't wrestle with their place in society *as* Arabs. There is in fact a lot of pride. The questions are around class, lifestyle and religion, all of which influence how they live and see themselves. And in these respects, there can be very clear markers of division, though not necessarily conflict. Jordan, perhaps, is one place where shades of nationalism can cause identity issues. For a long time, Palestinians, who now outnumber native Jordanians living in Jordan, have identified strongly as Jordanian, yet it seems that the conflicts in the region are paring away at this easy alliance. During my time in the country, it was common to hear a Palestinian–Jordanian say they see themselves as Jordanian, but others will ask them, 'Are you *Jordanian*–Jordanian?'

Jordan is growing economically, but countries bearing a sizeable influx of refugees experience tension among their residents – it was spoken about in Lebanon and in Jordan. Aisha, a media officer for Oxfam Jordan, accompanied me on a trip to the Zaatari refugee camp, which is home to 80,000 Syrian refugees. One of the challenges she identified in her work is addressing Jordanians who are worried about the impact of refugees – on their country's infrastructure and economy – and to foster greater understanding around the needs of refugees, and the realities of their lives.

So the women I spoke to in the Arab world may have experienced their hardships, but they knew who they were, even if they didn't always like who they were expected to be. If they were fighting for justice or equality or feminism, their battles were clear – corruption, societal expectations and misogyny.

In Australia, however, many of the women I met with were very conflicted culturally, personally and sometimes religiously, or at least had been at some stage of their lives. The difficulties of understanding or stepping into your place in society, discovering purpose or your role in life, and ascertaining what you truly believe were all amplified. Many of these women were confident and self-assured, even change-makers in their chosen professions. But they had also been battered by years of mistrust, discrimination, uncertainty about where they belong, and conflicting expectations from their families and wider societies.

So if the civil war was the resounding undercurrent of life in Lebanon, and the occupation in Palestine, identity became a familiar topic of discussion with many of the Arab–Australian women I interviewed. You don't need to be an activist or even outspoken to demonstrate identity confusion in Australia.

Life coach Hanan told me that a primary reason younger women enlist her services is because they struggle when it comes to belonging – women who were either born in Australia or 'moved here late'.

'I can definitely resonate with that on many aspects. For example, I struggled with belonging for a while because ... I wore a headscarf so I looked different. I look Middle Eastern, I pray five times a day, I have an accent. I don't belong to the mainstream society or community,' she said.

'But then on the other side I also don't belong to the Muslim community and I find it very difficult to find good friends that I could belong to. So that was also another challenge. I didn't belong here and I didn't belong there and I definitely didn't belong back home. The belonging was one of the biggest challenges that I have. And sometimes you go to places, you see people, but you don't really actually belong.'

Hanan eventually made a discovery: 'that belonging doesn't have anything to do with the culture or religion or where you come from or what's your mother tongue. It has everything to do with what's in your head and who can actually talk to you from the head that makes you feel like "we bond here". It has nothing to do with culture.

'It's very nice to have a cup of coffee with a friend and you just pour your heart out and you know that it's in a sacred place. You can do that. That was one thing. And I also have two mentors [who are] Aussie to the core.'

Hanan's approach is similar to mine. It's taken me years to reach the point where I feel comfortable being a multitude of ideas, beliefs; to feel attached to culture and religion but not be defined by them. It's a place you reach when you find yourself and realise that the relationship you have with yourself is the most important one you'll ever have. That the gaps don't have to be filled by anger and rage as an antidote to the hate others feel for you.

I know what it's like to wear your identities like armour, oddly proud and defensive even as you search for personal meaning. It never bothered me when people asked me where I was from. In fact, I tended to proudly proclaim my heritage growing up. Nor have I minded more recently when CEOs prolong interviews because they want to talk earnestly about their personal views on Islam or the migrant experience. But some consider such enquiries and conversations distasteful because the curiosity can seem like an insinuation, or an affirmation, that you're from somewhere else and therefore not really an Australian. If it's a power play, and often it is, it can be problematic.

This is why I understand but don't subscribe to the manic identity politics so many people are latching on to at the moment. For every proud Australian-born 'person of colour', there is a racist Australian 'reclaimer' who doesn't think you belong in the sun-drenched land of Oz.

Of course, racism in Australia is embedded in its history, but the way in which migrants have experienced it has shifted over the years. A new generation of post-9/11 youth is pouring its anger into poetry slams, academic writing and opinion pieces. The rise of identity politics has seen a remarkable change in how we address racism. People are angry, and it's breeding more rage. I understand it: I may have white skin, but years of wearing a hijab and having an Arab name have exposed me to some insidious racism, and for most of my life, being subject to this racism defined me. So I can appreciate the relief that comes with clutching your identity labels as a way to feel safe, in order to claim a sense of belonging. Indeed, in some cases I think marking a clear identity is important. No one should have to deny parts of themselves. But a damaging side effect is that in the name of defending a community, other important issues can be overlooked. In Australia, for example, Arab women might neglect internal community issues for the sake of unity against a nationalist antagonist, invoking the very labels that in some ways constrict them, to address backlash.

So I no longer see it as helpful or useful to be too firmly entrenched in identity politics, which can make you sound as racist as the people who are trying to oppress you. Whether the devotion to such politics is driven by a desire to stem personal confusion or is a reaction to discrimination, in my experiences it can be more harmful than helpful. It's not always a mentality that is interested in creating a new way forward.

RELIGION AND CULTURE

I am not what happened to me.
I am what I choose to become.

– Carl Jung

Growing up Arab Muslim, I've experienced the ebbs and flows of interrogating my religion, and the confusion of where it meets culture. There were times in my life when I had no clue that they had merged, at times in an unholy communion. With so much forbidden, it was rarely clear to me what was problematic from a religious point of view versus collective Arab culture.

Palestine, the land that brought to mind affectionate relatives, olive trees, plump figs and endless cups of sage tea, could also be a stern principal. At any moment, it could be conjured up, an energy that pressed down on me when I started to become too 'Western'. It wasn't always an explicit ordeal. It became normal to experience conflicting desires, but I can't say it was ever easy. Where it was particularly difficult was in differentiating between 'right' and 'wrong'. Take, for example, the very human desire to seek out connection, particularly in a romantic sense. How to reconcile your parents' belief that it's *haram* to be intimate before marriage, a perfectly common desire? How to cope with the proscription of something so utterly normal?

It's not 'Western' to want love or physical connection. Yet this is what we deal with growing up in the cultural-religious bubble.

Not that it was all doom-and-gloom. Between prayers, which I would complete in a swift, fiercely whispered cycle, my brothers and I would watch television or read our favourite magazines like any kids. I read a lot of books, happily immersed in the fictional worlds of others. When I think of my childhood, I don't regress to a faint image of myself filled with longing. I think of playing with best friends, of a slip-and-slide in the backyard with my brothers, of watching video clips and the boundless obsession with leg warmers.

I was, for a time at least, fiercely proud of the way my mother dressed me because she bought me lovely dresses. I even had my ears pierced, which for some reason was a major milestone for my Anglo-Australian friends. They could go to boys' parties, but they weren't allowed to wear earrings until they hit puberty. To my young mind, it was a strange restriction to place on someone who could swim at the beach in bathers, mix freely with boys and easily get permission to go to the movies. Having their ears pierced would happen when they went out on their first dates; I had one thing over them in the childhood liberty stakes, I suppose.

But I have never been at odds with my heritage, no matter how frustrating some of the side effects of being raised in it can be. Indeed, a lot of the women I spoke to expressed deep love of their Arab background and all it has to offer. We're not the shiny belly dancers in the desert but we love to dance, we love our music, we are at one with the land, and food and hospitality merge to create beauty in the home.

While I didn't always quite know as a girl, and later a young woman, where religion began and culture ended, I found comfort in the rituals they offered. They felt safe, like a warm hug, and even though I found it difficult to separate religion from fear, I benefited a great deal from having parents who instilled in us a belief in God. I have always taken comfort from my belief in the unseen divine forces. It has helped me immeasurably throughout my life, dealing with the ordinary but still challenging things people can experience.

But to my mind, it must be acknowledged that this safety stems, in part, from the safety you feel when you harbour this kind of fear. Rules, often unpopular, are sterile because they are calculated, designed to maintain order and to keep people safe from harm. Because I had been raised on a diet of restriction in many ways, I didn't get into trouble. But it might be argued that this also stifled the potential in me to develop into whoever my unique self could be.

Nowadays, I tend to regard myself in terms more spiritual, which I know irritates a lot of people. But I'm not bothered by the semantics of it – I care about how I feel when I think of those forces at play in my life. I have moved away from fear, because regardless of the intent, Sunday school lessons drill into you a fear of God, not a love of Him, and with that a sense of powerlessness, that you're constantly being judged and life is not meant to be easy. You learn to suffer in a lot of ways.

Hardly unique to Muslims – even Arab Christians feel the Guilt. These are also scenes from the life of Catholics, Jews, Hindus. Where it gets difficult is when religion merges with culture and they become so intertwined you can't tell them apart.

RELIGIOUS OR CONSERVATIVE?

A young Muslim university student in Melbourne, Shaimaa* was readying herself for a trip overseas when we met, her long-held desire to see the world made possible because she was travelling with her sister. Going with a sibling is the 'get-out-of-jail-free' card you need with ethnic parents to be able to do things when you don't have a husband. According to Islamic rulings, Muslim women who travel a long distance are required to be accompanied by a *mahram* (a male relative you can't marry).

Shaimaa described her family dynamic as 'very, very complicated' – a blend of Lebanese cultural conservatism and religiousness. 'It's a mix of both because often it's very cultural and we don't pay too much attention to what we're supposed to be doing religiously. But having said that, my parents do pray five times a day. We're expected to fast [during the holy month of Ramadan].'

Shaimaa said she wasn't as strict about prayer. She, like Saudi-born Lujayn from Brisbane, went through a significant change in her early twenties. 'I did an undergrad in Islamic Studies and it kind of opened up my mind to how the way we're manifesting our religion could be just what we're taught, and I was learning a lot about myself and thinking, "Maybe this is not right." But I've never ever doubted the existence of God. I just think that the way I feel it or practise it has changed dramatically. I see it as more spiritual and a lot more individual than I was brought up [with]. So my views on religion [are] probably very different to my parents and some more conservative members of my family.'

'Do you think that's something you have to keep to yourself?' I said, appreciating that sometimes we don't even find it easy to express different ideas to close friends, let alone family.

'Yeah, I do, because some of [my points of view are] a bit polemic and could go against what a lot of people think is not Islamic at all, but they're just my points of view.' Engaging family members on controversial topics hasn't ended well, she added. 'So I figure that maybe it's just better to keep it to myself and not involve others. I'm more confident with what I believe, even if it goes against the grain. But I am mindful and respect-ful of certain members in my family.'

Shaimaa said she's butted heads with her more conservative siblings on 'small things' like listening to music or going out. And when she started high school, she said there was pressure on her to wear hijab, her father suggesting that because it was a new environment, the transition would be easier.

'I adamantly refused. The hijab is one of those polemical issues I was alluding to earlier.'

Like so many others I spoke to, Shaimaa expressed frustra-tion at how women are so defined by the way they dress. She went on to tell me that she had in fact worn hijab for about six months when she was twenty-one. 'I was going through changes; I'll put it down to supernatural, irrational feelings and whatever. I've gone back and read a little bit and I'm pretty sure it was an episode of sleep paralysis. I felt something come on top of me and I couldn't move. So it was a sensation where my mind was fully awake but I couldn't get my body to move.'

It was terrifying for Shaimaa, and at the time she took it as a sign from God. 'I thought my death or something was imminent,' she said, with a chuckle. 'But that was when I was still a bit naïve and into the whole superstition thing. So I did wear it for a little bit, but I think that was very vital in my understanding of the religion.'

Like Shaimaa, I've seen more 'religious' days that involved fear of punishment in the afterlife, though not necessarily so marked by superstition. Periods when I would obsess over little details in my life to make sure they matched a particular school of Islamic thought. Something as minor as how you walk into the bathroom can be dictated by scholars (left before right), and there is a prayer for every situation. At university, a friend gave me a little book of these prayers – an invocation being a '*dua*'. To this day, I make *dua* before undertaking any form of transport, for example. I learned also that in Islamic thought, the prayer of a traveller is always answered.

It was only recently, while idly listening to a segment on ABC about obsessive compulsive disorder (OCD) and intrusive thoughts that I realised how religion, being fear-based, can raise your sensitivities to wrong-doing and fertilise obsessive thinking. My whole life I've peppered my language with expressions like *insha'Allah* (God willing), *masha'Allah* (praise God) and *la'sa-mahallah* (God forbid). Innocuous, strengthening phrases that can accommodate and breed obsessive fears at the same time. It's not something limited to Islam. In fact, on the program I listened to, the specialist talked specifically about Christians who obsessively attend Confession. Religion isn't the cause, she explained, but it facilitates OCD tendencies. But the same could be applied to me: I carried a huge amount of fear around jinxing. If I didn't say *insha'Allah* for an event, it wouldn't happen. If I forgot to say 'God forbid' after a bad thought, it would happen. No one drilled this into me – it's a learned behaviour, stirring up some already deep-rooted anxiety.

I do remember some funny things about this, in particular the obsessiveness that comes from needing to be pure for prayer. Muslims have to make ablutions – *wu'du* – before they pray, a ritual that is nullified by passing gas. Growing up, my friends and I joked about this a lot, not turned off by an elder relative's reassurance that the devil was just trying to take us away from our prayers if we lost our *wu'du*. One friend guffawed about the time she had to stop prayer and make *wu'du* again because she kept farting. It happened three times before her mother told her to give up.

As an adult, those silly conversations continued but the intention behind them grew more serious. A woman I was friends with for a few years, from a strict Salafi-leaning family, found many things to obsess about. Being super-strict, she relied solely on interpretations of the Quran, rather than following a school of thought. In some ways such Islamic rulings were simpler, but in other respects it could do your head in to listen to her. There was no malleability – you *don't* do this, you *don't* do that. One time, when I attended a scripture class with her, the teacher talked about the rewards of heaven, which included the ability to watch people you hate in hell. I sat quietly while people around me roared with laughter. I told my friend that I felt uncomfortable with the idea of taking pleasure in another's suffering. Islam, after all, is a religion that emphasises mercy and compassion. 'Oh, come on,' she said. 'Wouldn't you want to see George Bush pay for all he's done?'

I have no issue with devout observance of religion, but I find the inflexibility of some Muslims more challenging. In my experience, personal connections to very dogmatic followers who leave little room for human frailty, who see suffering as a ladder to heaven, are not long-lasting. There are common side effects – inflexibility and superiority, the same symptoms of overzealous thought in any religion. Faith is fluid, and I don't think it's the whole story to simply believe in God and pray without feeling. Religion isn't a rewards system. My most meaningful connection has always come in moments of true faith, not blind ritual.

*

That my Arab heritage is connected to Islam was not some-thing I thought about for many of my younger years; they were complementary to each other, or simply combined to form one super element. When I asked a close friend about being 'reli-gious' – she wears the hijab and is a strict observer of the practices of Islam – she said that as an adult she makes no connection between religion and culture. They're entirely separate for her.

But this is a luxury for contemporary generations of Arab Muslim women in Australia who, in adulthood, seek the truth of what Islam dictates about their rights and responsibilities. This freedom didn't come in our childhood. As an adult, I can see that many of the restrictions my parents placed on me and my brothers when we were growing up were informed more by cultural traditions and sensitivities than religious ones, though my parents wouldn't necessarily see it that way, even if they weren't deeply religious the way some families around me were. While we prayed and fasted, and things were consis-tently deemed *haram*, there was no real distinction made between conservative cultural norms and religious practice. Even now, if my parents talk about religion, it's not with the weight of fear I've witnessed in many 'devout' Muslims. It's not difficult for them to pray – in fact, it gives them peace.

Of the Arab women I spoke to in Australia, many of them described an upbringing that was conservative. They weren't allowed to go out with friends on the weekend in the evening; they didn't date boys; they had strict curfews. Quite often, the only real mixing of the sexes happened at school or within the family – a lot of them were very close to their cousins.

But their parents were more 'Arab' than 'religious'. I know this because a lot of these descriptions came out of the mouths of Christian women or atheists, not just Muslims. And it was always harder for the girls than the guys, though not necessarily by much.

Rita*, for example, is a Melbourne woman in her thirties, born to Lebanese-Christian parents who came to Australia during the civil war, and who, she said, brought their culture with them. They instilled in her certain values, like hospitality, which for Arabs is a concept that runs far deeper than just opening your home to strangers.

She described her restrictions: 'I was not allowed to sleep [away from] the house, which I think is very common for Middle Eastern parents. I was not allowed to have boyfriends – *no waaaay*.' Rita said the notion of finding someone later wasn't even discussed. Indeed, she added, her mother never wanted her to get married. 'My mum said, "I want you to travel, don't ever fall in love, love never lasts." That was the message I got growing up.'

A Sydney woman in her mid-thirties, Warda* didn't get that message from her Muslim parents, but she did grow up to be a lover of travel. The road to the freedom it offered her was, however, paved with hesitation. When she moved out of home she lived with a sibling and felt obligated to visit her parents every weekend. She didn't go out as much as she thought she would. 'It's almost because I suddenly had the freedom, that desire to do it wasn't there anymore,' she told me.

It didn't bother her until she began to travel in her late twenties. 'At the time I was just fed up with everything. I didn't know what I wanted to do with my career, my life. I was single. I think I was feeling frustrated because I was living away from home, but I wasn't. I had freedom, but I didn't. I was constantly going back to my parents' house,' Warda said.

She felt it related completely to her Arab upbringing. 'I don't think the religion was a big part of it because my parents were never that practising. So it wasn't a religious thing, it was an Arab thing.'

Warda thinks both she and her husband will be more flexible if they have children – they're not as attached to their culture, but, she said, it relates to a sense of obligation. 'I actually don't mind our culture. There are some beautiful, great things about our culture that I love. The sense of family and belonging, I love all that. It's just come with a lot of restrictions.'

She said her parents trusted her as an adult. 'Surprisingly, when I told them I was travelling on my own, and for months, my dad was more okay with it than my mum.'

But when she was younger, there were growing pains. At twenty-two, Warda went through a period of mild anxiety and depression. 'I was constantly lying to my parents, and then I was constantly on edge about getting busted. Personally, I think that's what caused it.' It's not that she was really doing anything 'wrong', she was just hiding things from them. Innocent stuff – lying about work shifts that were really days out with friends to the movies or shopping, for example.

And she identified another possible reason: the glaring contrast between her life and that of her many non-Arab, non-Muslim friends. They did anything they wanted – having boyfriends and so on – and didn't share her hang-ups.

Warda eventually saw a psychologist. 'I think a big part of what I was going through was not understanding, and fearing, what I was going through. Back then I didn't know what anxiety was.' She tried to hide her feelings from her parents and everyone around her, but this only amplified the problem. 'I was trying so hard to pretend everything was okay, which kind of exacerbated it,' she said. 'But I remember when I did tell my parents, it was almost like I instantly felt better because [they] knew now and they were supportive.'

'What made you tell them?' I said.

'I broke down. I basically broke down.' She wasn't eating or sleeping, constantly nervous, finding herself in tears at work.

'Do you think you struggled to have these two identities, to grow into the woman you are, versus being the good Arab girl?'

Warda didn't quite answer the question directly. 'As I've gotten older, I think I've learned to appreciate and value my parents more than I ever have, because I look back and I realise how good I had it,' she said. 'Even though I had these struggles, compared to so many other girls in our culture I am so blessed to have been able to do what I did.'

This is an important aspect of being in an Arab family – you're tight. It can be suffocating but there is love and support. Education is a must. The restrictions, though difficult when you're young, are rarely the work of parents who want to make you miserable. They just want to protect you. Like Warda, it's a realisation many of us come to more fully appreciate as an adult: we understand our parents better. We get how terrifying it must be to have children. And for me, I discovered that from a deep place of love they will almost always let you have your way if it means you're happy.

Years after I moved out of home, for example, I queried my mother on why she allowed it.

'I didn't,' she said. 'I was against it.'

'You would've made it really hard if you were against it, and you didn't,' I replied.

Mum paused, thoughtful. 'I looked at you coming home to that little room, and I felt you weren't growing up.'

Interestingly, truly religious Muslim families are often more easygoing, allowing their daughters more freedom, not as burdened by arguments that the outside world can't be trusted.

A couple of interviewees looked puzzled when I asked them if their parents were strict about going out. They had restrictions – they weren't dating boys, for example – but curfews were flexible, so long as their parents knew where they were. The friend with Salafi leanings, for example, easily came and went without questions being asked, it being accepted that she was guided by religious scripture.

A powerful example of this cultural/religious dissonance in childhood came out in conversation with Jamila*, a Sydney-sider who grew up in a big family in which the boys were given special treatment by her mother. Her parents were strict.

'Like very, very strict,' she told me.

Jamila and her siblings were brought up with faith, but her parents weren't particularly observant Muslims and, says Jamila, their homeland of Lebanon was a mystery to her. Nor did they 'trust anyone' after they migrated to Australia, which meant Jamila and her sisters weren't allowed to do much outside of school. 'My father would always say, "I trust you, but I don't trust people,"' Jamila said.

Every Arab kid has heard this or a variation of it. In the pre-meme era, we could have made bumper stickers out of this phrase and sold it at community events. It was the statement that capped any plans you were presenting to your parents.

'Were there things you wanted to do that you couldn't?' I said to Jamila.

'I just had the most boring childhood, I think,' she said, matter-of-factly. 'I was just really fucking bored.' She laughed. 'Let's be real here: you go to school, you come home, you go to school, you come home. I literally did nothing other than, like, hobbies ... We were together, the sisters, we watched *Young Talent Time.*'

Meanwhile, her brothers enjoyed extra-curricular activities, like sports. Jamila was one of several girls and she said they were together all the time, visiting people with their parents. 'We were obsessed with New Kids on the Block. We cried for a week for our dad to let us go to the concert. We ended up going then we got in trouble afterwards because I ran out like an idiot.' Jamila erupted into laughter.

'My dad was waiting outside with his hands crossed, and all the girls ran out at the end of the concert and I'm like, aaaaah-hhhhhhh!' Jamila recounted, imitating a diehard fan girl. 'And my dad's there like, what the hell is my daughter doing? And then my older sister got into trouble. Like, when we got home my dad slapped her in the face, ripped the posters off the wall – and we were crying more over the posters, not being slapped. I didn't get hit; my oldest sister always got hit because I was the second eldest. My oldest sister, she had the most pressure out of all of us. She got it hard, man.'

Jamila is a creative, but it's something she does for love not money. She has grown immeasurably from the experiences of her childhood and, later, a divorce in her twenties. But it was studying a creative pursuit in an area of Sydney far from her childhood home that helped break open her life to new possibilities.

'Being in this progressive kind of environment, but me myself being an absolute conservative, the way that I've been brought up, I didn't really interact with a lot of people, I only had a couple of friends. And then for my birthday, I wanted to go to the beach – just Bondi Beach with my two friends – and my mum wouldn't let me, out of all people.' Jamila was around twenty-one at the time. 'On the day my mum forced me to stay at home. I was crying and crying, and I had done nothing at that point – never gone out, never been anywhere, I wouldn't even ask to go to dinner with my friends. My life went from school–home, school–home, school–home to now uni–home, uni–home, uni–home. I got a job, finally, at a take-away shop so that was uni–take-away shop–home. That's all I had. I had nothing else,' Jamila recounted.

'And I'm like, why the fuck did they have such a rein on me? What did I do that was so bad that they thought they had to hold me back, that they couldn't even trust me to go to fucking dinner with my friends, or to the beach? And my mum was like, "I don't like girls going to the beach." I argued, I tried. And I could've gone but she would have been disappointed and if something did happen, she would have been like, "I told you so."'

I recognised that feeling of longing and angst, and the heavy price that comes with getting what you want. Usually you'd be in trouble afterwards, if you were allowed to go at all. But all the while there was this sort of dizzying confusion about why so many things that seemed so normal weren't allowed. You didn't stick posters of your heart throbs on the wall – that was totally forbidden. Parties on the weekend were fine ... if it was an all-girls thing. Music wasn't encouraged, though my mother never stopped me from spending pocket money on cassingles (are you old enough to remember those?).

Concerts were generally off-bounds for me – a monumental effort saw my brother Alex convince my parents to let me go to a Bon Jovi concert for my birthday when I was a pre-teen. It was the late eighties, long hair in boy bands was a thing, and I vacillated between my love of music and of movies. My mother would give me pocket money and I'd buy pop culture magazines like *Smash Hits* and *Hit Songwords*. Reading *TV Week* in my family involved a system of hierarchy – eldest to youngest to have your turn. I had the biggest crush on Jon Bon Jovi, and while I never divulged this to my parents, I was convinced that when I was older our paths would cross and he would just be drawn to me. Being allowed to attend the concert was like a surreal dream come true. I'm not sure how Alex convinced my father, but Mum was always more lenient about events and somehow the stars aligned.

After the Bon Jovi concert, Alex and I hung back in the parking lot to watch the band leave. I think he knew it was a hugely important event for me, so he didn't want me to miss out on anything. Even though he'd had his share of curfews and interrupted nights, Alex was a concert-goer and knew the joy of seeing and listening to an artist you love in person. An impromptu set in the parking lot by Jon Bon Jovi and guitarist Richie Sambora took the outing into the early morning, and the next day my father asked me about my night. I told him with measured excitement that I'd had a good time.

'You were late,' he said.

'That's because Jon Bon Jovi came outside and played some more.'

Dad was calm but unimpressed. 'Okay. But no more "Jon Bon Jon" after this.'

That was what it was like. Everything enjoyable, desirable, seemed ephemeral and to necessitate rebellion, to be antagonistic to our religious or cultural practices.

Sometimes the lack of a robust social life really didn't matter. I had enough imagination to push through the worry that I was missing out on things I liked. I could live in my mind without limit, creating new realities for myself.

Still, curfews were the bane of my existence – right into

my early thirties. My mother was a guardian of the clock. We argued about it a lot. I didn't know anyone else of my age who had to be home well before midnight. She was unapologetic: she didn't want me to ever be in danger, driving alone at night with all the 'crazies' on the roads.

Aliya Khalidi, a playwright from Lebanon with a strong feminist streak, talked about the idea of conservativism versus religion, and the difference between them. 'Do you think that there are a lot of families that are just really conservative but not religious?' I asked her.

'Yes, absolutely. There are. They would allow their girls to go out but they would not allow them out after nine pm, for example. After nine pm, you are not to go out, but they could go out wearing shorts up to here,' said Aliya, pointing to her thighs.

It's '*ayb*,' she added. 'That word *ayb*, my grandmother used to say "*ayb*" does not exist in my dictionary. There's nothing called *ayb*, because if what you feel is right, you do it, if you're doing something that is within reason. But *ayb* cannot be a word in our dictionary. She told us that when we were kids.'

This is something the Brisbane women I met with also acknowledged. Earth-conscious and artistic social worker Salam said her family was 'religious' but not conservative. For example, birthdays weren't forbidden in her family, but they were in more conservative families. Salam could comfortably wear shorts in front of her brother, but she knew people who weren't religious but frowned on this.

And I have encountered many supposedly strict Muslims and Christians who approach religious rulings like they're a pick-and-mix lolly bar. Many of these 'devout' observers lived on internet chat rooms during my uni days, easily exchanging flirtations and details with members of the opposite sex. This was pre-Facebook. Community events, even when segregated, were an opportunity to catch a glimpse or even share a brief conversation with someone you liked. A woman I befriended at uni, who wore a hijab and met all her prayer obligations, was one girl among a lot of guys and though she loved attention never bothered to attend class. 'I want everyone's eyes on me when I enter a room,' she told me with a laugh, though she was completely serious.

Then there were the university social groups that trembled with the rise and fall of religiosity among their members. In my first year, not having been in a mixed environment since primary school, I bonded with other Arab Muslims, finding solace and ease in our shared experiences. I never had to explain myself or why I couldn't do something, until one day a guy in my year (on a different course) requested a meeting. He had previously expressed interest in me romantically (in a *halal* way, meaning he emailed me with a pick-up quote from *The Fresh Prince of Bel Air*) but I didn't reciprocate and things were awkward between us. But the purpose of this conversation wasn't to talk about love; it was to check in with me about my religious observance.

'Do you know the difference between *haram* and *makrouh*?' he said, completely straight-faced, his posture relaxed. '*Haram* is when something is completely forbidden. *Makrouh* is something that isn't exactly forbidden but it's not desirable.' He sounded like a Sunday school teacher, but with an Australian accent. 'Which do you think your interactions with guys falls under?' he said.

Vibrating with anger, I told him in a low voice to mind his own business. I already felt conflicted about how to interact with guys at uni, though it was easy to see how harmless it all was. Still, I was a pretty naïve, innocent person, and mocked for being so. The attempt to humiliate me into 'behaving' had the opposite effect to the one he'd intended: I became more sure of myself.

His behaviour was demonstrative of the spiritual wrestling I saw in so many Arab guys brought up in Australia, though not so much in the ones who had come from overseas to study (who were either suddenly and wholeheartedly 'Australian' or fiercely dedicated to their religion).

One time, a Lebanese friend, who'd grown up in Australia and oscillated between speaking freely to girls (positively flirting, even) and refusing to make eye contact, returned a Mariah Carey CD to me that he had borrowed. He had wrapped it in an A4 sheet of paper and mumbled a prayer of forgiveness as he handed it over, his face etched in disappointment. It wasn't enough that he was sorry he'd taken something that featured a woman in a revealing outfit on the cover. The brief exchange felt like a reprimand: I shouldn't be buying CDs like that and lending them out.

When I think about it, it was exhausting being his friend.

NAVIGATING SPIRITUAL PATHWAYS

One of the most resounding clichés about the Middle East is that all Arabs are Muslim, and, moreover, religiously conservative to the core. Where to even begin in unpicking this almighty falsehood? It completely denies Arabs the complexity of a spiritual pathway, in particular women who are often identifiably Muslim if they veil. And what of the women who are not Muslim or who reject religion entirely? So much is assumed about them based solely on their cultural heritage.

Religion is one of the most contentious issues for Arabs around the world, and one of the most fiercely discussed in the West. With Muslim migrants inhabiting their lands, there is a constant need by Westerners for reassurance that Islam, a religion so scrutinised and misunderstood, won't take over their country, as though rulings under Islamic law (sharia) can be easily packaged and delivered to parliaments the world over. It's worth emphasising that Muslims do not advocate implementing an Islamic system of law in the West. What is also easily overlooked is that sharia is a system of laws that influence a Muslim's daily life.

In Egypt, tensions exist between Muslims and Coptics. Lebanon, a country that many would argue once peacefully protected the practice of various faiths, is now identifiably sectarian. In other parts of the Arab world, minority sects are outnumbered by Muslims and targeted for their beliefs. In a time where ISIS has become an enemy to all – Muslims included – how is the power dynamic of religion shifting? Moreover, what does it mean for an Arab woman to be Christian or Muslim or Alawi? Is the conservatism at the heart of many Arab families ultimately cultural?

ISIS, in the minds of so many Muslims, does not represent their faith. That the organisation's criminality is taken by many as Islamically acceptable says more about widespread misconceptions about Muslim beliefs and ways of life than anything else. When questioned on television about whether Islam promotes violence, historian Reza Aslan offered a succinct response: 'Islam doesn't promote violence or peace. Islam is just a religion and like every religion in the world it depends on what you bring to it. If you're a violent person, your Islam, your Judaism, your Christianity, your Hinduism is going to be violent. There are marauding Buddhist monks in Myanmar slaughtering women and children. Does Buddhism promote violence? Of course not. People are violent or peaceful and that depends on their politics, their social world, the ways that they see their communities.'

In hindsight, it wasn't surprising that religion was not a central concern for a lot of women I spoke to, though it was discussed. And when it did come up, religion became more than an identity marker or a clash between East and West. It was a symbol, a life path, a vast idea to navigate and find peace with. Others rejected it entirely.

Where some might not have seen religion as an essential part of their lives, there was no escaping it. But what's missing from meaningful dissections of this is that Arab women undertake faith journeys, and that these are thoughtful, agonising, empowering, beautiful, and don't revolve around how they're perceived. It's an inner journey that delivers a personal outcome; we don't exist for the masses.

You can see this in the rise of the 'cultural Muslim', a term increasingly used by people born into Muslim families who identify with the religion but do not practise it. Another term is 'Ramadan Muslim', but this is a critical label applied by practising Muslims to those who do not follow the religion but for fasting during the holy month of Ramadan.

Jennine Khalik, a young journalist from Sydney of Palestinian heritage, offered herself as an example of a 'cultural Muslim' in a panel for ABC's *Religion and Ethics* on Radio National in 2015. In her words, Jennine 'came out', such is the stigma and difficulty of vocalising your rejection of religious practice.

I can't overstate how significant this is for many people born into Muslim families. In the Middle East, one of the observations women offered during conversation was that, as Greek

Orthodox or Christian, say, they were in a minority in a Muslim country, the *culture* of which was predominantly Muslim (and, just quietly, deeply conservative). Listening to these women made me revisit the concept of the 'cultural Muslim'. I had first thought it was an ambitious description, given the word 'Islam' is essentially a reference to surrender to God. How can you be Muslim – one who submits – and not believe? This wasn't a judgement – I was genuinely intrigued by the idea of it.

So it was interesting to meet with Jennine a year after she had publicly identified herself as a 'cultural Muslim' and hear that she had abandoned the label. She was now, simply, agnostic about religion; more firmly oriented on an existential pathway. 'We create meaning in our lives,' she told me in her soft voice. 'There will always be cultural Muslim elements about me ... but I can't sit there and tell someone that I am Muslim ... Islam and religion, I feel, has let me down.'

It's not uncommon to hear people express a loss of faith or disappointment when things don't work out. Jennine did what many of us do: place our faith in a set of beliefs that we think is going to make our lives better. Given there can be a distinct difference between belief and faith, I wanted to understand better what happened along the way that led to the loss of hers.

Jennine explained that it was primarily the idea of *naseeb* (destiny/fate) – which so many Muslims and Arabs cling to in order to explain life experiences, and to give hope when something desired (like a marriage) fails to manifest – that had turned her away from her faith. And the suffering humans experience also played into it; that no matter what we do, we're destined to suffer, a sentiment similar to the learned helplessness Myra talked about.

'I can't fight against that and I felt it just doesn't make sense to me.'

In our conversation, Jennine described a youth that involved a catalogue of identity badges: Arab, Muslim, cultural Muslim. Now she's dispatched with religion completely, though being Arab remains important to her, particularly as an activist for Palestine.

This wasn't always the case for her. She recalled feeling confused in her early years when asked about her background. That she was Arab-Muslim never came up at home. 'It was never there. I didn't even hear the word "Palestinian".'

Her parents sent her to Saturday school to learn Quran and Arabic and it was through these classes that Jennine understood she wasn't like everyone else – she wouldn't be bringing a boy home after a date one day, for example.

Jennine's emerging passion is to defend those who have made an active choice to unsubscribe from faith. It's notable, given being Muslim is a significant identity marker for so many people in Australia.

'We're all a product of our circumstances, and where we were born, what families we were born into, our geographical locations ... I just feel like I don't have the answers and I like kind of letting go.'

It struck me that the greatest difficulty in doing so would be not to play into the hands of racists and bigots. At a time when so many Muslims and Arabs feel under attack, it would be easy for Muslims to take it personally, rather than see it for the personal experience that it is.

On the other side of that transformation is the experience of rediscovering faith. Brisbane social worker Lamisse has a Muslim father, and her Australian mother converted when

Lamisse was eight or nine. Up until that point they had been a pretty secular household. Nowadays, Lamisse said, Islam guides her work and the sort of character she wants to have, and the person she wants to be: someone who is committed to social justice. 'I see Islam as a religion that's very grounded in a sense of justice. That's something I try to infuse into my everyday.'

I thought back to my conversation with Jennine, in which we dissected the atheist argument that if God exists, why does He let humans suffer? I wondered if Lamisse ever experienced internal conflict about this.

'Yeah, I did. When I was twenty, I actually left Islam and I stopped practising. I didn't identify anymore, I didn't want anything to do with it. It was a big thing for my family at the time.'

'I can imagine. How did they feel?'

'Not very happy.' She laughed.

'Did they accept you, though?'

'Yeah, they did. Despite faith playing such a huge role in my family's lives, my parents are quite compassionate, and ultimately they were like, "You're still our daughter, we just fear for you and we want the best for you, and we thought that Islam was the best thing that we could give you."'

Lamisse's rejection stemmed from anger at the Muslim community and people's shortcomings. She was upset about the hypocrisy she saw in the community. 'Islam gave us such an ideal way to live and I hated the way it just kept getting bastardised and manipulated and used for ill intent and really just negative ends.'

For the women I spoke to who had grappled with religion, peace came with finding an alliance between what personally motivates them and how it fits in with faithfulness to God.

Shaimaa, the young student from Melbourne, told me that she was now at a point where it was easy for her to reject culture and religion when they didn't serve her well-being. Lujayn, the student who partly found her identity in veganism, said studying Islam has opened her mind to its possibilities and truth.

'I feel what I grew up with, what I was taught, is so ... it's just the facts, what's written in a book ... don't question it, don't question God.'

Lujayn now feels safe questioning everything, with a critical mind, no longer directed by a fear of 'going to hell'.

'Do you still believe in God?' I asked her.

'Yes, definitely. I believe in a higher power. But I don't feel like prayer and fasting is as important as the Arabs make it out to be.'

These ideas strengthened for Lujayn when she participated in a Muslim world study tour of Malaysia, Turkey, Morocco and Spain. Her visit to Turkey, where Muslims drink alcohol, and Morocco, where people smoke marijuana, made her realise that majority-Muslim countries engage in things she was taught are *haram*.

'There's another entire perspective. I talked to the locals and they had a whole different interpretation and take on religion ... I became a bit confused. I was like, what am I? What am I believing in? Am I believing in what I grew up with? Am I following Islam just because that's what I've been told to follow? Or am I following it because I truly believe in it?'

For Lamisse, the answer lay in separating people, culture and religion. 'And my issues were women's rights, community participation, ownership over the public space, being silenced, or women's voices are supposedly *awrah*, so I'm not allowed to talk in public.' *Awrah* is the term applied to the private parts of men and women that should not be displayed in public. Many Muslims believe that a woman's voice is, like genitalia, something that should not be exposed freely to just anyone. It's something that's challenged daily by Muslim women who don't take this literally.

'Have you reconciled yourself with the faith now to know you do have a place?'

'Oh, definitely.'

While Lamisse said she differentiated between what was said by others and what the religion actually says, it took her several years to unpack, to explore Islam on her own terms without the influence of others.

Belief and faith slowly crept back up on her. 'I always believed in a higher power.'

These women's stories represented deep, personal investigations into the meaning of life and what their purposes in life might be. Tied to identity and belonging, sure, but in no way purely a symptom of them.

Throughout my travels in the Middle East, the idea of the conservative Arab woman was subverted. It's not that the women I met in Australia weren't exploring and interrogating their beliefs and expressions of faith. It just seemed to me that they were less confident about stepping away from the ideas they grew up with, or, as Lamisse had, completely rejecting them for a time.

In the Middle East, women tended not to speak about religion unless it was a central point in their lives, and more often than not Muslim women declared their faith, or exhibited it in the way they dressed or spoke, lacing their language with common Islamic expressions of faith like '*insha'Allah*' (God willing) and '*alhamdulillah*' (praise God).

In Jordan, one woman I met with was planning to divorce her husband following the *eid* holiday after two decades of marriage because she simply didn't love him. Her friends told her she was crazy to give up a man who didn't treat her badly. But Naajidah* knew that she was out-growing her husband, whom she had chosen due to pressure to get married, not because she was in love with him. What really bothered her, she said, was that they had nothing in common. When I asked her if she wanted love in her life, she hesitated.

'Sometimes I feel that love, it's like marriage – it's against your freedom in some ways. Because love also, in our society, to be a good lover means you want to give your freedom to the other one. Because you love him, you need to give him everything.'

For Naajidah, being a practising Muslim didn't inhibit her ability to be free. It was being needed by a husband she didn't love that made her feel trapped, hence her decision, finally, to pursue the divorce she'd been considering for years.

'I always use this term [trapped], even in English not in Arabic. I feel trapped. I think it's better in English,' she said.

She went on to muse on the concept of freedom. 'In our society, or any society, even if you think it philosophically, who is free? Sometimes you choose things because they're the options you have. You think you chose him freely but you are [choosing based] on your circumstances.

'Sometimes I talk about myself as a free spirit actually; it's more than a free person. Because even when I wear hijab, I wear it because I understand that it's an obligation as a Muslim.'

'Do you like wearing it?'

'No. If it's not an obligation, I will not wear it.' She suggested that her ease with wearing it was because of her faith in God. The same belief that propelled her to pray and fast enabled her dedication to hijab. 'Religious beliefs – you don't go to it freely. I was born a Muslim, I didn't have a choice.'

In Lebanon, women were as forthright in talking about belief. Aliya, the playwright born into a Muslim family, easily declared herself an atheist, saying she supports a secular society. It's not difficult in Lebanon, she told me, to live this way – her friends, for example, know how she feels. However, she added, 'I don't tell my students I'm an atheist because it really does piss off some people.'

THE MODEST MUSLIMA

There is no denying that Arabs can be extremely conservative, regardless of their religious beliefs. Immigrants bring with them to a foreign land a set of ideas frozen in time, which are then repackaged for their children. The beliefs of Arabs who remain in the homeland may change – becoming either more or less progressive – but in either case, with Muslims outnumbering minorities in the Middle East, these countries are culturally Muslim.

The best example of how this affects women is in discussions of female modesty. The modern '*Muslima*' (female Muslim) is brought up to be respectable and demure, without being a flirt. And the ways she dresses and interacts with boys are loaded with meaning, crucial to how she is perceived.

In Australia, Jennine decried the obsession with gender interaction and how women dress, starting in scripture class. 'Some of the things male scripture teachers would say were just outrageous to the feminist who was brewing in me.'

She gave the example of a teacher who said that when he's at the shops, the onus rests on him to not be enticed by women around him, so he keeps his head lowered. 'I hadn't studied feminist literature or anything like that, but I was like, "That's really fucked up. Just chill out. You're walking through a shop."'

When a man talks about having to lower his gaze, it amplifies the burden many women feel they must shoulder, to be the perfect modest woman – even when you're not Muslim.

Take, for example, the experiences of Sabine Choucair, Lebanese storyteller and clown, who, despite being raised in a Christian family, doesn't subscribe to a religion. She told me stories of religious men lecturing or abusing her. Though she's based in Beirut, she performs around the world, including other countries in the Middle East. She experienced a particularly memorable incident in downtown Amman, Jordan.

'I was performing on the street. I wasn't in my clown costume, I was just doing street theatre. And I had everyone surrounding me. Then there was this sheikh who came and started telling me off and going, "You Shi'ites, Christians, you're all going to hell."'

'Wow, so no one was safe,' I replied with a laugh.

'Except the Sunnis.'

'How did he even know what you are?'

'Well, because he called me a *saafira*. A *saafira* in the Quran is when you don't put a veil on. So a *saafira* is, I don't know if it means a whore? But it's a bad thing, it's an insult.'

Sabine indicated her wildly curly hair. 'I was all over the place there,' she said, with a huge laugh.

And the sheikh's response?

'I just listened to him and when he was done, I was like, "Thank you, that was a great performance," and then I clapped.'

Sabine clapped for me again. 'And then everybody clapped and he just lost it. He kept shouting, then left.

'I always have faith in people,' Sabine continued. 'I only perform on the streets, and I have faith that, always, people will help me. And they did. I had two choices: either I fight him back, and I will lose. Or I'll just thank him for whatever he had to say.'

I wondered if Sabine felt afraid in moments like that, but she shook her head. 'Not really. And things like that happen to me all the time. In some places people get really aggressive.'

It doesn't much happen to her in Lebanon, she noted, but Sabine did describe one incident while on tour in the Bekaa Valley with her show by Syrian refugees, *The Caravan*, which saw her work with three hundred people in five different camps in Lebanon – women, men, teens and kids, all Syrians. Sabine collected stories through storytelling workshops using social therapy.

'We had a caravan, a bus. We would go, stop the caravan, perform.'

They performed it forty times for more than nine thousand people and even took it to Tunisia. The Bekaa Valley performance took place during Ramadan.

'I do not change,' Sabine declared. Meaning she dressed the way she would anywhere else. While the initial feeling of being judged by the conservatives (men and women) of the camp passed, one man approached Sabine and asked her to cover her shoulders – he was fasting and her appearance was causing him to sin, he told her.

Sabine didn't take it well, responding to the man's request with: '"I'm very happy, I hope you go to hell then." Why do I have to ... and I was in the middle of a souk. Either look somewhere else or see it as normal.'

The man, Sabine continued, lost it, praying for forgiveness and calling her a sinner.

'Anyway, we had this big fight and all men came – and I'm known for having fights with men in the middle of the souk. It's terrible,' she said, her tone growing cheeky. The men who came to her defence were Lebanese and the offender was Syrian, she said.

'I think we're more used to accepting the differences. You could go to a pub here [in Beirut] and find a girl wearing the hijab, not drinking but being there,' Sabine continued.

I asked Sabine if there were any limits on what she would do out of respect?

'No. I took a very conscious decision that if I accept somebody wearing the hijab, if I accept somebody wearing the niqab, then they should also accept me. If I believe that I'm equal to men, then I want men to know this … I'm just being myself.'

Sabine has worked with women in refugee camps who she said wore hijab due to social pressure. At a visit to Zaatari refugee camp, I noticed there were a lot of women wearing niqab. I asked someone about this later and she explained that it was common – they wouldn't dress that way in Syria, but being in a new country there was more pressure to cover up and be hidden.

We're obsessed with women and how they're dressed, I told Sabine. Seeing women dress a certain way doesn't really reveal a society, yet women are used all the time to define the elements of one – its liberalism, its conservativism, its progress.

'It's the case everywhere in the world,' she responded. 'People always have something to say. I started to throw back.' If a man tells her what to wear, she does the same. 'I'm with equality. If that's how you want to talk to me, that's how I'm going to talk to you.'

'Why do you think you get into so many fights with men?' I asked her.

'I think I'm too free. I'm very, very free. I'm very in peace with my body. I've always sat in the most ridiculous ways. And it shows, and some people get really frustrated by that. Some people hate seeing freedom in others, so they get really pissed off.'

Sabine straddled the bench, she propped one leg up, the other touching the ground; she embodied ease. But Arabs have pretty fixed ideas on behaviour and propriety. You don't loll about on a couch, especially not in front of guests. You don't sit with your legs apart, even if you're wearing trousers. It's a *thing*, and Sabine clearly doesn't engage with that thing. This would frustrate many people in a society that is concerned with appearances, especially that of women, who are meant to be modest.

But as more conversations would uncover, many people, both in the Arab world and outside of it, place too much importance on a woman's modesty as a marker of faith. And they're not always adept at differentiating between culture and religion.

THE VEILED CLICHÉS

Don't wanna be your exotic
like some dark, fragile, colorful bird,
imprisoned, caged
in a land foreign to the stretch of her wings.

Suheir Hammad,
'Not Your Erotic, Not Your Exotic'

I've been the girl you praise for her piety. I have quietened myself to fulfil others' expectations of me. I have stemmed desires that contradict cultural and religious customs. I've dressed myself down so that I won't disappoint anyone. And I've worn hijab under self-imposed pressure to avoid judgement or influence from others.

I don't know if men really appreciate how privileged they are to rarely be questioned on how they dress. To exist without the burden of judgement that a particular outfit makes them look like a 'slut'. To not worry that wanting to wear a t-shirt in summer is a direct path to hell.

I now appreciate veiling for what it is – an aspect of true faith for many, an obligation towards God; and an unconscious symbol of power for others – men over women, in particular. And when I was younger, it was a huge part of my life. Even though I grew up in a household of boys, and my mother didn't wear traditional hijab, I always knew I would have to think about veiling one day because I was observant. I completed my prayers every day; I read Quran; I didn't break the rules. And

I was already dressing as though I covered up – I never wore short skirts or singlet tops. I was a Good Arab Muslim Girl.

My mother has long covered her hair, but she has never adopted the large scarves typically worn by hijabis. Instead, she wears a small bandanna-sized scarf that she ties behind her neck, gypsy-style. It suits her, but I always knew that when or if the day came that I veiled, I wouldn't take the same approach, if only because it didn't suit me in the same way.

When I was about fifteen, a conversation with my father about hijab prompted me to make a swift decision: I would wear it part-time, outside of school hours. There was nothing fire-and-brimstone about my father's hijab sell; it was more an expression of how it's good and proper and so on. Certainly my father wasn't going to force me; he never, for example, influenced my mother's approach to veiling.

The question of whether or not I should wear hijab at school was not raised: it was unlikely that the Church of England private school I attended would permit it and my parents didn't ask. That it was an all-girls' school probably helped in this regard. My father was fine with this approach, but my mother wasn't as keen on me veiling so young, if at all. Despite her deeply conservative streak and modesty requirements in the dress department, she didn't approve of wearing veils as large as bedsheets and especially not ones in muted colours, and she understood that living in a Western country would be challenging for a hijabi.

I was a teenager with nowhere to put her energy and angst, and I think I partly wanted my father's approval. Even though not everyone was on board with the change, I found strength in the fact that ultimately it was a personal act. Seeing negative reactions only strengthened my resolve, hardly unusual when you're a stubborn teenager.

And this is something I will emphasise: the decision to wear hijab was in the end mine.

At school, I wore the normal uniform – albeit the baggy, below-the-knees version my mum made me wear. But on the weekends I would slide into a second skin, trying to fit a mould to impress and please the people around me. When I was wearing a headscarf I couldn't get into any trouble with my parents about how I dressed.

I took off the headscarf a year later, no longer so in love with being different. I'd had enough of being a 'part-timer'. I wanted to look like everyone else, to not stand out.

It was in my first year of uni that I was confronted again with the prospect of hijab. I was meeting suitors at my home, and a random remark from my father drove home the point that hijab may come up if I were to get engaged. 'He might want you to wear it,' Dad said. This time he wasn't advocating it for himself, but he wanted me to understand that it might be a deal-breaker for some suitors.

It lingered in my mind, and I realised that I didn't want anybody pushing me into doing anything. If I was to continue on my spiritual path as a Muslim, modesty was something *I* had to care about, and I wanted to care about it on my own terms.

At university I was surrounded by Muslim women who not only covered their hair, but did so with a level of style. These women looked bold and colourful, draped in fabrics with vibrant prints. Most importantly, they were at peace with themselves on a spiritual level. It was so much a part of who they were, and I found this appealing at a time when my non-Muslim friends were on life journeys that I felt weren't appropriate for me. In fact, I even felt out of place among some of my Muslim friends who prayed and fasted but didn't share my hang-ups around clothing or going out.

I can see now how I made my world unnecessarily smaller when I put on the headscarf the second time around. But it hurt too much to want things that felt out of reach and I didn't want my twenties to be as challenging as my teens. My high school years had been marked with disappointments: a longing to participate in creative pursuits that were *haram*. I couldn't do theatre because my all-girls' school always partnered with boys' schools. And even participating in extra-curricular activities could be difficult if they involved staying back after school. Mum didn't want me coming home by myself after dark; with Dad always working late, there was no one to collect me.

As a teenager I had an intense interest in musicals. I wonder now how much of that was shaped by my life-long love of singing (I was in school choirs, including a selective one), and how much of it was influenced by the idea of an exciting career on stage, one that meant working at night.

I didn't trouble myself too deeply with the difficulties a life in theatre would pose for a hijab-clad, practising Muslim. I didn't burden myself with considerations about revealing outfits or having to embrace a male co-star on stage. It was enough to enjoy music and drift deeply into an imaginative world, where I was always, always free to do as I pleased.

A trip to Jordan in my teens had reminded me that I had boundaries to consider. A relative had asked me about my career aspirations during a visit. I wasn't about to tell her about my love of musical theatre when I didn't even know how it would work. So I went to one of my default answers, a journalist, mentally affirming to myself that I would be working in the spirit of the feisty types you saw in old black-and-white movies.

My other default answer was lawyer, because humanities were my strength, not maths and science.

The relative – a middle-aged woman who had spent many years living in Australia – baulked. Was I not aware that I should be realistic? What would my family/husband/the shop-keeper-down-the-road think if I had to travel without (gulp) a husband? It was a mortifying, soul-crushing conversation I have never forgotten.

She apologised the next day for being so blunt. 'I was just worried that you didn't realise you have restrictions.'

Fast-forward to my university days, undertaking an Arts/Law degree, for which I felt a lack of passion; I had failed to sell the communications degree to my father, who'd urged me to do law.

Though university introduced interesting people into my life, and even romantic prospects, I was bored, frustrated, full of desires I couldn't distil in any meaningful way. The only thing that made sense was my heritage, and I was surrounded by people struggling with the same religious/cultural battles. So all this led to my decision when I turned twenty-one to wear hijab a second time, full-time. I had found my tribe, and I wanted every part of that belonging. Again, my mother wasn't ecstatic about it. 'Dress differently this time,' she told me, alluding to my part-timer days in high school when I'd emulated women three times my age on the weekends. 'Be young. Wear bright colours,' she said.

I partly listened to her. And for several years it felt good. I didn't care about dressing like everyone else anymore. I faded into the background, and it felt safe and comfortable. But I can't look at photos of myself during that time without wishing I could reach out to the young woman in the photo. I don't exactly regret wearing hijab, but I could have done it better in some ways. I could have been more creative and colourful. I might have opted to wear shorter, more flattering veils that maintained modesty but didn't take away all of my shape. I could have given myself time to ask if I really needed it the way I thought I did.

I could also have made better use of my twenties, but they were by no means a wasted decade. A lot of interesting things happened to me. In no particular order, I fell in love for the first time; I got engaged briefly (but not to the guy I was in love with); I discovered that I could write humorous observations on life and get them published (*vale* Heckler in the *Sydney Morning Herald*); I began to interrogate faith in a new way; and I educated myself on story, devouring films and their commentaries, and novels.

I learned so much about myself and the kind of life I didn't want to lead.

MEDITATIONS ON MODESTY

Aliya Khalidi, the Lebanese playwright, was remembering the six years she endured in Saudi Arabia – for her husband, who had a job there.

'In the first six months, I covered my head and then I said, "I'm not doing this anymore. I'm not doing this and I'm going to pretend that I'm foreign. I don't care. I don't give a flying."'

Aliya could pass as a foreigner. Flame-haired and pale-skinned, she wouldn't stick out in a regional town of Australia. It's something she lamented: 'I only aspired to be a Western woman when I lived in Saudi Arabia but since then, never again. I wish I was the typical Arab woman who had black hair and dark eyes.'

'They excuse foreigners in Saudi, don't they?'

'They do with the headscarf, but you have to wear the black cloak.'

The 'black cloak' is the abaya, common in many parts of the Middle East, but not in Beirut.

'I used the same black cloak for six years in Saudi Arabia ... I used to tie it up. It used to be haggard and disgusting because I refused the idea that I'm actually taking care of this thing. I would wash it but not give it any other [care] ... Six years, the same abaya because I thought to myself, "I'm never going to go out and buy a new abaya."'

From our first interaction, it was clear that she was a woman of depth and passion. We were in a hipster-influenced café in Hamra, which also featured a small bookshop. She looked me in the eye and asked me what I was trying to achieve with the book. 'Because I'm not your typical Arab woman,' Aliya said. She began to draw a graph on some notepaper. 'I'm here,' she said, crossing the lowest part of a newly illustrated bell curve.

I was used to queries about what I was looking for with my interviews, but Aliya had taken those a step further with her suggestion that speaking to her wouldn't illustrate the life of a typical Arab woman. The next day I met with a similar query from another woman, who used identical wording – 'I'm not a typical Arab woman.' By then I was truly wondering what constituted 'a typical Arab woman' in their eyes. Because I'm yet to figure out what she is supposed to look like.

Although I had no doubt that these women were identifying relevant and genuine differences (privilege in wealth, class and education, to name a few), the more I engaged with them – even those one might have been able to typecast as 'typical' – the more I appreciated the complexity of being a woman, and an Arab one at that. Every experience, even if you're tribal, is singular.

Back at the café that day, I explained that the book was an exploration, and I had no agenda for what women should tell me.

Aliyah and I sat for an hour talking, almost breathlessly, finding connection in our experiences, as vastly different as they were. And it quickly became apparent to what she had been alluding with her 'typical woman' statement. Aliya has a family legacy rich in activism and justice. And her devout feminism stood out, particularly her aversion to women veiling.

Aliya had recently directed a play called *Anbara*, about her grandmother, Anbara Salam Khalidi. 'My grandmother stood up to give a lecture at the American University of Beirut [in 1927] and, just before giving the lecture, she removed her veil and said, "I'm not doing this. I'm not giving this lecture with a veil on my face." And she continued and, of course, all hell broke loose and whatever. Many people left the room. A lot of people applauded her. The main issue was she made a statement and she lived by it. I grew up in the shadow of this woman, who was the first woman in the Levant area to remove her veil in public.'

'What a legacy,' I said.

Aliya agreed. 'I don't consider myself typical, in the sense that me and most of my family have been violently anti-veiling, and who in the world has the right to tell me what to wear and when and how, and so on. So, this is my family heritage.'

It made sense, then, that Aliya had struggled living in Saudi Arabia, a country she said 'infringes on one's privacy'.

'It tells you what to wear. It doesn't allow you to drive and there's absolutely no freedom of speech. As an Arab woman, I was devastated.'

She's not the only woman to express distress over the way Saudi Arabia directs women's lives. One woman I spoke to in Dubai, who'd had a similar stint living in Saudi due to her husband's work, expressed frustration at how something as simple as shopping was affected by the laws of the country. If you were waiting in line at a store to pay for something and the call to prayer sounded, everything stopped, she told me.

'There's no trust,' she said. And in Qatar, a feminist I met with made comparisons between her country and Saudi Arabia, saying it was much better to be a woman in Qatar, though she wanted to see her government do away with the remaining guardianship laws around travel.

I told Aliya about my experience with hijab; that I had adopted it twice, and the second time had worn it for nine years before I decided to take it off.

'I was a bit worried over the phone whether you were going to be with hijab or not, because it would have been very difficult for me to express myself [if you'd been wearing it],' confessed Aliya.

'I outgrew it,' I told her, admitting that it had started to feel disingenuous, even if it had been very sincere at the start.

She seemed genuinely surprised.

'I didn't do what your grandmother did. It was very slow,' I said, adding that I'd suspected our conversation might have been affected had I appeared wearing hijab.

'I wouldn't have been as comfortable but I would have said exactly what I [think],' said Aliya.

Hijab suggests many things about how the wearer sees the world, but more than that, it can impact behaviour. In some ways, hijab, as a modesty requirement, is designed to limit.

'It's a male-imposed limit. It's not a female-imposed limit,' said Aliya.

I suggested that every religion is a manifestation of spiritual beliefs. Islam isn't unique in that sense.

'If there's a purpose for my living, it's to tell women to take off the hijab,' Aliya said, firmly.

'But some women really love it,' I replied. Aliya agreed, but wasn't swayed by my suggestion that hijab is truly a symbol of faith.

'If I were in a position to tell people, I would,' she said.

When I told her that it does me bother if a woman is forced, she interrupted me in a matter-of-fact tone. 'Most women are forced to wear it.'

I don't believe this to be true for Arab Muslims in Australia. So many are driven by a desire for completion and wholeness, and in the case of devout Muslims, it's completely understandable that modesty for a woman is something she sees as honouring God's command. And for women in Australia, hijab can be a statement of identity and compliance with newfound faith. I've seen many young Muslims invest in learning about Islam, free of cultural interpretations, separate from the mores that shaped their childhood, digging out a purer interpretation of a way of a life that offers deeper meaning than the version-lite in which they were raised. I knew only one woman in my early adulthood who was forced into wearing hijab, her mother declaring she had to start covering up the day she got her period.

Aliya and I agreed that somewhere along the way, women who are coerced or influenced into a particular lifestyle might learn to embrace it. In the same way you come to accept the odd cultural–religious fusion your parents dispensed throughout your youth, you either embrace it so that it becomes easier, or you reject it and rebel, which can be painful and destructive. I came to hear more about the social pressures around veiling in the Arab world; even if women aren't forced, it's just what you do in some parts of the region. It can be learned because it's what you see everywhere, it's what you're shown is the correct way. This shaping of the ideal female begins young – in the Arab world even school curricula suggest the ideal woman. In Amman, a few women commented on recent changes to textbooks that meant females were only depicted in hijab. Moreover, they are depicted in only a couple of professions, and as housewives or praying. 'People should see that it is a choice that you make,' said Rula Quawas, a professor at the University of Jordan. 'For instance, why do they have to shame a woman who is not wearing the hijab? I don't accept it.'

And consider Fulla. She is the Muslim world's answer to Barbie: a plastic doll kitted out in modest clothing, with accessories such as veils, a prayer mat and prayer clothes. Fulla is the predictably modest, good Muslim woman – stick thin and pretty, inoffensively ambitious. She is no model/astronaut. She is a mother, or perhaps a teacher, life paths widely considered suitable for females in the Middle East. She represents the type of woman girls should aspire to be, an antidote to her scantily dressed Western counterpart.

In some ways Aliya's feelings on hijab surprised me. I was used to hearing women say they chose not to wear it, and that they didn't even like it. But it was rare I was told so clearly that it should be outright banned, and from an Arab woman.

I didn't just come bundled with my own experiences. I was familiar with the sentiments of many hijab-wearing women in

Australia. I thought of Salam, the Brisbane social worker I had met with her two friends, Ebby and Silda, all of whom wore hijab. Salam talked about her path to veiling, saying she had made the choice with the support of her parents. 'I could never ever have asked for better parents. And my mum has always supported the decision that I wanted to come to one day to actually wear the hijab.'

But it wasn't common among her parents' families to veil. 'It was not even part of the Lebanese culture in Lebanon. People looked down on people who wore hijab at that time.' That was seventeen years ago, when Salam was twelve. Summer in Lebanon meant going to the beach, but Salam reached puberty and decided it was time to consider hijab.

'Mum went out and bought me all these beautiful, colourful scarves, and she said to me, "They're there if you decide to wear it." And it was a big thing for me because all my cousins were on the beach, wearing bikinis, swimming, and there I was sitting in shorts [down] to my knees and a t-shirt, thinking, "Do I really want this? Do I want to continue living this way? Do I want to enjoy the beach [and engage in] all the worldly matters that we do?" And I sat there every single week, every day, in front of the beach, reflecting. And I wouldn't go into the water. I could go in my shorts ... but I felt that I couldn't really jump into that water until I actually came to a decision internally on what I really want.'

At the time, Salam's family lived in Saudi Arabia and her time in Lebanon was a family holiday over the three-month summer break. The week before they left Lebanon that summer, Salam made the decision to wear it. 'I just woke up with this immense internal amazing feeling. You can't describe it.'

She wondered how it would affect her position as captain of the basketball team; how would she wear the uniform. 'But something told me that I could tailor it. Something hit me: why am I thinking of my world more than my *akhira* [afterlife]?'

Not all of her relatives supported her decision, one aunt advising her she was too young. Salam was the only one in her class in Saudi Arabia who wore hijab. Later, however, her adoption of it had a ripple effect – now all the women in her mother's family wear it, she said, a complete reversal of how they viewed such matters in Lebanon seventeen years ago.

Living in Australia, Salam has been physically and verbally abused about her appearance. 'And it's fine with me. And the reason for that is because I do have inner peace with the hijab,' she said.

Salam's friend Silda, a twenty-four-year-old of Iraqi/Syrian descent, who also wears hijab, said it has multiple interpretations. 'It's so diverse in what it means to people. For some people it's just cultural – women of their family wear it and everyone in their village or town wears it. So it's just something that's expected, not a lot of thought goes into it. And for some people, it's incredibly spiritual, and it's so personal and [a lot of thought goes] into it. Even women who wear hijab, it differs in how they wear it and their philosophies and their theories on it. Even though Islamically there is a core of what hijab [is] … how people interpret it, their idea of modesty differs.'

Silda offered a further consideration: the literal meaning of hijab is protection/barrier, she said. 'So it's as important internally as it is externally.'

'I actually have nightmares where I go out of the house without a hijab. Or I'm butt naked,' confided Ebby.

When I met with Aliya and we dissected the patriarchy of veiling women, in the Arab world in particular, I was fresh off a similar hearty discussion in Dubai, where I had met with two Palestinian women who run a book club together. They were friends, mothers and both working women. Rahmeh and Ghalia were fairly matter-of-fact in how they talked about their lives, including the assumptions made about them, and in particular wearing hijab, which they wore in a trendy way – colourful and fashionable, but modest. They didn't shrink back when challenged on it.

Rahmeh was quietly confident and sweet, declaring, 'Work first, then marriage,' when I asked her how she approached her life. 'I was lucky because my father was really supportive of women ... Since childhood we were playing sport – tennis, karate, swimming. It wasn't unusual [for our circle]. But it's not common across Jordan,' she explained. Both women had lived in Jordan for much of their lives.

At this point Ghalia, similarly soft-spoken, joined in. Though she wasn't exactly shy, she would almost whisper her opinions, as though they were confessions – what she likes and doesn't like – giggling to herself as she went.

'You will reach a point where you are a girl, not a boy,' said Ghalia, meaning the rules for boys and girls are different.

It relates to education, the women told me. But Rahmeh said she's always wanted to challenge society. 'You want to prove to the world that you can do it, and I want to prove to my dad that I can do it.' Her father had faith in Rahmeh and she didn't want to disappoint him.

Still, despite her father's aspirations for her to become a doctor, Rahmeh opted for the new 'fancy thing' in Jordan – IT. Ghalia and Rahmeh met through work, and Ghalia revealed that neither liked IT, which is why they had subsequently transitioned into other careers.

'[In Jordan] we have a lot of women who are educated,' said Ghalia. In Amman, women are given more opportunities and choices, agreed Rahmeh. 'Outside the capital you can see that the women are discriminated against. This is not [so] in the capital. If you want to see the sad stories, these are outside.'

Hijab is not an inhibitor to education or work in Jordan, and in certain places it's as common to see women with hijab as without. It's really the level of modesty that will change: in Amman, and if you want to focus in further, in certain affluent suburbs of Amman, there were many women who don't veil at all. In other areas, longer black veils are common. In more urban areas, hijab tends more towards being on trend.

Hijab turned out to be a central part of my conversation with Rahmeh and Ghalia. They both chose to wear it, an act they acknowledged can be hard. It had taken Ghalia years to work up the courage to adopt it; she had started thinking about it as a teenager. 'I was not able to do it. I felt that whenever I go out from home, everyone will say, "This is Ghalia, she's putting a scarf on."'

Rahmeh explained people might think you're no longer 'cool', a big deal when you're a teenager.

'But when I put it on, no one recognised me, no one cared about me [wearing it],' said Ghalia. She said the greater worry than external judgement was about the hijab changing her lifestyle. As many hijabis will tell you, it's not simply about covering up. It affects all aspects of your life, the activities you undertake. Identifiably Muslim, judgement is easily laid against you however you dress, what you do, how you behave. Rahmeh and Ghalia talked easily about this, but there was a confidence about them. I wondered if it was also because it's easier to wear a scarf in the Arab world. What appeals to them about hijab?

'It's a nice feeling,' said Ghalia, going on to explain that dressing *halal* leaves you free of guilt.

'Another thing, people will start looking into your brains instead of looking at the outside,' said Rahmeh. 'When you sit in a meeting, you're very comfortable that you're discussing purely work. For me, I like that.'

'But you're still attractive,' I said.

Rahmeh looked momentarily ruffled, but it was a light moment as Ghalia giggled. And I wanted to go deeper on that argument: I've heard it so many times – how wearing hijab puts the onus on women to hold off men from objectifying them. Women still get attention when wearing the veil. Even women in shapeless abayas pretty up their outfits by opting for ones with sequins or stitched patterns. Some apply heavy make-up, their veils loose on their heads, leaving space for an ambitious fringe to peek through. I later found out in Jordan that some stores even sell veils with fake fringes attached to them.

'It's stages. For me, the right thing of wearing hijab may be different to this,' Rahmeh said, pointing to how she was dressed. 'We shouldn't put make-up on … But it's steps. On my way to the perfect way of wearing a hijab, I can tolerate this, and on the way I may change.'

'It takes time,' I agreed.

The stages element that Rahmeh talked about made sense. When I adopted hijab, the more devout among my friends were as giddy as bridesmaids at a wedding. I had arrived. I was one of them now. I was cashing in my ticket to greater heavenly rewards (in their eyes, not mine). And, as I came to understand much later when I took it off, I had validated their own lifestyle. But I needed to update my wardrobe. A friend took me shopping to find clothes and I learned quickly that finding skirts and tops that fulfil the modesty requirements of veiling would be more difficult than I thought. This is why so many Muslim women become experts at layering clothing – we're never without a cardigan, and thin singlets to go under a top are a wardrobe staple. Then again, I know women who are completely committed to wearing hijab, but unable to stop dressing as though they weren't covered. The conversion from tight jeans and short tops can be a slow burn.

'People will judge you on the way to you deciding,' said Rahmeh. 'All the way.'

Ghalia said that getting older helps. 'Now I don't care even if anyone tells me this is not hijab, this is hijab,' she said.

And it's not actually about being directed by others – the women said they know they're not wearing hijab 'the right way'. 'I feel it's about behaviour,' said Ghalia. 'It's just that I'm a good Muslim in the end.'

'It's supposed to be difficult,' added Rahmeh. 'It shouldn't be easy.'

Ghalia, sounding frustrated, interrupted. 'It's modern, Islam is modern. *Wallah.* You can choose Islam *mu'assab* [strict] or not.'

Of course, some women I spoke to who wore hijab in Australia and the Arab world either didn't see a need to discuss it at all, or when they did it was to talk about the discrimination they experienced.

'We do face racism. We do, especially the ones who do cover,' said Susan, a social worker and community leader from Brisbane. She said misconceptions surrounded her, especially at university, not only about the hijab she wore but also because she's Arab – everyone thinks that with an Arab husband, you're oppressed. In fact, Susan's Jordanian husband has been a stay-at-home dad.

Before September 11, Susan lived in Redcliff, what she described as a 'red-neck' area of Brisbane. 'I'd just graduated from grade twelve, and I decided to wear the hijab because I did an oral presentation of women's rights, and I was going to bag Islam so much,' she laughed, explaining that she came from a family that was 'very cultured'.

'I did my research and found out ... we actually have a lot of rights. So I did my oral presentation and after that I was like, "That's it, I want to wear it." When I did wear it, and it was literally just myself and my mum in this whole place [Redcliff], you'd get old men take off their hats. You'd get guys you walk past, they're swearing, they'd stop – "Shhh, shhh," you know. The respect was amazing.'

Susan worried her friends at school might shun her, but 'they were so beautiful and respectful,' she said. 'I loved it. After 9/11 and we still live with the times, you see the difference. You see the way people look at you and you see the way people throw remarks. For me, I'm more fearful, not for myself, but for my girls, because they do cover, and they go to uni.'

You're not allowed to have a bad day when you're a Muslim woman in hijab, Susan added. 'Make sure your clothes are clean because the remarks I get from some people is, "You're not like [other] ladies." I'm like, "What's the difference? We look exactly ..." "No, no, you smile. They don't smile."'

Susan admitted it's tiring being so wholly defined by others, and needing to exhibit her Australianness. 'It pisses me off.' Some people don't think she speaks English, for starters. Even at interfaith events, she feels the need to disarm people, telling them, for example, that she went to a local high school to soften their defences and find a point of connection.

'Which is tiring because it's like you're trying to prove "I'm not who you think I am,"' Susan said. 'And it takes a lot of energy. Sometimes you just don't want to do it.'

I recall the frustrations I have felt because of other people's assumptions about me as a Muslim, especially when I wore the hijab. As one friend recently remarked, it's easy to see a woman in hijab and think she has no interests outside of religion, or indeed even in freedom. When I took off the hijab, a co-worker who described herself as agnostic told me that my experience had broadened her perspective on veiling. Seeing that I had struggled with it, mining my own spirituality to make sense of my way of life, had helped her to understand that there was complexity to the experience of being Muslim. In the aftermath of taking off the hijab, I was not interested in validation from others on 'de-jabbing' (the phrase used to describe this act). To this day, I appreciate the nuances of spiritual devotion and how it can play out differently for everyone. But I have witnessed a tendency among Muslim women who don't wear hijab to make assumptions about those who do. A Muslim interviewee in Jordan suggested that she knew what to expect with many of the women she knows who cover. 'It tells you how they think.'

There is some integrity to the idea that Muslim women in hijab see the world in a certain way – to an extent, there will be commonalities. All the same, there is no cookie-cutter Muslim woman.

Hanan, the life coach from Brisbane, wears hijab, and talked about how she's battled with faith and, consequently, wearing the veil.

'I did have my questions ... Big questions. Because one of the things that I really didn't like is [it's like] ... why do you ask a person to go to the gym if another person is fat? That didn't make sense to me. Why am I asked to put a headscarf because another creation that you made ...'

'Can't turn his eyes away?'

'Exactly. That didn't make sense to me.' Hanan remembered the words of a Muslim man, a 'beautiful guy'. 'He said that the purpose of the hijab is for people to see a woman as a person, not as an object, and I loved that. I thought, "I could do with that." And, really, the word hijab, even, became much more than just a headpiece. It became: "How do you present yourself?" I mean, you could have a headpiece on, but you present yourself as someone objectified ...'

Hanan's raw honesty was important. She acknowledged that hijab can be hard, and many women who wear it feel they're constantly required to defend it.

'I want my body to be bathed under the sun on beaches. And this is one of the things I really, really miss. But that's fine, I made a commitment,' she said. 'And I really, really also respect myself and my body, and I feel like it's a way of me going, "You will never see me as an object. I am a person and you will always see me as a person."'

In our dissections on the veil and the intricacy of making that sacrifice (because in many ways, that's what it is), we don't always make room for the sort of complexity Hanan expressed. That it's okay to feel conflicted and still hold true to your faith, because you are tied to a larger purpose. That you can go so far as to take it off entirely and still submit yourself to God.

In Qatar, I met with a feminist named Haya, who was passionate about Islam but also felt comfortable challenging some of the beliefs Muslims usually accept without question. She was dressed in traditional Emirati clothing – a black abaya, a thin veil known as a *shaal*, which sits loosely around the head but does not cover the face. It's not quite like hijab.

'It's only one verse in the Quran,' she said, in reference to the ruling that women must veil. 'There are so many other verses people disregard, or they change to suit their mentality, or how they want it to be, how they want their Islam to look.'

Haya constantly played with her *shaal* while she spoke, adjusting it over and over. 'But this is a *shaal*,' she explained, pointing to her veil. 'Some people say it's hijab, it's culture. It's not in Qatar. It was never in Qatari culture.' It's a recent addition, she argued, and this formed the basis of a research paper she was writing at the time we met.

'My grandmother, to this day, she does not wear the abaya, she does not wear the hijab. She does not. She refuses and she tells my mom and she tells me, "It's not Islam." Abaya ... only came in the 1970s, 1980s.'

Haya cited a protest in Kuwait in the early 1980s that saw women burning their abayas. You won't see a lot of them in Kuwait now, she told me. 'Because they said it's not religion. It's not law, and society accepts [that]. If you want to wear it, you can wear it; if you don't, you don't. Most women don't wear it.'

For many, it's indisputable that veiling is a requirement. What does get dissected is the extent to which it's necessary – what is a woman's *awrah*? She must cover her hair, but what about her face? Her hands? Her feet?

There's no doubt that women's dress can ignite passionate debates among Muslims, and very often men. At uni, before I had adopted hijab, I veiled only for prayer. I remember a Muslim man casually asking me at lunch if I felt bad taking off the veil when I'd completed my prayers. 'Does it feel weird?' he said, feigning curiosity. He was trying to shame me and it was obvious. I can tolerate a lot of things when it comes to discussing women's dress, but the consistent interruption by men in the conversation is not one of them.

But perhaps one of the most defining moments I had wearing hijab in my twenties came at an Islamic camp run by a youth organisation. A friend enticed me to go along with her with promises of endless hours of swimming. (This was before the *burkini* was on the market, though if I'm being honest I doubt I would have worn it even had it been available.)

At the time, I was increasingly behaving like a hermit, something my brother Hossam had even picked up and warned me about. A lot of relationships in my life, once so formative and important to me, had shifted or dissipated entirely, and I wanted to be alone. I wasn't lonely, which was the problem. Anyway, the prospect of this camp – a sleepover in the country – didn't hold a lot of appeal for me. It took a lot of convincing on my friend's part for me to finally relent. (My parents had no problem with it.)

But the camp didn't look how the brochure had sounded. When we arrived, we discovered that women had to have a *mahram* – a male relative as chaperone. I had no one. My friend, who had come with her siblings, including a brother, advised, 'Just tell them you're my sister,' as we drove up to the entrance.

It was a scorching hot day. I remember this clearly because we were baking in our full-length clothing after a long drive. I was looking forward to a swim, so I didn't let the *mahram* issue temper my excitement. However, we hadn't even got to our cabins before we were delivered the news that, because men and women were attending the camp and the pools were all outdoors, women would not be permitted to swim.

I was crushed, and connected to a deep reserve of resentment and anger I didn't know existed in me. As we made our way to our cabin, we passed one of the pools and saw more than a dozen men and their sons there. We stopped and looked longingly towards it. A man, towelling himself off, his son beside him, looked up at us, his face creasing into an expression of what seemed like smug bemusement at the congregation. Something in me changed that day. It didn't feel right or fair, and the complete lack of compassion and empathy towards the females sat heavy on me.

We spent the next few days cycling, kayaking, even horse-riding. But in my mind I was in an entirely new territory. No matter how strict my parents had been, this energy was different. This was a new level of authority and I had difficulty accepting it.

NO POSING

In Dubai, Emiratis stood out for their uniformity: many women wore the long black abaya, draped in either a veil or *shaal* (some wearing niqab); men wore long white robes, and on their heads sat the traditional *hata* with a coiled black rope to keep it in place. Others dressed as they pleased. At Dubai Mall it was common to see women dressed in short skirts. I even saw a woman trail leisurely past in a top that exposed her entire back. No one blinked.

Nevertheless, on a trip to the Sheikh Zayed mosque in Abu Dhabi, I went prepared. It was a typically hot day, even for the end of September, but I dutifully put on a long-sleeved cardigan and wrapped a pink floral shawl around my head upon entering the mosque. I had no qualms covering up, though I ended up wishing I'd dressed lighter.

I walked through the expansive grounds of the mosque, taking in its tall ceilings, elaborate walls and columns, its white space offering sparse relief in the punishing heat. Around me were women in hijab taking selfies, beaming for the camera, their 'camel bumps' protruding beneath colourful headscarves. There were so many Muslims clearly alive to their surroundings, women dressed like they cared about how they looked, not letting modesty requirements diminish their individuality. And there was absolutely nothing remarkable about it. It was just life.

We took a free tour delivered in English, led capably by a young woman named Safa, who had a penetrating gaze, Hollywood make-up and an air of authority. She knew her script by heart, delivering it with an assertiveness that would challenge anyone's perception of the meek, subjugated Arab woman. Her ease extended to male co-workers. For all of the expectations of conservatism in the UAE, men and women were casual in their interactions.

Dressed in traditional black abaya and headscarf, Safa didn't smile except for the occasional joke. She emphasised the now-deceased Sheikh Zayed's goals: to make the UAE a place of peace, tolerance and co-existence. She told us that photos were allowed, except for Sheikh Zayed's tomb, which was enclosed in a small building beside the mosque.

When the tour was over and we were free to look around, Chris took out the camera. I told him to get my best side, lifting an arm up. I was joking, of course. I was more interested in exploring than taking pictures. I didn't get far before a security guard approached Chris and asked him to bring up the photos in the camera.

'Sure. But I've only taken one,' Chris told him, pressing a button to display the album.

The security guard, an expat, stared blankly at the screen then indicated with his hand for Chris to continue scrolling through the photos.

'What exactly are you looking for?' I pressed.

'No posing,' came his reply.

'Pardon?'

'No posing. You were posing.'

It took me a few moments to make sense of what he was saying. I realised he thought Chris was taking glamour-type shots of me. I wanted to laugh. I was dressed in comfortable, loose clothing, baking in a thick black cardigan and draped in a floral scarf that didn't match my clothes. If I was ever going to pose, this wasn't the time for it.

'Obviously I didn't, though, did I? As you can see there are no photos,' I told the guard.

He stepped back and shrugged, looking more amused than stern, then wandered off.

A moment later I saw him wave a woman away from the courtyard, where she stood posing for her companion like she was at a magazine shoot. The women were dressed head-to-toe in black, but I couldn't decipher whether they were visitors to the Middle East wearing borrowed robes, or locals.

I thought of the scandal the pop singer Rihanna had caused a few years back when she visited the region and posed, quite seductively, in niqab. People were understandably offended that she had appropriated a garment that held deep spiritual meaning for many on the one hand, but which was a sign of oppression for some on the other.

We walked off and it wasn't long before we encountered more 'posers'. All around us, women were taking pictures of themselves and each other, a lot of them hijabis, their expressions coy and flirty, their headscarves wrapped around that common 'camel bump' bun, which makes it look like there's a small soccer ball at the back of your head.

It seems many hijabis have no difficulty defining for themselves what constitutes modesty and acceptable behaviour. When I thought of the bored expat guard taking his decree to these vivacious women and wondered what their reactions were, I doubted they'd have been surprised or even rattled. Somehow they make it work, this push-and-pull of being a full-spirited woman in a region that places high expectations and demands on their looks and behaviour.

THE WAR OVER WOMEN'S CLOTHING

When it comes to the veil, women are very often spoken about as though they are bystanders of, rather than the main characters in, their own lives. Certainly the influence of patriarchal systems colours the subject, but the fact that many men actively promote the hijab is not a reason for a woman to disown her own decision about wearing it, and it's all too easy to underestimate just how thoughtful discussion around the veil is among women in the Middle East and Australia.

Hijab is, and has always been, a hot topic. Feelings around it are strong. In most cases, the women I spoke to had a clear perspective on it. Some expressed concerns about the rise of veiling. Curiously, it was most often the women who don't wear a veil of any kind, either by personal conviction or because they're not Muslim, who were fixed on it as a subject of discussion.

This became most apparent during a roundtable at the Australian Embassy in Amman, Jordan, arranged tirelessly by my contact there, Manal, with a local activist named Lara, raised in England but now settled in Jordan. Lara launched the first Jordanian Arabic independent newspaper, *Alghad*, whose website was award-winning, even though she said her 'Arabic sucked'.

They invited to the roundtable women who were carving innovative pathways in the Arab world. Manal and Lara had approached more than fifteen women with diverse backgrounds. Of those who attended, some were Muslim but none of them veiled. Lina Hundaileh recounted an inspiring journey into becoming a successful chocolate manufacturer and mentoring others in business. Reem Aslan worked for the International Labour Organization and was spearheading the payment of fair wages in private schools. She's a women's rights activist, with a focus on labour rights. Rana Husseini was also present, a highly regarded Jordanian journalist and a gender expert, who has spent the better part of her career documenting and writing about so-called honour killings.

Rana is a charming woman with an athletic build and larger-than-life personality. She loves sports. She had just returned from Thailand, where she'd been heading an under-sixteen female football team. There are around four hundred female football players in Jordan. She was another to describe herself as 'not a typical Arab woman'.

'I'm a very practical woman. With all respect, I'm not saying I'm right, but I've always lived the practical life and this is not acceptable in this part of the world. Even regular people [say], "Oh, you don't wear dresses, you don't wear make-up."'

'How does that judgement affect you?' I said. Other people's preoccupation with appearance is rarely just about covering up; it's about being feminine, too. 'Does it hurt at all?'

'It used to hurt but eventually – *tamahat* – I don't know how you say ... I became like a crocodile.'

'*Tamsahat!*' one of the women laughed.

116

Rana laughed. 'I crocodiled!'

We all laughed. 'So thick-skinned?' I said.

'Exactly, thick-skinned,' interjected Reem.

Earlier Rana had pointed out something more worrying than the many accusations regularly thrown her way as an activist for women. 'I don't know if you ladies experience it, [but] I go places and immediately they think that I'm foreign. So if I'm not covered, this means I'm foreign or a Christian,' she said. 'The perception is that you're either Muslim and you're covered, or you are a Christian, or you are a loose woman.'

Rana raised the lack of solidarity she's seen at times among feminists, who, she said, are all pretty much against her. 'If you don't talk in a certain way that people believe in, then you are rubbish.'

'In the past it was competition among women as well,' Reem later pointed out.

'Competition and jealousy, I don't want to tell you,' agreed Rana.

I mentioned I'd experienced a taste of this when I wrote a couple of years earlier about taking off the hijab. The women seemed startled – intrigued, perhaps.

'Well, that's interesting,' said Lara, who was beside me at the table. Her face lit up. 'Now we're talking.'

'Were you forced [to wear it]?' Rana asked.

'No,' I said.

My parents were strict, I explained. 'You don't know how to be yourself anymore. So I put on the hijab because I felt really safe in it. It helped me hide from the world, then one day I realised I was over it, this isn't who I am. It lost its meaning. It wasn't even like, "I feel guilty that I'm wearing something that doesn't mean anything." I just felt suffocated. And you're not allowed to say that. Because if you say that, you're saying Islam is wrong. That's how they hear it.'

I told them about the fall-out from an article I'd written about my experience. How I had become *persona non grata* among local Muslims because, with only a handful of Muslim people in the media in Australia, they wanted you to be someone they could agree with all the time. 'When I wrote about things they could agree with, they loved me. The minute I said something they didn't like, it was like, "You're not Muslim."'

'The problem is it's a tangible thing,' offered Lara. 'People could see it, they could touch it.'

I told them how an anonymous person had written to me to ask if I felt bad 'leaving Islam', something I never declared, after I'd hosted a panel event for an Arab–Islamic organisation. It was a strange email in which this person claimed his sister was a long-time fan of my writing, and that she was crushed to discover I had taken off the hijab – an odd claim given my mainstream writing career only really began after I had stopped covering my hair. He seemed to assume, incorrectly, that my feelings about myself relied on others' perceptions of right and wrong.

'Wow, as if the cover is the only thing that matters,' said Reem.

Lara spoke up, saying that, as a Greek Orthodox Arab Christian living in a Muslim country, she didn't feel intimidated. What media and pop culture portray about Arab society, and women in particular, 'is not what we live'. 'Just recently, in the last five years, it's taking a different toll,' she said. 'There's a new trend that women are letting go of religion, or this visual of hijab.'

Reem said she's had the opposite experience. She went to a missionary Christian girls' school. Around twelve of the women who were in her grade are now covered. But her mother-in-law, who is in her eighties, doesn't wear it, even though she's a practising Muslim. 'Older women think we're going backwards, because the hijab doesn't mean anything.'

It was an interesting point. As Haya, the feminist I met with in Qatar, pointed out, many of our mothers never veiled until it started to trend. My mother once wore skirts and dresses that were even shorter than the ones Anglo women around her wore; things she never would have allowed me to wear at the same age. In her youth, Muslim women didn't wear hijab. Veiling wasn't a 'thing'. But in the seventies, she adopted her form of veiling, that gypsy-style headscarf.

Lara said that when they were younger her mother and her friends would wear revealing clothes, but if they saw an uncle in the street, they wouldn't say hello to him. She looked thoughtful. 'I'd wear shorts, but not to the supermarket.'

Rana pointed out that in the eighties wearing hijab wasn't common. 'We used to go, "Oh, wow, she's wearing hijab."'

She suggested there are a few reasons for its rise: the Iranian Revolution; the rise of the Muslim Brotherhood in Egypt; and Saudi Arabia paying mosques to run religious classes.

'In Jordan, there were several families – girls from rich families – who were giving religious classes. Originally Syrians. And people are so stupid who used to go – I'm sorry, with all due respect – they would talk to them and then they would tell them, "Oh, you have to wear the hijab," and then they tell them, "My hijab is the right one so you have to buy from me." If I went to a religious class and somebody told me that, I would tell her to go to hell, and leave.'

Reem said she went to one of these classes when she was younger. She wanted to learn more about religion, because she wasn't taught about it in school, so she went with a colleague who wasn't covered at the time.

'The first class was fine. They usually have gatherings in a house and, again, it was a Syrian family. Anyway, so I went. Very nice women. Most of them are covered, but that's fine; I went for a purpose, to learn about Quran. Then the second class I went there and they were telling me, "You know, you're our sister in Islam, you need to cover yourself, blah blah blah."'

A cacophony of jokes about making a swift exit followed Reem's story. 'Exactly,' said Reem. 'See ya!'

I told them about a man who had approached me and my friends at university to tell us to spend a bit of money on hijab, as though money was the thing holding us back. But Rana said it's relevant in the Arab world. 'Some women [veil] for economic reasons. It's cheaper. You wear the same *jilbab* [robe], who cares? It's like a uniform. And some women wear it and go to religious classes because her chances of getting married will increase. Because women will see her there and they will tell their brothers, "Oh, this woman is good, she's coming to religious classes, she's covered, marry her." This is what happens.'

Reem agreed, adding that when she was at university in the eighties, many wore hijab for financial reasons. Rana said one of the leading Arabic newspapers once even led a campaign to cover women. 'Donate a *jilbab* and we'll give two *jilbabs* for somebody.'

'This was a newspaper?' I said in shock.

'A newspaper, yes, in Jordan.' She wouldn't say on the record which one. The campaign had been initiated by a government ministry and the newspaper was very vocal about it. 'These places selling hijab you never saw in Jordan. All of a sudden you started having all this. With all due respect, if somebody is really doing it for conviction, fine, good for them.'

'It should be a choice,' said Reem.

'It should be a choice,' agreed Rana. 'But they either force you – I have known several women who were forced, and ... they're afraid to take it off now. I have two who worked with me at the newspaper. Their father forced them to wear it.'

Beside me, Lara asked if I was afraid the first day I left the house without the scarf on.

'I felt exposed, not naked. I felt weird. I could feel the wind blowing against my hair, and I'd forgotten what that feels like.'

Manal expressed curiosity about the level of discomfort around hijab.

'What makes you so uncomfortable?'

Manal said her mother is Muslim and her father is Christian; her mother insisted she'd never wear it. For her mother it was a symbol of oppression and not the thing that identified her. 'Why have we spent ten minutes talking about it?'

'Because it's a symbol,' said Reem. 'It's not part of the religion, in my opinion.' She said she'd watched a television program in which a scholar had declared there is nothing in the Quran or Islamic religion that says you have to wear the hijab. This man had told his daughter and daughter-in-law to take it off. 'He kept forcing the family members to take it off. And to me, my classmates, when you dig deeper, our way of thinking is different. When we chat on Whatsapp, there is something that became a bit different in our way of thinking.'

We're tribal. It's that simple and that complex. When you wear hijab, you can self-censor; sometimes you don't feel you can be completely free, aware that your actions are amplified, for better or worse, because you are visibly Muslim.

A common example is the mindfulness you have about committing a sin in public – playing music in your car (the music being *haram*, not the driving); modesty levels in how you dress is a more obvious one. And not surprisingly, you find it easiest to be among women who dress and behave like you, or at least feel the same pressure to do so. 'I always felt like I was outside of myself, I wasn't inside,' I said.

'Interesting,' said Reem.

But I cautioned against making too many assumptions about women in hijab.

Rana interjected: 'My problem with this issue, all in all, is that people are connecting Islam to hijab as if Islam is only hijab. And, you know, when I started working for the *Jordan Times*, I had some people – not journalists, typesetters – and they come from a lower class, and a few months after working [they asked me], "Ah, why don't you wear the hijab?" The first time I ignored it. Then after two years, "Ah, why don't you wear the hijab?"

'Then four years ago, this one guy says, "You know, Rana, everything is so good about you. What's only left is for you to wear the hijab. So I told him, "Excuse me, I want to ask you something: is Islam only about hijab? Why don't you talk to me about treatment, good manners, to be good at my job, to be honest at my job? Islam is not only about hijab." That's it,' she said, wiping her hands together. 'He never talked to me again about hijab.'

Rana's story didn't surprise me. I'd witnessed similar ideas infiltrate the lives of women around me in the past – hijab is not personal to the woman, it's a subject on which everyone has a say; it's a symbol that must be upheld, often to the isolation of other life factors. As a result, some people – men and women – fearful of rejection, become too wedded to the practice of veiling, which inhibits thinking around it.

Hearing these women speak at length about something they have chosen not to adopt, or have not needed to consider, hijab grew into a spectacle of sorts, though a respectable one. It was a ball being tossed around, but in the Middle East the narratives held greater meaning, its effects on women in general being potentially more damaging, or at least influential, than in the West, where women in hijab are a minority and often make the decision to veil without pressure. What was confirmed for me at the roundtable was the undue pressure society has on a woman's basic right to choose how she presents herself to the world.

Rana offered a final declaration on why women wear hijab: 'Marriage. Being a good girl. Wanting to learn more about the religion.'

WAS IT SOMETHING I SAID?

When I first began to write confessional pieces in the media, I learned quickly that difference 'sells'. In Australia, the transition from acknowledging the mysterious 'other' to accepting diversity has been wobbly – either it's met with great resistance to the idea of 'pandering to' minorities, or it's overblown in its acceptance. We're not yet at a point of effortless diversity.

In my case, growing up Arab Muslim in the West gave me a lot of mileage. I exhausted years of experiences pretty quickly when I wrote columns for a few online websites. I didn't do this to capitalise on my life; I was writing what I knew, as writers do. Muslim 'dating' – all based on true experiences – filled more than a column or two; it was also the basis of my first novel, and led eventually into the second. Teetotalling came next: how to survive being a non-drinker in a culture that celebrates alcohol, and being in a profession that practically has it as a leitmotif.

But the big one, for me, was writing about taking off the hijab. How to deal with such a sensitive subject, which matters more to Muslim women than general Australian society? How to write about it without seeming like a sell-out who's airing dirty laundry?

I did so only when I was truly ready. I stripped away my fears about discussing such a sensitive subject. Women, the subject of so many interrogations in life – always being told how to dress, how to behave, how to live. I understood that no matter how I dealt with it, I would be regarded by many as a traitor to the religion.

When I wrote about it for Fairfax's feminist website *Daily Life* it had been three years since I'd taken off the headscarf. I felt I could put into words some of the mental conflict I'd experienced when I was trying to decide if I should remain in hijab so clearly feeling no connection to it. I wasn't wearing it 'correctly'; the scarves had got shorter and once I was mistaken for an Orthodox Jew in Sydney's eastern suburbs.

It was an apt time for my piece as the Powerhouse Museum was launching an exhibition called 'Faith, Fashion, Fusion', which put on colourful display the fashionable and unique ways Muslim women dress in line with modesty. I was disturbed but not surprised by the amount of criticism the exhibition was already attracting from Muslims, both men and women. The comments online ranged from the sin of dressing to attract, to the fact that such an exhibition existed: who exactly did Muslims need to please?

When my article was published, no one cared that I'd written it in support of women who, like me, have experienced a lifetime of challenging relationships to one's body, while also dealing with appearance and modesty. Nasty comments were shared liberally in Facebook groups. I was swiftly condemned. People I had once been friends with inserted themselves into the story, rejecting my version of events despite there being no mention of them in the piece. One, a high-profile Muslim woman, conservative in dress, outspoken on social media, a 'community leader' to many Muslims, was a conduit for the negative reactions. She encouraged me to come onto a thread to 'defend' myself against my critics, but I had no intention of defending myself. I had spoken my truth and had faith that not only had I done it respectfully and in a balanced manner – I'm still a Muslim, after all – but also that I'd done so because I wanted to throw light on to an area of darkness for many women I knew who struggled with the hijab and the weight of expectations of modesty.

My inbox had more private messages of gratitude and appreciation than hate. But that people wrote privately to me said a lot: more than one said she wasn't willing to express her thoughts in public because she knew her sentiments wouldn't be met with understanding. Another woman commended my 'courage' in speaking about it, saying she herself could never do it. One message even came from a young man who thanked me for offering insight into what his sister went through.

On my own Facebook page, I had a few messages of support when I caved and wrote about the abuse I was getting. One person I had considered a friend told me I should have expected it. I was being harassed by a Muslim man, who went so far as to hint in a Muslim youth group on Facebook that he'd like to shoot me with a golden gun. He did it in a roundabout way, his tone mocking but threatening. On my public thread, he warned me that he would let me get away with talking about hijab this time but I shouldn't do it again. I sensed that he was young and obsessed with the behaviour of others rather than invested in his own.

My brother Hossam attempted to be a voice of reason. On a thread that was descending into a cloud of negativity on my Facebook page, he wrote, 'The majority of Western society assumes that Muslim women are forced to wear a hijab against their own will and this stereotype reinforces the obscured image that Muslim women are oppressed. It takes a lot of courage to wear a hijab in a Western society and just as much courage to not wear a hijab in the eyes of the Muslim community.'

Of course, the piece triggered strong negative reactions from men, who projected back to me their 'battles' with the beard. It's not that I discounted the significance of having a beard for a man – particularly given this was pre-hipster days when beards became fashionable – but the comments were dripping with sarcasm. They implied that I'm a bad Muslim because I couldn't stick it out. Attitudes like that reveal a deep insecurity in many people when it comes to their own faith. Religious bullies are hardly a new phenomenon, but in the online stratosphere they're certainly a rising one.

I really began to understand the damage fear can do, especially in a crowd.

One of the biggest sources of conflict when it comes to hijab is not purely whether or not it's *fard* (compulsory), but, in light of that debate, the use of the word 'choice' in relation to it. *Is* it still a choice, for example, when many scholars say women are obligated to wear it?

It's all a matter of personal opinion, of course.

With the *Daily Life* piece, I was ambitious. I wanted to convey a lot but didn't have a great deal of space to do so. And writing it for a mainstream audience relieved me of the need to offer conclusions from an academic perspective. This was confessional writing at its most personal.

The only aspect over which I was slightly adventurous was my suggestion that, regardless of the word of scholars who say veiling is – in some way – compulsory, many Muslim women do ultimately have a choice. 'Choice' is such a loaded concept – not even merely a word – when it comes to religion, but to me many of us do have a choice, even if it's in the acceptance, rejection, or indifference to a religious obligation.

Mona Eltahawy, a feminist writer of Egyptian heritage, has been outspoken on the subject of hijab, writing about her experiences once wearing it and her later rejection of it. In her book *Headscarves and Hymens* she makes an interesting point about 'choice'. She convinced herself that she had chosen to wear hijab, and continued to hold true to this idea, even though she began to find it suffocating and felt pressure from family to continue wearing it. Then an Egyptian feminist accused her of pushing back the cause. Eltahawy in turn pushed back, denying that was the case because her veiling was a choice. But when a man observed that her hijab made her marriageable, she did a one-eighty. 'Then I understood ... that I wasn't the Hijab Poster Girl I thought I was. I was just a hijab.'

Mona relayed the immense guilt she felt for years for taking off hijab, and her attempt to assuage it by remaining modest. She seems less conflicted now, critical of the Muslim mansplaining that occurs around hijab, and positing, somewhat controversially, a belief that niqab, in concealing a woman's face, erases her as a person.

I think hijab is a personal choice, but the sometimes-glib dismissals of concern about choice by Muslim women who have the ability to actually choose – particularly in the West – and by left-leaning liberals interested in supporting minorities, are not helpful. It's clearly not a choice for many women in certain parts of the world; nor, depending on whose opinions you subscribe to, is choice really a significant factor when it comes to being an obedient Muslim woman. Some of this does stem from the attacks on veiling by feminists, and the West. This is most insidious when hijabis are used as pawns in public battles. Take, for instance, an example with which Shakira Hussein opens her book *From Victims to Suspects: Muslim Women Since 9/11*: Oprah Winfrey, before a crowd of 18,000, unveils a woman in burqa in a highly charged moment that came to symbolise a persistent motif – that of the Western woman saving the oppressed Muslim woman. Despite being viewed as helpless, the burqa-clad woman, a member of the Revolutionary Association of the Women of Afghanistan, gave a speech about oppression under the Taliban. Hussein goes on to talk about a photo of another woman swathed in black, which was seized upon by right-wingers, who used her image to terrify people into believing she was a security threat. In fact, she was an Afghan police woman.

'How has the woman beneath the burqa been transformed from a helpless victim unable to cast off her own shroud into a menacing terrorist who must be brought under control "for security reasons"?' asks Hussein.

There are numerous examples of women's rights being invoked when discriminating against Arabs, and particularly

Muslims. Racism disguised as concern is a common occurrence in Australia. When people attack Islam, they inevitably suggest it's because of how it views women. In arguments against Islam or Muslim women who defend the religion's perspectives on women, it's not long before women are asked: 'But what about your rights?'

Regardless of the noise around veiling, it is the woman wearing it who bears the brunt of censure, and women who wore hijab then took it off will tell you the latter is more difficult than the former. I found this to be true. I felt like I was going to disappoint people. In the process of shedding the garment, I was going to lose friends.

But I wanted to be anonymous again; to blend in. I wanted to be a blank slate in my professional life, too, and not have CEOs stare at me for a few seconds before warming up. But in all of that was a succinct and simple desire to be myself and to do so honestly – I just wasn't that 'religious' anymore.

In what should be news to nobody, not wanting to wear a headscarf doesn't mean you have no faith, that you hate religion, that you have a desire to burn in hell, or that you are a traitor. Hijab is a personal act of faith, not a communal one.

Much of the rhetoric around women and the veil – it's rarely a conversation – reduces the experience of covering your hair and your body to simple platitudes of right and wrong. If it's not men telling us that good Muslimas should wear hijab, we're fighting the censure of feminists who are telling us we're oppressed in doing so. As I've been told in conversations with other women, anyone who chooses to cover up 'just doesn't know any better'.

And in the Middle East it was abundantly clear that Arab women can get as passionate or as pissed off about the issue as anyone. The difference between their anger and the anger of someone not affected by veiling is that it has a huge bearing on them how hijab – or women's modesty in general – evolves in society. The conversations I had with these women showed me that, even if they don't agree on the necessity or purity of veiling, nor always easily accept it, it's clear that the matter is not one that can be simplified.

ONE DAY, LOVE (AND SEX)

Sexual attitudes and behaviors are intimately bound up in
religion, tradition, culture, politics, and economics.

Shereen El Feki, *Sex and the Citadel: Intimate Life in a
Changing Arab World*

As Arab females, many of us grow up knowing that we have to behave a certain way with the opposite sex. Guys do as well, but the rules for them are more malleable. Quite simply, the burden of shame is placed on us.

Forget dating or romantic courtships. As girls, we had our own version of these to one day look forward to – a respectful, more cautious process that involves family. At eighteen, I began to meet suitors in my living room on awkward visits that ended in disappointment or, eventually, indifference and boredom.

All of this shapes not only how young Arab girls view and feel about sex, but also how we engage in relationships, friendly or romantic. No one teaches you to hate men or be afraid of loving someone from the opposite sex. Interaction between the sexes is simply draped in limiting, hushed ideas of what is proper; everything is okay when you're married and only when you're married. So in the end many of us explore romantic longings or just plain old sexual urges in a parallel world, often hidden.

THE BIRDS AND THE BEES

When I was young and impressionable, my understanding of love, romance and sex was shaped by various sources. These included, in no particular order, Hollywood, and romance books I read secretly between feel-good, age-appropriate R. L. Stine horror novels. I read voraciously, and often above my prescribed age group. When I told my Year 7 English teacher that I'd enjoyed *The Accidental Tourist*, she stared down at me with a look of amusement and pondered out loud whether I was mature enough to appreciate its nuances. I was a little discouraged, but I felt sure I had understood the book well enough.

What I couldn't learn from books or people, I could glean from the occasional peek into women's magazines and late-night movies on SBS. My mother was never going to pull me aside for a 'talk' like you see in American sitcoms. I didn't even tell her when they started to teach us about sex and masturbation at school (in Year 8, for the record). If we were watching television as a family and the couple onscreen so much as looked at each other with intense longing, the discomfort would be palpable and someone would have to change the channel.

My vision of love in the Arab world (including Arabs in the diaspora) was reinforced by what I saw of couples in their wedding videos. These were popular – it wasn't unusual to watch the wedding of complete strangers if you knew someone in common. Every wedding put a happy couple on display. A beaming bride, a groom with a smile so wide it looked like he'd slept with a coat hanger in his mouth. There was smoke, an unusually large cake that would be cut with an elaborate sword, and a slow dance to an American ballad ('Tonight, I Celebrate My Love' was a resounding hit at weddings in the eighties).

This suggested to me that Arabs weren't completely shy about romance, but it was always a very discreet form of love that was demonstrated. No kisses on the lips, only on the forehead. The couple might hold hands the entire night, but there was restraint in their affection.

This syrupy offering eventually clashed with other stories I heard. While I wasn't naïve about sex, nor completely lacking access to information about what it involved, my understanding was clouded by anecdotes of poor unsuspecting brides who had no idea what awaited them in the marital bedroom. These were uncomfortably juxtaposed beside the romantic vision of relationships and intimacy offered by fiction, pop's latest heart-throbs and those wedding videos.

The tradition, I gathered after hearing many tales, was that mothers and aunts pulled the bride aside the night before the wedding, waxed her until she was bare, and explained – potentially with the use of phallic-shaped vegetables – what was going to occur with her husband after the drumming and dancing had stopped. I have never forgotten one person telling me the sorts of things being advised, including, 'If he asks you to spread your legs wider, spread them wider.'

In hindsight, I don't know how much of this was old wives' tales. The stories were all very hushed and conspiratorial, retold with a flourish to emphasise that not all was as it seemed. After all, most girls aren't afraid of sex – we all think it's going to be fabulous and romantic – but you could certainly learn to be afraid of men.

I remember with great clarity a visit to family friends with my parents when I was around ten years old that gave me early exposure to what happens when real life turns dark. I got along with one of the daughters, who was around my age. They had other guests over, including an Arab couple who were completely mismatched. She was young, pretty and had recently arrived in the country. Her husband, too, was an immigrant, but much older and less friendly.

On this visit, my friend and I went off to play. At one point she leaned over, a wisdom in her expression belying her years. 'See that woman in there?' she said, indicating to the door of her room. 'I feel so sorry for her. She hates her husband. I heard her telling my mum that she doesn't like having sex with him because he doesn't care about her when they do it.'

Wide-eyed I listened, intrigued and inexplicably sad. 'What do you mean?'

'She said she just lies there and can't wait for it to be over.'

I was scarred a little. Suddenly the poetic Arabic love songs and wedding videos depicting impossibly happy couples were not to be believed.

While I had evidence of seemingly content couples around me, my parents included, they didn't exhibit affection the way my Anglo friends' parents did. I nearly fell over when my best friend's mother and father made up in front of me and their kids after a fight with a playful series of kisses on the lips. That stuff happened in the real world, not just on television?

The fact that romantic interaction with men, let alone actual sex, must occur within certain confines (marriage) did add a layer of excitement when I was young, because I'd been raised on fairytales and idealised princes who would sweep me away one day to a land where curfews were non-existent and no one would ever say 'haram' or 'ayb'. It also created a sense of forbidden longing. The downside was that any intimacy or sexual act outside of marriage, and perhaps even thoughts of them, was considered shameful.

*

As I got older, I gradually shed the instinctive ease I'd had around boys: I went to a public school until I was twelve and grew up the only girl among four boys, so for a long time I didn't see them in any special light. Eventually I would; for many of us, dealing with the opposite sex was fraught with challenges.

'This is one of my favourite topics,' guffawed Shadia*, a Melbourne woman of Arab heritage. 'This is something that I've always found really interesting. As a kid, I was petrified of boys, like cripplingly petrified of boys. I couldn't bear talking to them, I would stutter, I would blush. I thought, "You can't just talk to boys, they're just scary and they all want to rape you."'

Shadia attended public schools until about Year 9. She was a tomboy in primary school and was also shy; she didn't feel the need to interact with boys. Her parents also warned her against playing with them. 'I wasn't allowed to have any male friends. No mixed parties. I went to one mixed party in grade six and I didn't tell my dad it was mixed, and then he came back an hour later and dragged me out.' She broke out into laughter again but admitted it was scarring as a kid.

From Year 6, I went to a girls' school, had little interaction with guys and later grew fearful of being caught even looking at one. This was a far cry from Arab girls I knew who lived in the Western suburbs and had a stronger cultural congregation. They secretly dated boys, unperturbed by the need to hide these relationships from their Muslim parents. I was a little in awe of them.

Shadia spent a few years at an all-girls' school but she also attended an Islamic school, which she described as having a complicated environment. It was co-ed but the playground was segregated and it was *haram* to talk to boys. Despite this, boys and girls did interact, but Shadia said she 'was so scared' of the boys, teenagers by then who could be 'little shits'.

'At the time, to learn to overcome my fear of talking to them, I would watch the flirty girls and then mimic. I'd be like, "How do they do it? Why are they so confident? What do they say when they talk to boys?" It was a terrible way to learn but I saw no other role model who was teaching me how to talk to the opposite sex,' said Shadia.

It would be easy to assume strictness between the sexes is the result of Islam's influence, but, as we've discussed, Arab countries are conservative in general so it's not unusual for Christian families to be as restrained when it comes to dating and sexuality. I know and have spoken to women of all religious backgrounds who dated on the quiet and even lost their virginity outside of marriage. Similarly, there are women who will wait because they adhere to traditions or religious scripture. Then, of course, there are people who get married but it's unspoken that they have been secretly dating for ages – accepted, but still hushed.

Though guilt may plague a woman for bending the rules of her family, natural desires may outweigh the demands of culture. It's a strange kind of 'normal' that gets easier, though it is always burdensome.

DOOR-KNOCK APPEALS AND THE DREAM OF LOVE

Even though growing up under strict rules was extremely difficult and isolating at times, I see now how much my parents did to keep me safe. They scrutinised every man who came for a suitor visit, an awkward ritual I called 'door-knock appeals'.

My father never tired of instilling in me the importance of a good education. Sending me to a private school came at great expense to my parents when it wasn't raining money. My father urged me into a law degree because he never wanted me to be reliant on anyone, especially not a man who could turn out to be a bad egg. Or, in Dad's case, a bad apple: 'Men are like fruit,' he'd tell me, every time a suitor was going to visit. On one occasion, we were in the kitchen so he held up an actual piece of fruit to demonstrate cracking it open. 'You don't know if it's rotten inside.'

My parents were, for the most part, discerning when it came to potential husbands. They never let anyone past our front door until I was at university, and even then nothing was ever forced upon me. They always simply asked, listing the man's credentials like a shopping list of positive attributes. I could say yes or no to meeting him. I usually said yes.

Mum did not make it easy on suitors. In hindsight, I kind of feel sorry for those guys – they never stood a chance. She rarely liked anyone because, with a keen intuition, she could detect insincerity or hidden agendas.

At one point I really liked suitor visits. Now the idea of them appalls me. I cringe thinking of the awkward banter, the audition process of serving tea and coffee. But I was young, shy around guys and not free to date whoever I wanted (and frankly, I wanted to date Brendan Fraser and, later, Richard Armitage). So when guys came around, it seemed exciting and as close to dating as I could imagine. And of course, the bonus was that if I had zero interest in the guy (this happened 95 per cent of the time), the refusal came directly from my mum and dad, and I never had to see him again. The downside was that inevitably at the first meeting all parents/guardians/supporters would sit with us, which, coupled with the requirement that I serve tea and fruit and sweets, made me very self-conscious. And probably aloof: to be too friendly wasn't a good idea as I knew it could be construed as flirting.

One man who had been particularly keen put me off with his cockiness. He'd been engaged a couple of times before and divulged at our meeting that he had asked a mutual acquaintance about me at university. This wasn't a reasonable enquiry about whether I was a nice, polite person who didn't walk around with parsley in her teeth. He wanted an assurance that I was a Good Arab Muslim Girl. He had asked a guy I barely knew, who apparently gave me the tick of approval. This suitor thought it was a good joke because I had passed the enquiry test, but I was completely turned off him.

By the time I was in my thirties, living out of home, my parents were flippantly suggesting that I was better off not getting married. Those in my generation who had married young were mothers now, juggling the demands of kids and work, and it wasn't easy. In fact, a lot changed in my thirties. Increasingly independent, travelling more and growing career-wise, I started to work on me. I didn't become hardened and resistant to love; it just didn't hold the same meaning for me. It was a part of my journey, not a destination.

I asked a much younger Arab–Australian Muslim woman about all of this, curious about whether suitor visits have sustained their relevance. Sara* is in her mid-twenties and single, still at home but without a shred of discomfort about it. Her Muslim family is not big on practice, but recognises Islam; her parents can be conservative but they're not bullish in placing restrictions.

I asked her if she ever had suitors coming to her door. She said she didn't, nor did many women around her. Only a cousin of hers had met her husband in the living room. She said her father wants her to get to know someone and pick him herself, not for them to choose someone for her.

On reflection, this wasn't a huge surprise. The longer I was single, the more feasible the idea of bringing a man to my parents became. This is how I first got engaged in my late twenties – a meeting through friends. However, rules remained firmly in place. I wasn't dating freely. At one point, following a string of failed suitor meetings, my father even queried me about online 'dating', something that he never would have approved of years before.

But Sara didn't seem super-keen on dating for the sake of it. The one boyfriend she had lasted a month – 'I thought he was a nice guy but it turned out he wasn't.'

While many of us aren't subject to huge pressure in the living room dating scene, for others the demand from parents to get married young can be far stronger. Kholoud, a woman who'd immigrated to Australia as a child, told me she was never interested in getting married when she was younger, let alone dating. 'I was interested in myself. I wanted to go out. I wanted to see the world.'

Kholoud fought for her education, railing against 'cultural' restrictions, but in her late twenties did succumb to pressure to get married. She wasn't even sure of the number of proposals her father had received for her. But the spectre of being an 'old maid' hung heavy above her. Her marriage to a man who was raised overseas but had moved to Australia didn't last. Despite the support of her family and community, getting a divorce proved traumatic because the man didn't want to grant one to her.

Kholoud said there's no regret because she is a mother of her beautiful children. 'Everything happens for a reason. I don't sit there and feel sorry for myself and I don't sit there and say, "Oh, why did I marry him?" – this and that. I've moved on. I moved on when I was married to him, actually.'

Many women I spoke to have emerged from a conservative childhood intact; others not so well. Some were single and others married. Some were happy in their relationships, so there was nothing to discuss. It just showed in how they talked about their relationships – your everyday couple stuff. Others were not in balanced relationships and this was always raised.

Meanwhile, regardless of religious background, parents were often central players when it came to marriage.

Like any kind of analysis on a group of women, there was a vast spectrum of experiences and beliefs about love, dating, marriage and sex. Some women drew me in with their recollections of past loves and tragedy. I found that women in their fifties and above had more romantic stories to tell. Loves lost and found; romantic, political idealism threaded throughout their experiences. How much of this stems from generational differences versus lived experience, I can't definitely conclude. But courting in the fifties and sixties was a vastly different proposition.

Take Chadia, a charming Lebanese woman, and a natural storyteller, who narrated a life rich in experiences – widowed at thirty, she eventually remarried. She languidly recalled growing up in Beirut when the only access to males was through school – so they crushed on their teachers. 'We never spoke about boys or sexuality or anything else. What we spoke about, at that time, was, which book did we read? Which music do we like? You know, and the only masculine figure we were exposed to were the teachers. You can imagine that all the teachers ... we all fell in love with them.'

Chadia said she was drawn to study French and comparative literature not only because she likes both Arabic and French literature, but because both teachers were excellent at their jobs.

'They had the personality, the charisma, the presence ... and they used to create dreams for us. I remember our teacher used to walk into the class ... and create some kind of romantic atmosphere and recite poems for us. He said, poetry, it's a voyage into space. He used to create for us this kind of escape behind the walls, you know? Going somewhere else. Where we can feel free and happy.'

Elsewhere I heard other complex tales: there were women who had married outside of their parents' expectations: to non-Arabs whose families' cultures at a cosmetic level differed wildly at times from that of Arabs; to men who weren't born Muslim. A Jordanian-Christian woman I met in Amman had chosen her family over love. She had fallen deeply for a black man from the US, and she knew her parents would have a difficult time accepting it. Racism is rife in the Arab world, with fair skin favoured over dark in many parts. This woman and her partner had broken up and then reunited numerous times. But she has a strong relationship with her parents and while she believed they would eventually come around to an inter-racial marriage, in the end she thought the road to such a destination would be paved with too much pain. In her eyes, it just wasn't worth it.

Her story was touching for many reasons, but what I found particularly moving was her love of her family. For this woman, trying to undo years of thinking would cause her parents hurt. She didn't express anger at their conservativism. Things just aren't that simple.

There were women who were content in being single, in no rush to partner with someone for the sake of it. Haya, the feminist from Qatar, said she had no interest in dating or marriage, and Hanan, a Palestinian woman who has lived in Jerusalem for most of her life, credits her parents as being exceptional: 'They raised me to be independent and they don't get into my business. They are very supportive, never tell us what to do, they are there to help; dream parents. They don't let family say anything.'

Hanan was raised in a Catholic village by nuns ('That's probably why I don't believe in God,' she quipped), and isn't sure if she wants to get married. 'I'm living my life.' But she has been in love, several times, including two serious relationships that lasted four years each. 'Each time I was like, "Thank God I didn't get married!" I can't believe I fell in love with that idiot.'

Some women talked openly about marriages that ended in divorce. There was Naajideh* from Jordan, who had decided to exit a marriage because she, quite simply, had got married under pressure to a man she didn't love and she now wanted her freedom; and Kholoud from Brisbane, who now counsels other women facing similar domestic challenges.

And then there's Jamila*, the Sydney woman in her thirties who spoke of her adolescent love for New Kids on the Block. She got married and divorced in her twenties. She grew up observing the double standard when it came to how boys could behave. 'But I just thought it was normal,' she admitted.

It was after her divorce, when she went back to her parents' home, that she began to question the norm. 'It was only then I realised, "Hold on, I'm the one with the secure job, with my own money, with the car and everything, and I'm worried about going out, even at twenty-four, for dinner with my friends."'

Jamila now lives alone, but she was frustrated to have to return to her parents' home like a little girl as a woman. But there was no other option. While it's more common now for

Arab women to live alone, fifteen or twenty years ago it was unheard of.

'Did you want another option or was it something you didn't even think about?'

'I didn't even think about it because I moved from ... obviously my parents were strict, then I got married and my husband was, you know, abusive.'

Jamila said he was both verbally and physically abusive, but clarified that he didn't hit her. 'I wasn't bashed, it wasn't that. But he'd push me or use a pillow and smash my head with it. He was very rough. And just an asshole. A fucking asshole, you know? A bully.'

Jamila was engaged by way of a ceremony Muslims call *fatiha*.

'I wasn't asked. I was never asked the first time if I wanted to get married. It was just like, you read the *fatiha*, so you're just going to get married.'

It's not actually an Islamic act, though it involves recitation of *Al Fatiha*, the opening verse of the Quran. Among ourselves, we call it the 'five-minute engagement' because it is just a loose agreement of courtship; easy enough to break off. The *nikah*, which is the actual Islamic marriage ceremony, is often done in advance of a wedding, allowing a couple to behave as they please with each other. It's the equivalent of dating, but technically you're married under Islamic law. This sort of arrangement is more difficult to exit. While the couple has got married, having sex is frowned upon because if the relationship ends before the wedding, a woman can be disadvantaged – she risks a sullied reputation. She might have been married, but she wasn't living with her husband yet, so ending it no longer a virgin could cause her issues.

I can't tell you how many stories I've heard about these sorts of situations, how many judgments were laid against women for sleeping with their husbands after *nikah* – *by other women*. This is why some wedded couples yet to move in together are still expected to interact carefully (even under supervision).

That it causes issues is a problem in itself, and it says a lot that I'm relieved I never did *nikah* when I was engaged briefly in my late twenties to a Jordanian man, whom I will call Hany*. We were introduced to each other through a mutual friend while Hany was in Sydney to study. We did *fatiha*, much to the reluctance of my parents. Even an uncle from Jordan called me to ask what I was doing. On paper, Hany wasn't ticking the right boxes – he was slightly younger than me, still studying, not financially stable and, importantly, didn't have a permanent visa (which meant I was breaking my own rule to never consider someone who could be using me to get citizenship). There were a few reasons behind my decision to get to know Hany; I was rebounding after a failed 'relationship'; Hany seemed the complete opposite to the types of guys I usually considered; and at first blush, he was sweet and we got along. Later, through long phone conversations, I would learn that his entire attitude towards women was a problem.

We got engaged for 'five minutes', and were barely alone except on the phone or at a coffee shop up the road from my dad's office. My brother Hossam urged me to take every step I could to get to know him better. I sensed that, like my uncle and my eldest brother Alex, Hossam was baffled by my choice of partner. They wanted the best for me and struggled to see it in this man. So Hossam went to every effort to give me more sanctioned opportunities to get to know Hany better. This included a night out, when finally I saw in small interactions how petulant and selfish Hany was; for example more concerned that his phone battery was flat than spending time with me. When it ended, I was glad that I had stuck by the rules. I didn't trust him and, still being at home, still in a headscarf and concerned with my parents' feelings, I didn't want Hany to have anything he could use against me in a court of shaming law.

Of course, the less observant the family, the less these rituals matter. For some, *fatiha* is a symbolic but weightless act, the engagement it produces easily broken. But for Jamila her engagement extended into preparation for the wedding. 'It was never a "this is a period to get to know each other". It just meant "you're betrothed".'

Jamila said she doesn't know where the pressure she felt came from; her parents wouldn't have forced her into a union. It was perhaps her naïvety. She had met her husband through family friends, knew of him, and that seemed enough to recommend him.

'Looking back now, you think your parents would have said, "You don't have to," if you had spoken up about your doubts then?'

'Yeah, if I was strong enough. But they didn't bring me up to be strong. I was brought up to obey and to listen, and when it came to boys it was embarrassing – you don't talk about that. And I was excited to move out,' she laughed. 'I thought it was going to be romantic. I had doubts but I pushed them away.

'That is a product of me not ever talking to boys my whole entire life; that being the first boy who's shown interest in me; not having any sense of who am I and thinking that I was just going to get married and everything was going to be perfect and I would leave my boring life behind and I can be my own woman in my own home. I thought I would have more freedom, this concept of freedom was so, "I need freedom" my whole life.'

It was the opposite.

'I went from one kind of male domination to another. It was sickening. It was fucking sickening.'

I think a lot of us were deluded that way: we saw marriage as a ticket to freedom, because a lot of women around us, born and raised in Australia, seemed happily paired off and independent as a result of it. Why wouldn't it be the same for us?

Jamila believes she wouldn't be the person she is today if she hadn't been through those experiences, though. 'I often joke about this with my other divorced friend. Without this divorce, I would not have this freedom. Can you imagine if I was stuck in that marriage? It was almost like my get-out-of-jail card.'

This, despite a challenging road of self-discovery. Jamila is someone who is still peeling away layers to uncover herself. An activist in her heart, it seems one of her greatest fights has been to claim her personal sovereignty. 'I'm in my late thirties and still fucked up. Can't have a relationship. Don't know how to be in a relationship. Don't know how to receive love,' she declared, acknowledging a sheltered home life as the major culprit. 'I've always been fun and outgoing and social, my whole life, but always outside of home,' said Jamila. 'Everything was a mystery. I had no life skills. What life skills do you have if you don't know how to talk to a man? If you're growing up and you don't know how to interact with people?'

Then: 'I wish my parents would have said, "Hey, tell us your goals," or talk to me about my future or what I wanted to be.'

Though Jamila in many ways is on a continuing journey of self-discovery, she indicated that there remains the spectre of being 'the odd one out'.

'I just want to be normal. Blending is not about being the same as everyone. It's just being allowed to be myself and not feel persecuted for it or made to be the other. I'm always the other.'

She won't show weakness. As a single woman living alone, she said it becomes ammunition against her.

'I embrace the hardness. I embrace hardship if it means I'm learning. But sometimes I want to say to my mum, "I miss you, can you come sleep over so I can spend time with you?" But I can't because if I ever show that I'm needy – *ever* – the first thing they'll do is be like, "Oh my God, you poor thing, come back home, you shouldn't be alone." It's like, "Oh, for fuck's sake, I just need some company, from my family." They never come visit me. I'm always visiting them.'

Where Jamila's independence truly lies is in how she increasingly makes choices for herself based on her own feelings: if she dates a man, for example. Being intimate with one. Making time for her creative passions.

'What would you want women to feel that you didn't get to feel?' I asked Jamila.

'To realise that they *can* break free and don't have to conform. I know girls who were rebels and went against their parents' wishes. I was brought up in a way where it wasn't part of me ... I am *rebellious*, don't get me wrong, in other ways. But I want girls to realise if they're not happy, you *can* question your parents, you *can* stand up for what you believe in. When we act weak – don't ask for permission. If you want to do something, do it. If you're at uni, just go out afterwards. Experience life. Have a boyfriend,' she said, ending with a laugh.

We shared the commonality of a childhood where very little was allowed, where we frequently got into trouble over things that didn't seem at all worthy of any sort of admonishment. Then again, it was impossible to know what was normal because everything felt wrong.

As I heard women's stories around the dream of love and marriage, I felt fresh appreciation for my parents. Although I think my mother resisted me finding my path in some ways, she never brutally took me off my natural course. I recall with great clarity a conversation with her about marriage when I was in my late twenties. I'd had enough of suitors and serving them tea and fruit. It was starting to feel like I was on display, a specimen for judging, something that had never occurred to me in the earlier days of door-knock appeals because I was scrutinising the suitor as well.

'You're just going to get married late,' said Mum, casually, with a shrug.

Her words fell hard on me; my gut affirmed my mother's words and I felt a sadness wash over me. Though I treasured my solitude, I had tasted my share of loneliness and hadn't yet come to understand the beauty of self-development.

Then, more recently, long after I did marry someone my parents never would have expected, came another revelation from my mother: 'I always knew you weren't going to be a typical housewife.' This was news to me, mainly because I had very few ambitions at twenty-one. Falling in love and maybe working on the side were the extent of them. Mum had never bothered to teach me how to cook. When I still lived at home, she never harangued me to clean the toilet. I never asked her to do my washing, but she would find a way to do it anyway.

Mum didn't see great housewife potential in me, clearly, so she knew better than to invest time and effort in a daughter who wasn't going to spend a day rolling vine leaves for dinner. And she had a point. That she sensed this in me before I did is worthy of note. I have to give Mum credit for not directing me onto a pathway that wasn't suitable, even if my preferred map went against so much of what she believes.

I was also lucky that I could break off the unsuitable attachment to Hany without issue. In fact, my father impatiently advised me to do it via email.

'Dad!' I gasped. 'I should at least call him.'

My mother, who was half-convinced that my engagement was the result of someone's dark magic, agreed with me.

It was difficult navigating a relationship, still formal and incomplete, under my parents' supervision. I never talked to my mother about falling in love; I tried once to express my frustration about our limited dating rituals, but I felt she was closed off. She knew there was nothing she could offer to assuage my feelings on the matter. Despite being my greatest defender against unsuitable men, I'm not sure who she thought would be the right match for her slightly wayward daughter.

It's difficult to know what truly fell away when I stopped meeting men in the living room: my belief in the 'dream of love' or my faith in the door-knock system altogether. I suppose the latter crushed the former.

Those awkward living room meetings eventually became awkward meetings in cafés or restaurants. I still remember the man who made me realise that I was too old and cynical for these rituals.

It was a disastrous courtship with a guy who told us he'd grown up in Kuwait and that he was a pilot. My mother, who tends towards suspicion, didn't believe him. She had spent some of her younger years living in Kuwait and knew the land well.

And there was something a little too forced about him. When I told my best friend Joanne about our first encounter, she asked, 'Was he well dressed?'

'So well dressed I think the clothes still had the tags on them.'

He was smart and a good conversationalist but something felt off. In a bid to prove his identity, he delivered a manila folder full of documents, including a scan of his passport. My mother took out her magnifying glass and decided that it was a different man in the photo. She wasn't imagining it – there did seem to be a difference.

The ridiculousness of it all clarified in my mind when Joanne offered unbiased perspective: 'Don't you think it's a bad start to the relationship if he has to prove his identity?'

At the time I met the pilot, I was weaning myself off full hijab. In the year before I completely unveiled, I began gradually to change how I covered. I tied my scarves around my head like a gypsy and began wearing hoop earrings again, similar to my mother's style, but closer to the hijab I had previously worn. Sometimes I exposed my neck. I always wore long sleeves and ankle-length clothing, though. Still, it wasn't 'proper hijab'. When the veil came up in conversation with the pilot suitor, I tested his feelings around my loose interpretation of hijab. 'I don't really wear it properly, I guess.'

'Ah yes, but we can talk about that later.'

We didn't, obviously.

I eventually felt completely happy to not investigate love in such a formal, awkward manner. Reflecting on it now, I feel for the young woman who had complete faith that she would find the right person in time, that obeying the rules would somehow compensate for the complications of getting to know someone in your parents' living room.

I remember my father checking in with me at one point, evidently frustrated that I refused everyone. 'What exactly are you looking for?'

'Someone special,' came my simple response.

'What does that mean?' my father replied, flustered.

Years later, an ex-love interest similarly queried me. 'It's not like Hollywood,' he lectured. 'Love comes later.'

In my case, love eventually came knocking in the most unexpected of ways, with Chris, a man I had previously worked with, who had been my mentor and had shown unrelenting faith in my professional and creative abilities; who had become a good friend and whom I got to know without the pressure of expectation.

One day, we met, both in strange, imperfect places in our lives, and in a single exchange, something shifted. Life had thrown us both challenges, but we were two people comfortable with who they were. And so, we were ready for each other.

I realised quickly that years of cultural and religious conditioning would affect how I approached getting to know Chris. But just as significantly, he arrived without this baggage. What would be more difficult? Reconciliations between culture and what I felt, or Chris having to deal with ideas he'd never had to deal with before?

'You know I'm Muslim,' I told Chris evenly, aware I would never ask him to convert for me.

'I know. But I figure, if we can put a man on the moon, we can make this work.'

This would be a new exploration of love.

And he would eventually meet my parents, but not in the living room.

SHAME

Shame is the lie someone told you about yourself.

Anaïs Nin

The sexuality of women is a global obsession. In the course of one morning, browsing social media and a few news outlets online, I came across no fewer than four stories, a couple with videos, that related to women, their bodies, how they dress, and their sexual behaviour. One video, by digital writer Maddy Butler, demonstrated the hypocrisy of criticising women for veiling while wider society still punishes a female for wearing a short skirt. It showed an Anglo girl covering up under pressure from a teacher, who then cried 'Oppression' when a girl in a veil walked past.

Meanwhile, a column for *Daily Life* considered what 'sex' actually means. Headlined 'In this day and age, why do we insist that "sex" still has to be penetrative?', the article, by writer Giselle A. Nguyen, talked about the limitations of heteronormative definitions. She described the difficulties she's experienced with sex, and the many judgements surrounding women who engage in sexual activity:

At my religious high school, we often gossiped behind locker doors about who was and wasn't a virgin in our grade. Some girls said they were 'saving themselves', but still engaged in oral sex. We counted them as virgins. They weren't sluts who went the whole way. That was what bad girls did, the ones who got pregnant and dropped out of school. Sure, our friends liked having fun, but they knew where the line was.

These reflections could apply to women anywhere, a point I emphasise because not many people seem to apply similar analysis when discussing Arab women and sex. Our impressions of sex in the Arab world are largely informed by the media, fiction and crimes against women committed in the name of 'honour'. In books written by non-Arab women from the West, we're treated to in-depth considerations of how sexual Arab women are and the consequences of it, or we're studied and analysed as though we haven't discovered the joys of intimacy or sexual attraction.

REPRESSION OF NATURAL INSTINCTS

In her film *Caramel*, Lebanese film-maker Nadine Labaki gives a nod to the restrictive hypocrisy of life for women in the Middle East, which could easily apply to Arab women in Australia or any other Western country. In the film, a young Muslim woman who is soon to be wed goes to a doctor who specialises in reconstructive surgery 'down there', something that has been well documented as a reality in the Arab world. This surgery – 'hymenoplasty' – doesn't 'restore' a woman's virginity, only the evidence of it. There are no accurate statistics, but it has been discussed and documented for many years now.

In another scene, this same character has a tender conversation with her mother, who has no idea that her daughter has been sexually active (and not even with her fiancé). As such, her mother tearfully farewells her daughter, whom she has sheltered until now, informing her obliquely that she is crossing from one stage into another, from a girl to a woman. The mother doesn't explicitly acknowledge that her daughter is going to become a sexual being, it's implied, as is the difficulty this can create if you're the naïve type. The daughter's guilt is plain to see.

So much can be extrapolated from this exchange. That her mother has never spoken to her about sex, and on the eve of her wedding can only speak about it in code, is to me an accurate depiction. Women of younger generations have told me that sex isn't a taboo subject. But I believe it's a generational thing. Women my age always saw it as off-bounds as I did – I never talked about it with my mother. Arabs are very accepting of traditions and ideas; we don't do change well. So what could she tell me? To ignore natural instincts? I think this is the case for many women – we're never told to repress; we just pretend it's not a problem.

My friends and I, however, could talk about sex with each other, and we did so, with relish. We obsessed over it, exposed as we were to Hollywood's treatment of it – tender or passionate love-making with a man who looked at you like you were his sun. Easy access to Mills & Boon-type romance novels further fostered our intense interest in boys and sex. Inside we were raging, hormonal, like anyone else our adolescent age. We crushed on the guys closest to us. But on the outside we showed no signs of it.

In Amman I had a particularly insightful and revealing conversation about this sexual tug-of-war, so familiar to Arab women everywhere. Yasmine*, a Christian Jordanian of Palestinian heritage, in her forties, is a women's rights activist. She identified the double standards that plague girls from a young age, but also pointed to the obsession with women's bodies.

'This is the problem: we raise our daughters that their bodies are sacred,' said Yasmine. 'Because we don't want them to have sex before marriage, we end up creating this fear of sex and men, and the sexual act. We make it a fearful thing until the day she's married and then suddenly, her life should flip 180 degrees and she should turn into a sexual person. And she's not only a sexual person, she has to be a seductress. [But] you've made her asexual her whole life. You made her fight her sexual feelings, her desires ...'

Yasmine brought up the example of a male cousin who had lots of girlfriends, slept with women, but was hard on his sister and her when they were together, peppering them with questions about where they would be going. She bolstered this example of double standards with another recollection, a conversation between her father and this cousin. Princess Diana had just died, and the topic of discussion was the shame of her affair with Dodi Al Fayed, the man who died in the same car crash.

'I said, "Her husband had an affair throughout their lives. And now you say no [that's acceptable], because the husband – if his wife is frigid, if she's not good in bed – has the right to search for it somewhere else,"' said Yasmine.

At the time Yasmine was a virgin, so felt she could express strong viewpoints. She told them: 'You want us to remain a virgin, not do anything,' she said, now hitting the table with her hand to emphasise each point. 'Not have experiences, and then you want to marry us and suddenly we have to turn into sexual ... How? And then you find that's why there are lots of marriages with lots of problems in the Arab world.'

Yasmine's frustration was also directed at another problem women face – we are easily shamed not only by men but also by older women in families who continue to uphold restrictive ideas about females and how they should behave. Women can be made responsible for something even when they're deemed as lacking rights or power. This is not an Arab problem, it's a universal one.

'You're responsible if you're raped. What were you wearing? How did you look at him?' said Yasmine, acknowledging that this happens everywhere.

This seems to get to the heart of the world's trouble with sex, but particularly the double standards lacing Arab communities' dealings with it. We like sex, and if you're Muslim you might even be handed down tales about how men must make sure their wives are satisfied through foreplay (sex is even considered an act of worship). But we're also told that it's sinful to reject a husband who wants sex. Sex revolves around men, and it's difficult to demystify this. Marriage does, too. So much of the relationship lore we're taught, either directly or by example, is about what a man wants, what a man approves of or likes.

During one courtship in my twenties, at a time when I was trying to embrace a more conservative lifestyle, I felt compelled to ask the man I had fallen for if he had any issue with me working if we got married. He didn't, but there were certain things he wouldn't approve of, he said. 'It would need to be a mainly female work environment, no working in teams with men.'

I eventually understood that I didn't need anyone's permission to pursue work opportunities or to have certain beliefs or feelings. While this man was a lovely, caring guy – extremely thoughtful and witty – I'm pretty sure we would have ended in divorce if we had got married. Because the truer parts of me were starting to emerge and demand my attention.

When he suggested an engagement, I found myself saying strange things like, 'I'm not sure if I'm ready to give up wearing sandals in the summer.'

He was strict and would have been the type of husband who expected his wife to cover everything but her feet and hands. I wore hijab at the time, but my family wasn't strict like that. *I* wasn't instinctively strict like that. I knew I was forcing aspects of our connection and I needed to be honest with myself.

'Are you afraid of smelly feet?' he quipped in response.

Silently I acknowledged my fears: that I would fall deeper into a way of life that didn't feel natural. Where I had to isolate my social interactions to the circle of women in this man's life; where music was forbidden; where my body had to be covered up in shapeless dresses, my head wrapped in scarves that were starting to feel a bit suffocating.

This is the problem: you start to feel like nothing about you belongs to you because it's all subject to a man's approval. The background hum was that I would go from the security of my parents to the security of a husband. But I had a mind I wanted to cultivate; by then I had a body I no longer felt compelled to swathe in unflattering clothes.

Jamila raised similar points in our conversation – that so much focus is placed on how men see us. She told me she never felt loved by her ex-husband.

'No. No, that's not love. He did nothing for me.'

'Do you wonder why he married you, then?'

'I think he married the idea of me, because he liked that I was a good Muslim girl. And he thought that I would be submissive. Our family had a reputation – the kids of my father, we're known for being good girls. We wouldn't do anything wrong.'

Jamila didn't think her ex cared to get to know her, he just liked the idea of her. 'I was there to love and be equal with him and to share a life and experience. I would do anything. The problem was that I was too submissive in the marriage. If I knew myself, if I was a stronger person, he wouldn't have treated me that way.'

Yasmine believes that Arab society is obsessed with sex and women's bodies because it's considered distasteful to discuss those things in public. 'For example, in [Arab] mainstream media, this is something that is taboo. It's not shown, it's not discussed.'

Moreover, if sex does come up, it comes across as 'wrong' because it's done outside of marriage, which always has consequences. Or it's adultery, also with consequences. In other words, sex is always connected to morality.

Salma Nims, the Secretary-General of the Jordanian National Commission for Women, also concerned with the legal rights of women – particularly in fighting for the reformation of laws around family issues that tend to negatively impact women – offered similarly candid insights, saying sexuality is not talked about or accepted openly in the Arab world.

'It's a private matter ... but we see it also, I think, generally speaking, as an act of power of men over women. By seeing it this way then it is connected to many issues, like, for example, when a woman is raped, it's not her body that is violated, her family's honour is violated. It's not her body. We're not protecting her from this violence, we're protecting the family, because it's an act of aggression towards the family,' said Salma.

'And then, if a woman has slept with a man also, it's the honour of the family that we're worried about ... nobody cares about her emotions.'

Jordan, which is constitutionally but not in practice an Islamic country, has a 'Muslim culture', Salma explained. Islamic law is selectively implemented, meaning it is only applied where women and family are concerned. And the way Islam is explained in the Arab world, Salma continued, is that the woman has to obey her husband in bed. She reiterated a point Yasmine made: 'If he wants sex, you have to sleep with him. You cannot not sleep with him.'

'Do you think women feel that pressure?' I queried.

'Yes. I know lots of women who have this problem.'

These women may love their husbands but the frequency is an issue: he wants it every day and she doesn't. For example, in Islam men and women are required to undertake a full ablution after sex – head to toe, which includes the hair – if you want to pray. Practising women complain about this: they might have just had their hair done, for example. It sounds minor, but it would be frustrating and unpleasant if your day-to-day life was punctuated by the needs of your partner.

Yasmine said that women might pretend they're already asleep to avoid sex. 'It's a sense that it's an obligation for a woman towards a man. Although she could enjoy it ... it's not like they don't talk about joy, but it's an obligation.'

She suggested that sometimes women refuse sex if they're angry with their husbands. She said her friends mock her for not doing the same, but that, 'It's emotional for me. I don't use it as a power thing. It's an expression of love. If there's no love, that's the problem. To me, I see shame if this is happening outside a meaningful relationship. It makes you feel shameful if you're not part of a meaningful relationship.

'I used to say, and I remember I used to say this when I was single, and in front of my parents and my father would have a heart attack ... "I find more honour in a woman who is in love with someone and sleeping with him outside of marriage than a woman who hates her husband and is sleeping with him." Because there's a lot of lying in that and to me that's not honest. Maybe my type of thinking is an exception.'

Yasmine said her mother told her never to sleep with her husband if she doesn't feel like it. 'Because you could end up hating him for the rest of your life because of that night ... It's amazing that these values come from my mother, not from books. Because this is something you should enjoy, and you want it.'

Meanwhile, having sex, or even dealing with sexual thoughts outside of marriage? That's just not allowed. *Haram*. So it's like sexual desire is a switch that gets turned on the moment you meet your 'person'.

This is something I, like many others, can relate to. I felt frustration growing up, particularly as the years stretched out before me and finding the right partner seemed like a distant impossibility based on divine decree. It's not that finding love is everything; but it is something. And it's another thing you have no say in, because, as Arabs love to remind us, such things are pre-determined.

THE WEDDING SHEETS

My concerns around relationships and sex only fermented when I heard more stories from the homeland via girls my age who had come in recent years to Australia when I was in my early teens. Matter of factly they talked about the requirement that a woman bleeds on her wedding night, the first I had heard about hymens. 'They're thin, like Glad Wrap,' one girl told me. 'You could rip it accidentally, but you have to bleed on your wedding night otherwise your husband will think you've already slept with someone.'

I was, obviously, a virgin, but suddenly paranoid that I had ripped my hymen when I was younger riding a bike or something, or that my private parts weren't normal. This fear deepened and grew wings when these girls went on to regale me with tales of how brides would be sent home to be dealt with by their parents if they didn't bleed. It was a fear that eventually fell away as I matured.

'But couldn't he just tell if she was a virgin?' I asked, confused how anyone could come across as being sexually active if she'd never had sex. How did a flimsy piece of flesh determine otherwise? And how could someone who loves you put you to the test?

Of course, my understanding of the hymen test has grown with age. Like clothing, it's the thing used to hold women to account, to unrealistic standards of piety, and is a way of instilling fear. A man can have sex, and his name and reputation remain unsullied, not even called into question. A man can travel without a companion, do whatever he wants, and easily marry no less than a virginal girl with no romantic past.

I have heard of engagements being cancelled, leading to a woman's integrity being called into question – her virginity needing to be determined before she can marry someone else; of mothers entering the bedroom the morning after a marriage has been consummated to check the sheets for blood. When a woman in Australia told me about this happening to her, she shrugged it off, though. She'd bled, so if anything it was in her favour to have her purity on record.

Rula Quawas, Professor of American Literature and Feminist Theory at the University of Jordan, shared a few stories of the purity exam that some brides are subjected to on their wedding nights. While she said that Arabs of course enjoy sex, and her students will even point to religious scripture that supports healthy sexual relationships, there's a big difference between 'having sex' and 'making love'.

'I tell it in the classroom … You make love, you have sex. They say, "What's the difference?"'

Rula went on to talk about 'rights' in marriage and a study on intimate partnership violence by among others Professor Cari Jo Clark from the Harvard School of Public Health, who interviewed women in Jordan who are married but were raped because they didn't want to have sex.

'When I met her [Professor Clark] said, "I can't believe it, because you have the right to say, You know what? I'm not in the mood for it. It's not going to happen tonight." But he says, "I'm in the mood for it, and you have no say in the matter. It's going to happen, it's going to happen right now." That is what we call rape.'

Rula has heard women say they won't initiate sex for fear of being called 'slutty'. She gave the example of a woman who told Rula that she loves sex, but her desire led to a separation from her husband; he left her, questioning, 'Where did you learn all about sex? The movement, the way you move, and things like that.'

'So you see? If you are ignorant, they say you are not good enough,' said Rula. 'You don't know what you're doing. If you know what to do: "Where did you learn it from? Did you have other relationships before me?"'

Rula provided a further example that brings us back to the

bloody sheets. A couple, both people from 'good' (meaning educated) families, who were madly in love, got married. On her wedding night, the woman bled and the man bundled up the evidence into a bag. Upon being asked why by his new wife, he told her that he wanted to show his parents. The woman, Rula said, cried her eyes out, at a loss as to why her husband, the proof of her virginity already established, would not think it's enough to know for himself.

'And you know, they divorced after three months,' said Rula.

Education meant nothing given his mindset, she added. Though he should have known better, 'Blood is really very important,' said Rula.

So important that women who don't have the option or desire for reconstructive surgery may find other means to 'prove' their virginity. For example, they might buy bags from Egypt, which get inserted into the vagina. Upon penetration, the bag rips, qualifying the woman as a 'virgin'.

And that whole argument about having witnesses to the blood on the sheets helping a woman? It's sadly true. The man who had bagged up the bloodied sheet to show his parents told people he was divorcing his wife because she was a slut who hadn't bled on her wedding night. For the woman, the bagged sheet was her 'alibi', at once her oppressor and her saviour.

While I abhor the 'hymen test', and I acknowledge it is an enduring problem, I think it's essential to point out that many people have moved beyond this poisonous tradition. I don't believe my perceptions of Arab men were highly influenced by it. Over time, it was something I didn't hear much about. By the time I was in my late twenties and briefly engaged to the Jordanian man, I didn't worry about it at all. However, holding women accountable or pinning their reputation on their virginity is a persistent issue, particularly in the Arab world. Most recently, we've seen how women in Egypt have been subjected to traumatic 'virginity tests' for their part in the Arab uprising, an exercise in humiliation.

The way people view women, sexuality and their engagement in sexual acts is, in general, skewed away from freedom and towards shame. The idea of the Good Girl is a universal one, as is the Good Girl Gone Bad. The hymen test is perhaps one of its most extreme manifestations.

EVERYTHING BUT SEX

Warda* married later than she expected to, well into her thirties when she partnered with the 'right guy'. She is an example of the frustrated longing and confusion many of us experience as we grow older and have to fight off natural desires around intimacy, companionship and sex.

Warda was a virgin when she met the man she would marry. They had fooled around, and she had dated men before him, so she wasn't inexperienced. But, like so many women, she had investigated and drawn up her own limits. Sex was not an option even if other things were, not an uncommon approach to dating for Arab women.

She described her Lebanese–Australian husband, raised Muslim like Warda, as an easygoing man who was aware that she had dated men before and ostensibly had no problem with it. But she admitted, with a level of discomfort, that her husband feels the need to share his past, while she doesn't.

'And when it does come up, I say to him, "The same way I don't question you about your past, please don't question me."

I don't think for him it's about wanting to know as such; I think he doesn't want to feel deceived,' Warda explained.

This became relevant when it came to Warda's virginity. She said her husband found it difficult to believe she hadn't slept with another man.

'I don't think I bled, and if I did it was very little. And I don't think I bled the first time; I bled a little bit more the second and third times we did it. Which is weird … I don't know.'

Ultimately, it wasn't an issue. In fact, overall, sex wasn't difficult for Warda at all. 'I think I was very comfortable with myself sexually. A big part of it was him. Not only was I comfortable with myself, I was very comfortable with him, and at that point in time we'd fooled around that much that that was all there was left to do.'

Warda explained that her husband allows her to be who she wants to be, sexually. They don't have a boring sex life. 'If anything, he's encouraging of stuff that I wouldn't even dream of,' she said. 'Even though he knows a little bit about my past, whilst a lot of Arab guys would be, "Oh, I can't believe you've ever done that," whilst he's a little bit like that, it almost turns him on. Like, really bizarre. It almost excites him.'

When Warda dated in the past, some of the men were not Arab or Muslim. She takes comfort in the fact that she ended up with an Arab Muslim man, because they can relate to each other culturally. But her road to connection with him was paved with disappointment and guilt. I can count on one hand the women who have not felt the burden of shame and guilt for their more intimate encounters with men (or women). I asked Warda if she ever *didn't* feel guilty secretly dating men.

'I always felt guilty. Always,' she said. 'It just made me feel shit, really. It made me feel shit.'

'Did you feel guilty because you really thought it was wrong, or deep down did you believe what you were doing was okay?'

'I think I really believed I was doing something wrong. From a religious perspective, not a cultural one. Actually ... it was probably both. Growing up, it was like this idea that the first man you would ever kiss would be your husband, let alone anything else.'

I understood Warda's disappointment. At the heart of her grievance was the heavy burden and expectation placed on people who are not married – to stem sexual desire and be patient. This applies to women and men, but we readily accept that for boys it's harder so it's often overlooked when they transgress. It's rarely overlooked when women do.

Warda acknowledged that the disappointment of not finding love and having that sexual freedom with a partner deepened as she got older.

'I got to the point where I went, "What if I don't meet him? Am I really going to live the rest of my life not knowing what it feels like to be with someone?"'

She said on occasion she was tempted to give in and have sex before marriage. 'I don't know if I ever would have done it though ... if I hadn't have gotten married. I don't know whether I would have gotten to a point in time where I would have said, "Fuck it, I'm just going to do it, I'm just going to live with the consequence."'

Some people might suggest that living in the West makes this all a whole lot harder, or easier, for Arab women, depending on how you look at it. On the one hand, we're surrounded by sex and couples who openly date, move in together, show affection in public and the like, so trying to be the modest, asexual being until marriage can create heightened anxiety around it. On the other hand, it can be easier because in such an open society, where mixing between sexes is not so loaded, women *can* date, even if it's in secret. That doesn't diminish the guilt around it but it allows for exploration.

Either way, what I find most troubling is the dilution of the natural desires that are inherent in human beings. Most of us desire connection, and this was true for Warda, too. It wasn't purely about sex, she told me, it was about intimacy in general.

I asked Warda, 'Did it feel unfair? With the Arab focus on *naseeb* [destiny], did it feel like a lotto and your numbers never came up?'

'Absolutely,' she said, going on to relate a story from her single days. She was sitting with a married female relative and they were talking about marriage. 'I don't know how it came up but I said to her – and I didn't mean it in a bad way and I wasn't directing it at her – "What gives you [you being anyone who's Arab and married] the right to think that just because you're married, you can do what you need to to relieve those feelings and those needs, yet I can't because I'm not married?" And I said, "The same way you've got needs, I've got needs."' Warda went on to reiterate that she found it unfair. 'She had never really seen it that way.'

Adding to the frustration is that no one really wants to talk about or admit how trying it can be to feel so sexually frustrated if you're eternally single. When it comes to getting to know your own body without a partner, it's considered normal to do so in the West.

'Oh no, it's not normal,' said Warda, in reference to Arab society. 'Like everything, we were never directly told [not to do something]. It was always insinuated. Like, "Don't ever let anybody touch you, or don't ever do anything with boys. You can't do that until you're married."'

169

I wondered if Warda was afraid of punishment or getting caught when she dated.

'I think it was just more the guilt within myself,' she said.

'Do you feel now that you did something wrong?'

'Sometimes I do. I don't know whether it is that I feel guilty. Sometimes I feel like maybe it takes away from the intimacy I now share with my husband. Sometimes I just wish he was the first person that I experienced certain things with.'

On the other hand, other women I spoke to signalled the opposite sentiment. They were relieved they had addressed their curiosity and attempted to fulfil their desires. One woman, in her mid-thirties, said she wished she'd been more carefree and just had fun with it. 'Who cares? You were going to get married eventually. Enjoy yourself.'

Another woman, Safa*, who was raised in Sydney and is also in her thirties, suggested that while she never completely felt at ease being with men, she enjoyed her explorations in romance and attraction. 'I had been so sheltered all my life. I was thirty and hadn't kissed a man. Then I met someone and the attraction was so strong, we ended up connecting. I think part of the appeal was that he wasn't Arab or Muslim. I could just be myself. I felt free.'

However, that freedom wasn't unfettered, she said. 'I just liked this guy but I think he was trying to "save" me a bit. He knew I was sort of innocent, and while I think we had genuine chemistry, I know part of his attraction to me was that he found me exotic.'

And unattainable. 'I wouldn't do anything with him for the longest time because I wasn't ready. It only made him want me more, but that wasn't my intention at all.'

Safa never had sex with any of the men she got to know;

she was a virgin when she got married. And the unfurling of her sexual desires didn't begin with her first kiss. 'I was very sexually charged. I really wanted to be with someone, to eventually have sex. But I knew it had to be in marriage. It just wasn't an option any other way. Eventually that becomes harder when no one you're suited to comes along.'

The larger issue for Safa was the feeling that she hadn't really *lived*. Meaning she wasn't like friends who had experienced the waves of pain and pleasure that come with relationships. 'Heartbreak isn't fun, but at least you're experiencing something. Everything I did in that area was innocent until I hit my thirties. I had been in love but we never did anything together. Then I fell for someone who wasn't Arab or Muslim and it took me down a more challenging but also very fulfilling path. I was a virgin but for the first time, I felt like a woman.'

She said she had no true sense of how electric connection to someone you're attracted to can be, and she never felt guilty about those rumblings. 'I felt conflicted about acting on them, though,' she said. 'The thing is, no one says sex is wrong. You're just meant to be this very pure and innocent woman until you get married. If you don't find love, well, it sucks to be you. And that got harder for me to stomach later. I mean, eventually I felt like I was going to burst.'

Safa tapped into something deeper here: a desire to break a pattern. 'Sometimes I feel my ancestry bearing down on me. Not disapproval. But like I've inherited the ways of the past that need to end. I don't want to continue the stories of the women before me, whatever they are. I just want to be me.'

She admitted to a period of deep shame later, after she met the man she would eventually marry. 'I felt dirty, like I should have held out. But my husband knew I wasn't "innocent" in that way and he didn't care. He told me I shouldn't either. And now I'm glad I did it because it's such a nice thing – having a connection, a first kiss. I wouldn't want to have just one first kiss. You know?'

And she believes attention from men helped her grow up. 'I enjoyed flirting sometimes. I discovered that I could banter with guys and it was pretty innocent but fun. I wish now I had enjoyed it more. I just think somewhere along the line I didn't like being a woman. I felt unsafe, like I couldn't trust my own feelings.'

The guilt, where it exists, seems mainly to relate to parents and wider society.

'I don't believe God is going to strike me down,' another woman told me. But she would hate for her parents, whom she truly loves and respects, to know that she has done things they would find shameful. Safa felt the same. 'It's like you're the perfect daughter until you do something they would consider shameful. And it makes you feel horrible, because you love your parents. They're not villains. They're just trying to protect you, but you have to grow up.'

In one interesting example, Suheir* related how she remained a virgin but sex initially proved a disappointment. 'It was excruciatingly painful. My husband is a good guy, very patient. But that first time was pretty awful. Afterwards, I think he needed more comforting than me. I felt so bad for him.'

Suheir married a convert to Islam, whom she described as more spiritual than religious. She said they were intimate before they married, but they had limits. But while Suheir said she was very comfortable with her husband, sex continued to be challenging for a while. 'I was like, is that how it goes? It doesn't feel like anything. Is he in me? I can't feel it. I thought something was wrong with me.'

When she got a 'honeymoon UTI' – 'No one tells you about that' – she felt crushed. 'I went to a healer a friend recommended because I had a couple of UTIs in a row. I'll try anything and I felt like something was out of whack. Anyway, this woman uses crystals and stood in the corner of the room yelling at invisible beings, telling them to leave me alone. She told me that I got the UTI because my ancestors were unhappy that I had married a non-Muslim man. I didn't go back after that. I didn't need another person voicing stupid ideas about women having sex.'

What Suheir was acknowledging, of course, was the deep guilt many women inevitably feel if they are intimate with a man before marriage – intimate, mind you; Suheir was a virgin, after all. This healer, for all of her best intentions, was suggesting that Suheir's guilt and shame about sex was manifesting in her physical body, in the same way many New Age believers will argue that illness is the result of trauma or a negative mental state.

'I was never at ease being with my husband before we got married, but I don't think I was a prude. I thought sex would be easy once I was married, but physically it wasn't, even without the guilt. I guess everyone's different, but that magical transformation didn't happen.'

I don't think Suheir's case is that unusual. I have heard from many women of all backgrounds over the years how difficult sex can be – if these women weren't tensing up and stressed in the first few months, even with their husbands, they weren't as enthralled by the act as they had expected to be. 'Overrated' is one word I've heard used a few times. A close second is the phrase: 'It gets better.' And, of course: 'I like the foreplay more than actual sex.'

Which left me wondering what my generation would teach their daughters, should they have any.

Safa said she was wary about having children. 'I think being a parent is a hard job. I don't know that I would be easier on my kids than my parents in the end, but I really hope I would be. I really hope I can tell my daughter that she can use her head to make decisions and if being intimate with someone outside of marriage feels right for her, then she can do that and she's not going to go to hell for it. I would want her to understand her own power.'

Warda's response was a simple one: 'I don't know.'

'Would you tell her that intimacy before marriage is okay?' I prompted.

'I honestly don't know.'

'Knowing what you went through, would you want her to go through the same thing?'

'I honestly don't know. There's part of me that thinks I'll raise her similar, there's part of me that thinks that I won't. Which is bizarre, because I always thought, "I don't want my daughter to go through what I went through." But at the same time ... And I don't know whether it goes back to the upbringing and the guilt thing,' she said, thoughtful. 'Okay – I think I'd be okay with my daughter kissing a boy; I don't know if I'd be okay with her losing her virginity before marriage. Which is ironic, I know.'

'What if she was in a loving relationship?'

'I think that would make it more acceptable for me. And I don't know whether it's a protective thing. I don't know whether ... it's so ingrained in us, and as much as we've moved away, a little bit, from the culture ... and lived our own lives, it's kind of still there.'

Warda said she *would* encourage her daughter to pack her bags and travel the world when she finishes school – even if her husband doesn't feel the same way. 'I will be like, "You do what you have to do; you finish uni if you want to before you settle down and have a career. Here's a one-way ticket, go and explore the world." I'm all for that. But for me, when it comes to the intimacy, I'm still a bit protective.'

Protective, but it's still progress.

SEXUAL AWAKENING

Of the women I spoke to, some talked about losing their virginity outside of marriage. One woman in Lebanon flippantly told me she had lost her virginity at sixteen – and her father, a religious man, had walked in on her. She didn't suffer punishment for it.

Yasmine, the women's rights activist from Jordan, said she slept with a long-term boyfriend in her twenties, then with the man who is now her husband. She demonstrated no hang-ups about sex. 'My mother, when I was fifteen or sixteen, gave me the books of Nawal El Saadawi to read.'

Saadawi is famous for her feminist books that openly and honestly detailed the lives of women in the Arab world without glossing over the difficult parts.

'To let me read about my right to masturbate – for a wife who got married into a very typical marriage … I think she really didn't want me to lead the life that she led,' said Yasmine. Then her voice lifted. 'By the way, my mother is very happily married. She was lucky. Even sexually they had an amazing relationship.'

Yasmine had sex with her boyfriend when she decided she was ready. 'I wanted to do it. And he wanted to marry me. He insisted, actually. We were together for five years and I didn't want to marry him for several reasons. He thought it was because he's a Muslim – it wasn't. And we broke up,' she said, her tone matter-of-fact.

When Yasmine met the man she ended up marrying, her friends warned her against sleeping with him, thinking that he would be turned off because she was not a virgin. But Yasmine exhibited strong self-awareness. 'You need to do things because you are comfortable with them. I wasn't thinking of my chances of marriage. I was liberated from that. When I slept with the first boyfriend, I knew I wasn't marrying him, yet it was something I wanted to do. I couldn't just keep thinking, "How am I going to find a husband in the future because I lost my virginity?" I want a husband who accepts me as not a virgin. Not as "not a virgin"; as a woman who has total control over her life and her decisions,' she continued.

'I think there are a lot of Jordanian women like this, and Lebanese and Egyptian. I think there are. And they find that type of man. I know women who actually lived with their boyfriends in Amman and ended up marrying them.

'I'm not saying that this is typical; it's not normal, it's not spoken of. It's between groups who are alike, quite accepted – not talked about but we know. We all know that we're comfortable with it.'

And it's not a large group, she acknowledged. They tend to be highly educated, very intellectual and they've moved ahead and away from the expectations of society.

Most interesting to me was Yasmine's candour in talking about the double standards that are applied to women.

'I believe that there is a lot of hypocrisy in the Arab world when it comes to sex,' she told me. 'Yes, the concept of shame is connected to women. But men want to have sex. Who are they having sex with, for God's sake?'

Yasmine believes – though it's not something that can easily be validated – that there are lots of men and women who are doing everything except going all the way. 'It's hypocritical. This concept of virginity is connected with honour, and the honour of the family ... The stories that I know of women just giving blow jobs to their boyfriends all the time.'

I wondered if there was any chance these women were eventually marrying the men they were intimate with outside of marriage.

'Sometimes they do!' said Yasmine. 'It depends. First of all, there are those who sleep with each other and end up getting married. So it's not like it's not there and it's not happening. Some don't go all the way, yet they know they're going to get married, and they get married. And some, he would never marry that woman. To him, she's not who should be the mother of his children.'

Yasmine said there are lots of men in Jordan who do what they want to do but have to find a virgin to marry.

'Oh my God, how many virgins lied to them,' said Yasmine, a little wickedly. 'I know women who got their hymens patched up. They reconstructed it to get married. So really, what kind of a marriage are you starting with a lie?'

Of course, if sex is a taboo, masturbation is non-existent, despite the best efforts of Nawal El Saadawi to normalise it decades ago.

Rula, the university professor in Jordan, said she demystifies it for students by simply telling them, if they ask, that it's okay to masturbate. They express their fears: going blind, not being able to have children.

'You're not going to die, and you're not going to be blind. And you're going to have babies. I tell my students that we do not have scientific evidence to back up what members of the family say.

'This false info is circulated and endorsed by women of the family,' she added.

'We accept it for men,' said Yasmine. 'I remember I had a friend who was going to get married and she was really scared, didn't know how to do it.'

Yasmine told her, 'I think you need to masturbate before you get married. You need to learn what your body wants. How do you like to be touched? Because you're going to guide him. And I think she was shocked when I said that. I was twenty maybe, actually. Now I have friends who are in marriages and still cannot have an orgasm.

'Their husbands are frustrated that they're not having an orgasm, by the way. There are open-minded men ... Of course, sometimes it's a reflection of his own macho-ness – "I can get her to have an orgasm. No, two!" So sometimes it's frustrating for men also because [they think] it's a reflection on their abilities as a sexual partner,' she said.

'And I tell them, "I think you need to masturbate." How can you convey the message of what you like and don't like to him if you're not comfortable with your body? You need to love your body. If you feel shame, you're not going to enjoy it.'

Whether we're talking about sex or masturbation, no matter how easily and ubiquitously pop culture conveys them, they remain controversial topics. And it starts with what we're not taught. Lamisse, the youth worker from Brisbane, told me she wrote a paper on sexuality in an attempt to deal with the lack of education around sex.

'You get this sexuality education, which is like: you don't have sex before you're married, and if you do you've got issues. And then no one talks about it. But it's happening, can we talk about it? Can we help young people? Can we do something about this, because they're doing stupid things and making mistakes and all that sort of stuff. Instead it's like: if we talk about it it'll just make them have more sex. But they're having sex anyway.'

QUEER VOICES

It is amazing how one single aspect of ourselves can arouse
and create much controversy, secrecy, disapproval and
difficulties.

Waqfet Banat, Personal Narrative, Aswat – Palestinian
Gay Women

The film *Bend It Like Beckham* has many great attributes but perhaps one of its strongest is how progressive it was. Not only did it deal with the challenge of being a young woman from a conservative immigrant family living in the West and wanting to play sports, it also acknowledged that you can come from an ethnic minority and be gay.

While *Bend It* focused on the pressures of straddling a traditional Indian community, and broader Anglo ideas and values, it was a very relatable struggle for me as an Arab woman brought up in the West. It dealt with being a minority within a minority extremely well. In one scene, a character admits to Jess, the (Indian) heroine of the story, that he's gay. 'But ... you're Indian,' she spluttered. It's not laboured and it was a moment that elicited a great deal of laughter from my Arab friends and me because, at the time, you could just as easily have replaced 'Indian' with 'Arab'. Arabs pride themselves on tradition, and our culture favours conventional marriage, no matter your religion.

The moment comes with a heaviness – of the burdens faced

by a young man navigating the cultural and perhaps religious expectations of his family, amplified by the realisation that he will struggle to live the traditional life expected of him.

I'm not gay, so I have no place dissecting how this must feel for a man or a woman. But I certainly want to include the voices of women who identify as lesbian or bisexual, or who can offer insight into life for an Arab dealing with sexuality issues.

OUTED

Mariam*, a Lebanese Muslim woman in her thirties, raised in Sydney in a close cultural and religious community, had barely come to terms with her sexuality when she was outed.

'Coming out is a choice,' she said. 'You do it on your terms, you choose who you tell. Being outed, you are stripped of all rights around things and are immediately put in danger.'

Mariam described being outed in her twenties as '*fucking terrible*'. She was suicidal, at one point hospitalised. Dealing with her sexuality 'wasn't the only thing happening' at the time, either. 'This is the thing that a lot of straight people, and straight white people, don't understand, is that for queer people of colour, the idea that you come out doesn't exist. You in fact invite people in,' Mariam explained.

'And that's the thing that people need to realise when they're talking about queer people of colour – being a child of migrants ... there are a number of things that influence a person's decision to necessarily invite someone in or not. You never really isolate your sexuality from the rest of the drama in your life.'

Speaking to Mariam, it was clear that she had struggled on multiple levels – being gay has its challenges in a society that doesn't always accept it; but add to this other differences – culture, religion, everyday life struggles – and sexuality is just one thing, it's not everything.

'It was surprising to me how racist the queer community could be. I guess I thought there would be some holistic understanding or camaraderie among queers, but in fact the queer community faces similar issues around sexism, racism and patriarchy.'

There was some relief – in part from the support she did receive from other circles.

'It's funny, a lot of people ended up extending their hands, people that I hadn't spoken to in years ended up making contact with me,' said Mariam.

'Muslims?'

'Muslims.'

'Is it more common than people realise?' I queried.

'Yes, extremely.'

It occurred to me how it might feel to have to justify a relationship, or sexuality in general. Most of us would want the option of privacy, a choice that seems to be rarer for LGBTQI people. And while Mariam had been outed, and it was a brutal time in her life, I wondered about how not having to hide has helped.

'I took my girlfriend to *eid* this year at home,' Mariam said. 'I told my mother that I was bringing a friend. But she knew that she wasn't just a friend. And everyone in my family, my extended family, my cousins and uncles – they're on my Facebook, I didn't defriend anyone … They accepted, they kept me in the loop because they wanted the ability to gossip. And it was really fucking amazing. There was no need to say that she was my girlfriend. We slept in separate rooms …'

It took a couple of years to get to this point for Mariam. For Melissa*, another Sydney woman of Lebanese background, that small form of acceptance is yet to occur. Melissa is in her forties and has a lesbian partner she can't take home to her mother, even though she joins her girlfriend's family for Sunday breakfast.

'I'm Christian and my family are not accepting of my sexuality, but my Muslim partner, whose family are very religious, accept me as their daughter's life partner. They accept me wholly into their family.

'I leave her then go home and have lunch with my family and pretend I'm a single woman. At least my girlfriend escapes the *wajbat* (duties) of a partner,' Melissa told me with a laugh.

It's humour laced with a bit of sadness, but Melissa wasn't playing the victim. Sitting in her kitchen, she offered me sweets and Lebanese coffee – one of those *wajbat* Arabs consider important – while she talked about sexuality in an ethnic minority. Melissa might have grown up in Sydney, but she's very 'Arab' when it comes to culture, and she loves it. But she said being a lesbian has its challenges in a tight-knit community.

'Generally, Arab lesbians aren't out. [At least] they're not out to their family, but they're out to their friends. There are very few women today who are totally in the closet … you know, the whole "only gay Arab in the village",' she said.

There has been a significant shift in recent years, however, with social media helping Arab queers to identify with each other. 'In the last five years, even,' she said. 'And I don't think you'll find people who aren't at least out to themselves.'

Melissa said trying to come out initially 'was really depressing'. 'I tried to tell my parents in different ways. I knew I could never win, and I never wanted them to die unhappy. I always thought it would take years to get used to and I didn't know if I had that luxury,' she told me.

She pondered whether coming out in her twenties would have changed her narrative. 'If I had come out when I was young, I wouldn't have cared, because I was quite rebellious. I would leave the house under my mother's screams and shoe-throwing. I'd get home at three am. If only I was a lesbian then,' she joked, in reference to the years she dated men.

But it wasn't something she struggled with as a teenager, and now she lives what resembles a divided life – one truth in front of her family, another in her private life.

Melissa said that it's harder for Arab women to come out because homosexuality is still illegal in many countries in the Arab world. But she sees progress, especially in the increasingly public acknowledgement that homosexuality is real for many Arabs. She cited Labaki's film *Caramel* as a good example of how you can deal with lesbian relationships in a country that doesn't accept them publicly.

While Australia has made great advances in this area in the past fifty years, we're yet to legalise gay marriage, and debate still rages on the 'permissibility' of being queer in various religious and/or conservative circles. Meanwhile, a popular web series, *I Luv U But*, by Sydney filmmaker Fadia Abboud, explores with humour and pathos being gay and Arab. In the show, two young Lebanese Australians get married to hide the fact that they're gay. It's raw and funny, and deals honestly with the struggle some face in straddling two lives – one lived openly, another more hidden.

'Whether I want to get married or not, the good thing about the public debate is that it brings up a conversation on TV. Because it's so visual and prominent, it dilutes the energy my mother would ordinarily expend. She used to swear at the TV and now it's less frequent. And I tell my mother; "Well, you're going to have to accept it – the rest of Australia is." We both know I'm talking about me.'

Where acceptance does come is from the queer community. As Mariam had noted, you invite people in, making it a chosen family. And certainly, being queer does not necessarily involve the same level of secrecy as it used to. Social media, as Melissa mentioned, has made it easier to be part of a community. And events for queer Arabs, such as dance parties, are more public. Nonetheless, as so many women I spoke to attested, dating is not something a lot of Arab women do openly; add to that the potential 'shame' of being gay and the pressure is amplified.

Rita, the woman I met from a Lebanese-Christian family, who was raised in Australia, brought this into sharp contrast during our meeting, halfway through which she 'outed' herself as someone who is interested in men and women.

We were talking about relationships and how open she could be in taking someone home to her parents. Rita had introduced them to an Australian boyfriend of a couple of years without an issue. She said she would move in with a guy. 'I would tell them. It would be difficult to tell them if I wanted to have a baby without being married. Maybe not, though. You know, when I think about it now, the lines are so blurred because I've done so much. I've moved overseas, I've had boyfriends that they've known about. I've travelled ... I moved out when I came home from overseas ... The rules have adjusted.'

I felt compelled to ask Rita: 'Could you ever see yourself with an Arab guy?'

'I can see myself with any man. I honest to God wouldn't care about his race. What I do care about is where his values lie within himself and do they align with my values. And while we're on the topic, does it have to be a man?'

'No.'

'There you go.'

'Are you happy to talk about that?'

'Yes, totally.'

'So, do you feel both ways?'

'Yes. I do swing both ways. I've felt that way for years, but I've only had experiences more recently, maybe in the last year.'

While being from an ethnic minority seemed less influential than for Mariam, Rita acknowledged the added burden of shame that queer women experience. 'I would say everywhere, but for the purposes of this, let's focus on Australia,' she said. 'I think the difference is, if you're a straight woman and you go out and get shamed and called a slut, it's almost like there is still some human in there. Whereas if you're a woman and you happen to fancy women, and you want to explore that ... as a woman being into women, I feel like I'm looked at by some people, not all people, but some people would look at me and say, "You're wrong, you're not even human – you're sub-human." It's almost like – and I do not use this term loosely – but for a "slut", she can come back from that and redeem herself. You know?'

Rita was speaking of people in general, not specifically Arabs.

'I deal with it by telling myself, first and foremost, that it isn't anything for me to deal with right now because it is not my shame or guilt. I don't feel that. That is not my experience that I'm living in my body, in my feelings and in my heart. That's someone else's. When someone else makes you feel guilt or shame, isn't it really theirs?

'The tragedy is that there are people everywhere who are paying with their own lives for that stupid way of thinking, at the expense of someone else's shame and guilt and fear. Someone else's shame and guilt and fear is literally killing people like me. And I live in a place where – what's the worst that would happen if my cultural community found out? They might outcast me, but I'm still going to live. No one's going to fucking kill me. What about every other Lebanese woman? I was just lucky enough to be born on Australian soil.'

Though many women, of all backgrounds, might not feel safe in Australia, Rita is right, especially in relation to Arab women. The shame and guilt we inherit is the product of others' fear. That in all the discussions on how to live, we still believe in collective and individual ideas of the *right* way to live. Such ideas are just that – concepts, beliefs, rather than lived realities. This is a burden placed on women of all backgrounds and experiences.

Rita said she doesn't feel like she has to tell her parents. 'I'm okay with it being for me. My sister knows.' And her sister was 'totally fine, high-fived me, was so happy', she said.

'Do you feel like you were battling that part of yourself for a long time?'

'Yeah, you could say I was, but not ...' Rita trailed off. Then she acknowledged that, sure, culturally being gay or bisexual is not accepted – but it wasn't about that. 'It was about both cultures. It was about the culture of world society in general – you don't have to have a specific race or religion. I think that we're so – especially in Australia – way too conservative, my God.'

'Can I tell you something really important about that?' she said, her tone more serious. 'It's good that you can have a sense of all Middle Eastern women ... because we don't fit into boxes.'

Rita said she 'had a complex upbringing and I am a complex person ... I'm not predictable. When I first explored this, I very, very, very quickly realised that gender was nothing. Gender is another category and another label we give ourselves, and of course there is our biology ... which gives us a point of difference between what we know as male and female. But with exploring our souls and exploring ourselves, gender is nothing. The only thing that separates us ... are our fucking genitals. It's not even a thing. Because I was with this woman and I didn't even think of her ... I just felt like I was with a person. And in that moment, I really understood how my gay friends felt and how my lesbian friends felt. I understood how they loved their partners; I understood what their own experiences meant to them.'

Rita will say she's 'bisexual' for everybody else's processes, she told me. 'But I don't feel like labelling myself with the sexuality that still refers to my gender or refers to what gender I'm attracted to, because it was really – and this is honest to God just how I feel – it was completely removed from gender and completely ... I just connected with that person.'

She said she believes in how people identify – physical attraction. But it wasn't the case for her. 'It was very much an awakening, too.'

I asked her if she felt she could ever take a female partner to her parents.

'Do you know, it's so weird, I feel like I'd be able to bring it to my parents before I could bring it to anybody else in my [extended] family. I would actually feel more comfortable telling my parents than I would my cousins or my aunties or my uncles.'

'Do you think your parents would accept it?'

'I feel like my parents would struggle, but I would hope that they'd accept it. I feel like maybe the gifts that we've all given each other are enough to help each other understand. And I've been expressive for most of my life and I would hope that, as my parents have taught me a lot, maybe they've learned something from their children. And maybe they have learned from me that different is okay.'

Rita's stories touched on another element of the queer Arab experience, namely the confusion that comes with identifying your sexuality.

Mariam described a long journey towards her realisation. She experienced her first crush when she was a teenager. 'At eighteen, when you start to think that you could potentially be gay, that's extremely fucking scary. And there were endless times when you stood in front of the mirror and said, "What is wrong with you?"'

But she wasn't lonely because Mariam knew she wasn't the only one. 'There were plenty of other closeted queer Muslim women around me, and non-Muslim women around me.'

Mariam said some of these women, older than her, were like mentors and took care of her. 'They helped me understand what was happening. [And] there were those who were my friends who would just hang around and feed me and just show me their support ... and forever pretend that they didn't know when they were constantly questioned by everyone.'

Mariam said that the queer Arab women around her pegged her as gay before she even knew. 'But me, because I'm fucking stubborn, for six years I knew I was gay and I wouldn't come out to these queer Arab women who were around me, who were part of my almost every day,' she said.

'They'd be like, "Oh, you remind me of me, I remember I used to wear the scarf ..."' Mariam had worn hijab for many years, but eventually took it off, cut her hair short and continued her journey with Islam in other practical ways.

Part of her resistance was the pressure she felt to come out to these women, all Arab but from different backgrounds and religions. It eventually happened at a queer Arab women's *iftar*, she recalled with a laugh. 'Everyone at this thing is gay. Everyone is Arab – Muslim or Christian ... It's a family. It's what we say is the chosen family.'

Mariam said it helped a lot that she was surrounded by women who were going through similar things. However, if you do come out or get outed, she added, it doesn't mean there will be a neat conclusion. Your mother will constantly be asking: don't you ever want to get married? To have kids? 'That's still a conversation that happens. You can't pull that out of someone who, that's their entire narrative of their life and their understanding of how a person grows and dies. You can't expect otherwise.'

Mariam accepts this, but said there are limits to what she will and won't tolerate.

When I asked her how being Arab and Muslim affected her experience, she responded that there's a fine line between culture and religion. 'It was definitely hard. A lot harder than if I was a white Christian girl. You grow up and you have a certain idea of what you will do and what you will become and what you stand for, and then you find that, regardless of what you try to do and how you try to live your life, there's this thing that constantly comes up.

'It was a massive struggle for a long time and I feel like even now there are moments of shame and guilt that come through when you are with your friends or when you are with other Muslims.'

Navigating relationships can be difficult with life's usual pressures, and the shame that many women experience around dating. I asked her what the difference is between shame for straight women versus lesbians, citing Rita's thoughts on slut-shaming.

'I think there's a change of late, more recently, for the better. I think the Muslim community is coming out and accepting the fact that there are queer Muslims,' said Mariam. 'I think the struggles around sexuality as a straight woman and the questions you'd be asking yourself are ever different to growing up in the Muslim community and the Arab community and having thoughts of being gay. Homosexuality is forbidden in Islam. There are few *shukha* [clerics] who will give any sort of movement on that.' (There are *some* who will, she acknowledged. In recent times, there has even been an emergence of gay sheikhs in the US, Australia, South Africa, Europe and Canada.)

'So when you're comparing it to a woman who is straight and wants to explore her sexuality as a straight woman, with men or herself, the questions she would be asking and the shame that she would be feeling is very different to when you know that your entire upbringing has been telling you, "This is disgusting. There is no way around this." Especially because I feel like, growing up, there were plenty of people who had boyfriends and girlfriends, and people understood that, and those people ended up marrying each other, and it doesn't matter.'

The closest you might come to the gay-shame experience as a straight Arab woman is falling for a non-Muslim man who doesn't convert.

It helped that Mariam's friends stood by her when she was outed – Muslim girls who knew Mariam was gay but played dumb when questioned by others; who didn't ask questions and covered for her when she needed to go out with someone.

Overall, however, Mariam said the Muslim community has a long way to go in relation to queer issues. Despite the support of these Muslim friends, at a wider level Mariam felt she was cut off when she was outed; invitations to community events were no longer extended. But she is a passionate activist for social justice and believes that no queer, Arab or Muslim will be able to get any form of justice or rights until the rights of First Nation people have been met.

'That to me is much more important that a sheikh saying it's okay for me to be in a relationship with a woman.'

RAISING LGBTQI VOICES

Hanan Wakim is working in her 'dream career'. The freelance culture manager, who comes from a small village in Galilee and has lived in Jerusalem most of her life, has taken the fruit of her studies in Barcelona to help run Aswat, a support organisation for queer Palestinian women.

'*Aswat* means voices,' she told me. 'We have a film festival, we have a yearly exhibition about gender and sexuality, and we also try to make talks and other cultural events.'

Working at Aswat sees Hanan combine her sociology studies and culture management, as well as her community and political views, into the organisation, as an educational program coordinator.

Aswat was established more than ten years ago by a group of working women. 'They were very active in the community politically and socially. And for a while they thought that they were alone – like each one thought she was the only queer woman working in Palestine.'

Over time, they realised they had a lot in common. 'Then the idea came that there is a need for such a place for queer women to have a safe place to talk and to share.'

The women started to meet frequently, creating Aswat to let the voices of queer women be heard. In 2004, up to twenty women from the West Bank founded the committee. Aswat's first conference was held in 2007. It was significant that the women were out in public as a group.

'Aswat Palestinian Lesbian Women – this is the official title for now. And there was a big deal [made] about it. Some people didn't accept it and there was a small demonstration from Islamic fanatics outside the doors – like, this is the end of the world, and stuff like this.'

The first conference was mainly foreigners and local Israelis who supported the idea; less of the local Palestinian community. 'There is a lot of LGBT and human rights activists from the Israeli side who supported the establishment of such a conference and movement.'

But while the women knew they would need the support of everyone, ultimately it was the Palestinian community they wanted to reach.

Aswat is well known for its publications, some of which are in English, not just Arabic. They have people downloading from all over the world – Arab speakers are desperate for trustworthy information about sexuality, Hanan said.

'If you Google "gay" in Arabic, you will see all of this rubbish or things that relate to how Islam sees it and it's all negative.' There is no back-up or basis for these beliefs, added Hanan. 'It was very important to produce knowledge in Arabic for people mainly in Palestine but also abroad.'

Aswat steadfastly worked on increasing its reach through the media, as well, holding workshops for journalists about sexuality and sexual identity in a bid for representation in, if not a positive light, at least a neutral one.

'It worked,' said Hanan. 'In 2009, the majority of the [conference] audience were Palestinian. Even one Palestinian Knesset member, which is the Israeli Parliament, attended and supported the conference. So for Aswat it was a major step to have people more ... from the community, not just gay or queer, but also people from the media, from the political and social community and activists ...'

They showed support and gave legitimacy to the group to continue working. Aswat also had the support of feminist organisation Kayan, which until recently had hosted Aswat as a project.

'Can a Palestinian woman come out to her family?' I asked Hanan.

'It's a personal choice in the end. And it depends ...'

At Aswat, Hanan doesn't encourage everyone to come out with an alluring offer that it will make their life easier. People living in the West Bank and especially people who live in Gaza don't have the same opportunities or freedom as people living in '48 areas. (Nineteen forty-eight was the year of *nakba* – 'the catastrophe' – when hundreds of thousands of Palestinians were expelled from their homes or fled, and the areas they left became what is known as Israel. The Arabs of '48 – Palestinian citizens of Israel – either lost their land and became refugees, or lost their land but remained in their houses if they were not destroyed.)

If a queer woman is working and independent, she will have more freedom to do as she pleases. 'We have people who live a double life; we have people who are fully out and everybody knows that they are out; and we have people in denial. So I can't talk about one type of queer woman living in Palestine.'

The important thing groups like Aswat and alQaws, another queer organisation in Palestine, strive to provide is 'a safe place for people who want to share and talk about their sexuality, or they have questions, or they just need a community to support and just do things together. This is very important.'

It's also about providing knowledge and championing dialogue in society about gender and sexuality. 'Let's talk about it. Queer people exist in every religion, every community, so what do we do about it? Let's just talk and put it all on the table.'

Aswat is also targeting proper sexual education in schools – it's missing, Hanan said. Under occupation, Palestinians aren't in control of what is being taught in schools. Add in Arab society's deeply rooted conservativism and reluctance to change, and many people don't want to have a conversation about being queer. 'So there's a lot to be done.'

In addition to operating a phone line, Aswat sees women approach them through the website and Facebook. 'And sometimes we can help, and sometimes we just listen.'

A recent case was for two women from Gaza, both married with children, but who are in love. They're trying to get out of Gaza, which is hard for anyone on a normal day. Aswat found support in an embassy, but the women would be forced to leave behind their children. Under Palestinian law, the children belong to the fathers.

'And you're in the middle. I don't know what to do,' said Hanan. 'I can't even physically go and meet [one of the women] and talk to her and try to help her. Sometimes we feel helpless and sometimes people approach and we try to provide a home, help with finding jobs, give support. So we do as much as we can.'

It's worth noting that Hanan is not queer herself, and has the support of her immediate family for her work. What matters for her is the difference she can potentially make for women who are struggling with their sexuality.

'What's special, I think, is our relationship with the law. In '48 [land], we are working with the Israeli law. It's a little bit [more] advanced than West Bank and Gaza, but still, it's not ours. It's a law that discriminates against Palestinians and Arabs, so it doesn't matter if you're queer or not queer – by default, if you're an Arab this whole system of law and politics is put there just to discriminate against you and make the settlers, the Israeli community, stronger.'

Because of the political situation, the feeling most of the time is that 'it's no-man's-land'. On paper there is law, but the system is vague and ruled by *wasta* – connections, political alliances, etc. Weak people are negatively affected in these situations, Hanan said: women, children, the poor.

'And Gaza, where to start? Poverty, and you also have Islamic rule.' Hanan sounded genuinely upset, helpless. 'A lot of people tell us, "You have to work on policy change and we will give you money," and I'm like, "What policy? You're talking about occupation and, like, the Wild West."'

Indeed, while Hanan did not talk about it, 'pinkwashing' by Israel has gained a great deal of attention in recent times. Writing for *Kohl: A Journal for Body and Gender Research*, Palestinian feminist Ghadir Shafie recounts her experience of moving to Tel Aviv, sold to her as 'the ultimate gay haven', in 'Pinkwashing: Israel's International Strategy and Internal Agenda'.

'I had been a Palestinian Arab my entire life, who simply happened to question her sexuality. I had come to Tel Aviv to be who I was, but it became clear to me that I was welcome there as a "lesbian", not as a Palestinian. In their world of alleged "freedoms" and rights, there was no place for my Palestinian-ness. I had to choose between being gay and being

Palestinian, but giving up a part of myself was impossible to bear.'

And while efforts have been made to improve understanding around sexuality in Israeli schools through funding Israeli LGBT organisations, 'Palestinian queer and LGBT organisations simply do not figure in the equation of LGBT resource distribution in Israel,' wrote Ghadir.

Of course, as Mariam explained, there is a huge difference between coming out and being outed, and in a conservative society, already burdened with economic and social issues, it poses a threat to not have the autonomy to make a decision on this yourself.

Not surprisingly, dealing with family is one of the primary concerns for queer women: 'Family, friends and how can I deal with my parents? What if they know? People tend to think that all Arab people will kill their children if they do something wrong – if a woman has sex before marriage or if they are gay, all Arab families will bring knives … But sometimes it's more profound. Their parents won't be proud, or they will be sad – "I don't want to upset my parents" … It's not always fear that makes people move; it's also that it's hard,' said Hanan.

'A lot of people come and ask how they can deal with their parents. The thing that we do is give them stories; not telling them what to do but let them meet others and talk about it and learn from each other's stories and experiences.'

However, Hanan said, not everyone suffers rejection; sometimes you'll be surprised by how loving and understanding parents can be for their children. 'We have a lot of out gay people who are welcomed in the community.'

'[And] we are trying to find the Palestinian voice ... the thing that works for us because we also have queer Palestinians who still believe in God and religion and they do want to pray and they do want to wear hijab ... There are several ways to be queer and we're trying to find this authenticity of how to be yourself and queer and to live in peace with it. If it's not coming out, it's fine. If you feel you want to come out, we will support you.'

I thought of Rita from Melbourne and her meditations on acceptance and fear. Like the women Hanan described, the struggle with sexuality, acceptance (self- and societal) eclipsed culture. The struggle wasn't about being Lebanese or Palestinian, it was about a woman's humanity.

THE SISTERHOOD

Give your daughters difficult names. Give your daughters
names that command the full use of tongue. My name makes
you want to tell me the truth. My name doesn't allow me to
trust anyone that cannot pronounce it right.

Warsan Shire

Despite our divergent views on life as a woman in some crucial aspects, my mother is the first person who taught me that women are strong, that we don't have to be silent. Her emotional muscle goes beyond the neat and precise characters we've come to associate with Arab women – the overwrought mother defending her cubs or the meek veiled servant who has no capacity for individual thought.

In the West, we suffer the same need to simplify strength as a form of rebellion, rather than a character trait. Here we have caricatures: the angry feminist who rallies followers on social media is considered 'strong', for example.

Of all the fables about Arab women, the ones that bother me the most are those stories that render us weak, or, worse, strong in a two-dimensional way – an Arab mother can wield a shoe and get you with it from a mile away; or she's helpless in the face of patriarchy, submissive, unthinking, a slave to her fate.

Arab women are three-dimensional, and not necessarily unusual in their struggles, even if cultural and religious influences are strong. The competing simplistic ideas about us barely scrape the surface of our true strength and complexity.

It's a belief that held true throughout my meetings with Arab women. When I met with Rula, the university professor in Jordan, she handed me a collection of stories written by her students: *The Voice of Being Enough: Young Jordanian Women Break Through Without Breaking Down.*

'We talk ... in my classrooms, we uncover, we peel away. We discover ... I do this in my feminist theory and it's a lot of fun.'

In the book, many journeys unfold, the narrators themselves unfurling, free-falling through their lives. 'Why me? Why not me?' writes Haya. 'My loud voice and bubbly personality are no longer shame.'

'I am enough because I live for myself and for my freedom,' writes Sjoud. 'I love life and I love freedom, but I do not forget that I am an Arab.'

It's not enough to talk about society's issues; for sustainable change to occur, cultural shifts must also transpire. This is why Rula's work with the students is so progressive and important.

'This book ... the women are writing themselves ... I tell my kids in the classroom whenever I teach them feminist theory, "Use your white ink. Use your white ink, according to the French feminists, and write. We have been told by the patriarchy that you cannot use the pen because the pen is part of the penis, and the penis is the 'pen is'. French feminists contest that notion ... we have the ink and our ink is white and we can do with it wonders. We can write who we are because we're enough and more than enough."'

Rula said it took a long time for her to utter this in the class-room. 'I used to write it on the whiteboard ... Now, I say it. I roar like thunder, and I say it.' Rula said the students will stare back at her in embarrassment. But she had more to say: 'We're in a classroom. A classroom is a site of education, a site of resistance. This is a safe space. We have a social contract. You can say what you really want to say. Don't be ashamed. Break the silence because your voice is not an *awrah*. Your voice is not vice.'

THE LOWER-CASE FEMINIST

I don't explicitly call myself a feminist, though I am one in belief, essence and action. I embody the energy of change feminism seeks, but I also see there is no one definition of what a feminist looks like, or what they stand for.

I'm a lower-case feminist. I'm certainly not a brand feminist, the hashtag warrior who feels the need to fight everything and everyone. I don't feel buoyed by Beyoncé taking to the stage in barely-there outfits, oozing defiance as she stands beside the word 'FEMINIST' in lights, but nor do I see her self-empowerment as an affront to feminist values. I don't see it as my place to decide what a woman's life should look like, though I naturally have beliefs that influence how I live mine. I don't see myself as less than a man, nor do I champion being his equal. In a world of confusion, where people do not all neatly fit into categories of male or female, how can we advocate for anything but authenticity that causes harm to none?

I'm an agent for change, but I focus on the outcome I desire, not the problem that compels me towards it. It's taken me years to appreciate the difference, and I'm not sure I get it right all the time.

But here's the thing: I just feel completely and utterly over-loaded with labels. I'm trying, somewhat unsuccessfully, to shed them – the words, not the meaning. I am Amal Awad, sometimes Amal Larsen née Awad. Yet I continue to struggle with the explanation of my odd-sounding name: I am Amal – an Arab–Australian Muslim. Add in feminist writer and it gets convoluted, burdensome and limiting – it tells you all the things I can be, not who I am. I am at once honoured and burdened by my odd-sounding name. I wouldn't change it. 'Amal' holds great meaning: *hope.* My mother gave me that name because she was hoping for a daughter.

Previous experience has taught me that feminism applies differently in Australia to women who aren't white. Having read this far, you would recognise my fractious relationship with identity, and my near-complete rejection of identity politics. But I do understand identity and the appeal it holds for marginalised people. I've played around with it enough myself.

THEY JUST DON'T KNOW ANY BETTER

Of all the women I engaged with, few of them outright called themselves feminists. In Beirut, Aliya, who spoke passionately about her desire for women to unveil themselves, never used the word feminist. I'd certainly consider her one. As I said, we can embody feminism without needing to declare it.

I think of all the female 'exceptions' to the clichés: Muriel Aboulrouss, the Arab world's first female cinematographer, a professional description she reluctantly embraces, knowing that it matters but that it's not how she wishes to define herself. Souad Al Hosani, a confident and highly successful entrepreneur in Abu Dhabi. Lubna Nasser, a Jordanian woman who is working with Dignity, a Danish organisation against torture. Nikita Shahbazi, a dancer who sweeps into refugee camps in Lebanon to help women unburden their bodies through movement, and hopefully, in some way, heal. Laudy Lahdo, an Australian–Lebanese woman now settled in Dubai who does important work mentoring young women professionally through a not-for-profit program called Reach.

I think of the women who bring their ancestors' stories to life. The women who are activists for change. All of them women who want to improve the lives of other women. In Beirut Sabine, the clown, was perhaps the most memorable rejecter of the title while standing out as a ground shaper: 'I'm not a feminist. And I believe that the feminist movements in the world have made a big difference. I have problems with some feminists who hate men, who attack others.'

Sabine does extraordinary work in refugee camps, assisting women as they open up about religion, culture and their relationships with their bodies.

'I worked with a group of women in the Zaatari camp in Jordan. I did social therapy with them, and it's actually like group therapy. But instead of me being the only therapist in the room, we're all therapists for each other.'

When Sabine left, the women would continue group sessions together.

'And the whole idea is for them find out what's bothering them as a group of women, find the solution and execute the solutions. And they opened a gym in the Zaatari camp. They all had problems with their husbands, because their husbands were not working, so they were just staying at home and being assholes to them.

'Women have such a great power and they can do things. If I want things to happen anywhere, I just go and talk to the women. That's it. I stopped talking to men on those matters. Women are doers.'

I was pleased to hear Sabine's thoughts on disturbing cultural norms and the importance of fixing 'our own shit'.

'We cannot have an agenda coming from outside because nobody understands.' She was referring to the curricula NGOs hand them when they offer funding: a sort of 'how-to' on making Arab women better off.

'I can't go empower a group of women and once I empower these women I know they're going back to their tents and disempowerment is going to work against them,' said Sabine. 'No, let's hear what they have to say, what their ideas are, because they know better than I do.'

Sabine's argument that it's necessary for this community to find the solutions from the inside is something that can be extended to other parts of the Middle East. Certainly in Jordan women expressed frustration that funding was subject to the cause of the day, or an outsider's interpretation of what an ideal life should look like for an Arab woman.

This is one of the biggest challenges: that people in the West so often talk down to Arab women, as though we can't be trusted to know what's best for ourselves. If we're not being infantilised by men, we're being infantilised by women in the West who think they know better. I hear it all the time, particularly in relation to Arab Muslim women. If you suggest that some women have made a choice to do things a certain way – in the West this is often the case – you are told, 'That's because they don't know any better.'

But we're capable of carving our own pathways, and of helping others to do so where their circumstances are more challenging. I acknowledge the many privileges of my life, but also the difficulties. I began to walk a path that wasn't given to me, but which I chose. And I did it for myself, not to make other people happy. In the same way, I didn't see it as rebellion – no one else was the basis of my life decisions.

On the other end of that are Arab women themselves who simplify the struggles of women. Some will argue that making a choice has nothing to do with 'not knowing better', but rather that many women are happy as they are. In other words: don't disrupt the narrative they're accustomed to, even if it means they won't see all that is possible.

Somewhere, a woman can start to think for herself and develop her own barometer for personal contentment. This is what frightens people. It's not what women can do for themselves, it's the impact it will have on men, on families and societies.

What Sabine is doing in camps is progressive: helping one woman to change her life will help many women.

'Of course. I just give tools, and I listen. I've studied seven years to really know how to listen. Listening is engaging in a productive conversation, where you give the other the power of finding the solution and executing the solution. And you just support. And then I feel so much better, because the answer isn't with me. I have no answers. I can barely save myself,' she said with a laugh.

BENEATH THE BLACK ABAYA

An undercurrent to all of my conversations with women was the pressure they have felt and continue to experience as females in male-dominated or male-favoured environments. You can want to forge a way forward without reference to men, but it's not easy because you didn't choose the setting in which you operate. Ultimately, many of us go from being daughters to wives, and perhaps mothers. Not moving on to either marriage or motherhood comes laced with its own unique set of judgement. We're meant to satisfy everyone, to fit conflicting ideas of how we should live.

It's certainly a difficult but formative time for women in the Middle East who are agitating for change. And there are plenty of women who are shaping new ground, searching for new ways forward, lighter pathways. Women who are working in a variety of areas that don't just help women, but men and children, too.

As I embarked on my journey, Saudi Arabian women were hash-tagging their dissent against the guardianship laws that can see them treated like children. A music video appeared on my Facebook feed featuring Saudi women demanding their rights. Entitled 'Oppression' it showed women completely covered but with colourful clothing beneath *abayas*, rollerblading and riding on scooters, playing basketball and even dancing. It mocked the laws governing their lives: in one scene, the women sit in the backseat of a car – they're forbidden to drive – and a boy no older than seven or eight takes the wheel. This is subversive progress and it's coming from Saudi women themselves.

'May all men disappear from the earth,' the women sing. 'They give us psychological illnesses. Damn, you feel none of them is sane.'

It's a flamboyant and irreverent indictment of the system, which requires women to seek permission from male relatives to go about many everyday aspects of their lives. It features men, who mock the freedoms afforded them in Saudi Arabia.

The dissent trended on social media, with women rejecting treatment as a man's property, rather than a person in their own right.

Years ago, I took note of a breast cancer awareness campaign in Saudi Arabia that was directed at men: it beseeched them to make sure women had check-ups because they were their daughters, sisters, wives and mothers. I wrote critically about it and the backlash was fierce. I wish I hadn't because I now feel it's a far deeper problem than a moment of online outrage can capture. And it's an issue requiring far more nuance than an 800-word column can afford it. It's also something for Saudi women to take on. And many suggested to me that the campaign was progress; while I found it unfortunate that even a health issue that primarily affects women (I was told that men can get breast cancer, too, of course) had to go through the man, I understood their point. To address inequities for women requires social change, which will take time. Because what women are up against are the sullying beliefs that any desire for change is a desire to Westernise, an accusation that can dampen if not outright halt a movement.

It's been damaging for activists like Jordan's Rana Husseini, who has been working in the area of so-called honour killings for years. Trying to reshape how wider society perceives the role of women, the shame attached to sexuality, and the previous acceptance that men may murder or injure 'in the name of honour' saw her accused of a great many things, including a desire to Westernise – the connotation being that Western women are overly sexual and 'open'.

I also touched on the Saudi women's rights movement in conversation with feminists in Qatar, where similar guardianship laws in relation to travel exist.

Nurah*, a student at Georgetown University in Doha, is in her twenties and passionate about improving the lot of women in Qatari society. She has experienced the inequities of guardianship laws that limit women's movement, including travelling abroad, and wants to see reforms to laws around divorce. A child of parents who split up, she learned firsthand that the difficulties of being a girl in such a situation are amplified. Her father had already left the country and her mother when Nurah was born, a situation that left them under the control of male relatives. Nurah explained that women can't leave the country without the permission of a male guardian throughout the Gulf region.

'It applies here in specific areas. It's more in Saudi Arabia,' she said.

The day before our meeting, Princess Noura University in Riyadh, the largest women's university in the world, had ended its guardianship rules, allowing women to join the gym and sports facilities without the permission of a male. Nurah thought it was 'pretty big news'.

'For Qatar, you can't leave the country without male permission until the woman is twenty-five or twenty-four years old.' Nurah said she experienced limitations due to her father's absence. 'It also affected my mum because she was married and he only divorced her four years after he left.'

Nurah's mother needed male relatives to contact people in government to get permission to leave. 'My mum and I were lucky, we had contacts. For other women, they can't, and that really affected me. It feels unfair to me. It felt unfair to me being in that position where I'm at the airport and I'm not allowed to leave just because a man didn't sign my permission. My mum was with me and she'd tell them, "I'm her mum, I'm not going to do anything to her," but they would turn us back.'

Nurah recalled the memory matter-of-factly but her pain was evident. It had been traumatic for her – she was very young. Eventually, when she was eighteen, the permission requirement shifted to her brother. 'I still can't leave the country without my brother's permission.' He gives her permission, but she resents it being necessary – she's not a child. 'It feels like my own government doesn't trust me.'

But Nurah said Qatar is an easier place to be a woman than Saudi Arabia in several aspects, even if only in the last couple of decades. She's done research on the history of women in Qatar and how society has changed for them. 'I've spoken to a couple of mums and elderly women and they keep telling me, "You are so lucky, you were born when Sheikh Hamad came to rule – the same year – because [we had it] hard." For elderly women [years back], Qatar society was much more liberal, it was much more open, they could go wherever they want. They were happy. It was only when petrol came and then in the seventies, the influence of the Iranian Revolution, and Saudi Arabia welcoming the Muslim Brotherhood, that things started to get conservative here. Like, back in the day, we would not wear the abaya, we would not wear the *shaal*.'

When Sheikh Hamad's father came to rule in 1970 he declared that Qatar would follow Saudi Arabia in almost every aspect of daily life. 'And women were so limited. I remember one elderly woman told me, "I would leave the house and walk to the other side of Qatar for the whole day, alone, without any supervision. But [from 1970] women were basically confined to their homes."'

We agreed that a huge issue is how deeply embedded the negative mentality towards women is – a young boy is going to grow up seeing his mother and sister as being less than him.

'That's what I'm seeing,' said Nurah, who thinks it's a psychological issue for women of the time; things changed for them. 'I don't blame them … But the men were taught since they were young, "You're a man, you're in charge of the females in your family, even if your sister is older than you."'

Nurah offered the example of a Saudi woman who lost her husband and father. Without brothers or uncles in her family, her male guardianship was given to her nine-year-old son. 'We don't have that here, thank God,' Nurah said, almost with a chuckle. 'But it's a mentality.'

Even though rules are more lenient in Qatar, Nurah said guardianship still annoys her. 'When I complain they tell me, "Just be glad you're not in Saudi Arabia."' But for Nurah that's not the point, and, she added, it's not Islamic.

Haya, another student whose focus is on politics and improving conditions for women, offered similar insight. She said guardianship is explained by invoking Islamic law; more specifically, there is a law that in court, a man's testimony is equivalent to that of two women. Yet guardianship didn't exist in the time of the Prophet Muhammad, Haya said. Women travelled by camel alone.

'Does it bother you that your testimony is deemed less trustworthy?' I asked Haya. 'It's hard for me to get my head around it.'

Haya didn't give an immediate response. 'It's hard for me to get my head around it, definitely. But ... when something bothers me about Islam, I always look into the background of it, the context of it. Because Islam came at a time when women were oppressed, and they gave women a lot of rights.'

Haya went on to explain that if she found stories in the Quran she deemed sexist, she'd ask someone knowledgeable about it. It's not enough to look at the Quran as a set of rules that you have to abide by; you have to understand where they come from.

Haya said she has no inherent issue with religion, it's the patriarchy she objects to. 'Because I'm studying Islamic history now and I'm still learning, but I have a professor who is amazing when it comes to women, the Middle East and Islamic law.'

She explains things to Haya, who said she doesn't believe Islam is sexist. She argued that the practice of Islam grew patriarchal around four hundred years ago, with the arrival of certain scholars.

Haya takes her study of Islam seriously and she doesn't shy away from the rougher elements of life. Before we met, she had been reading up on Islamic rape laws, which in the modern legal system are the same as those applied to fornication. 'If a woman reports rape, she's punished like she's fornicated. But when a woman reported rape to the Prophet, he executed the man.'

Haya declared she's about improving conditions for women, rather than comparisons to men. 'I'm trying to improve their lives, and the way I see it here – I can't speak for women in other parts of the Middle East, I can speak for women in the Gulf, especially Qatar – women here are strong. I don't like how we are labelled as weak. No, we're very strong. Sometimes they can be conformist, but it's because they're hiding because they're scared. They fear backlash, but when they get the support – and we have received the support – amazing things can happen.'

'Do you think one of the big problems women are facing is the older generation of women?'

'Definitely. Not just women, men as well.'

Haya added: 'I know a couple of Qatari guys who are feminists. They're in my university. Most of the Qataris, they say they're feminists, they say they believe in women's rights, but when it comes to them towards the end, they want the [upper hand]. I've even spoken to professors in class. Even when it's sexist and they don't know it's sexist – like if a woman talks in class, a guy will speak up for her and he'll be like, "I think she means ..." No, you don't know what I mean. Even those little things that's in their mindset, which is technically by the patriarchy. You know, your voice is more important than a woman's voice. Even when we get into debates, they kind of disregard us, like what you're saying is nonsense. But that's specific guys, not a lot of them.'

'Do you feel respected here as a woman?'

'Sometimes. [It's not that] as a woman I feel respected. When I feel disrespected, I think it's because I'm a woman.'

It's a crucial distinction. For example, Haya said, when voicing an opinion, she can be disregarded because she's female. Or if she's speaking and a guy is speaking, people will listen to the guy. Or usually when she's approaching someone, especially if they're a male, and she's with her brother, they will answer her brother.

Nurah pointed out another insidious aspect to being a woman in Qatari society – it's relatively small: around 200,000 Qataris and 1.7 million expats make up its population, so among Qataris everyone knows each other. Nurah explained that a lot of Qataris go to London and women there won't cover, which foments gossip back home, the insinuation being that they are immoral for not covering. 'Basically like a slut because she doesn't do it,' said Nurah. 'And it's ridiculous, honestly. Then they can start rumours ...' Like a woman, hair uncovered, going to a coffee shop means she was definitely going to meet a guy, even though she could be going to study.

'Women can be their own worst enemies,' I said.

'Exactly. Women don't help other women.'

And women face the most pressure in meeting society's expectations, said Nurah, for example, in relation to covering hair.

Nurah wore her *shaál* loosely around her head, not proper hijab per se. 'But I have to wear this. I don't wear it abroad. And some women don't.'

When we met, at Georgetown University, I noticed that pretty much all the women were dressed in black abayas and wore either headscarves or a *shaal* in a similarly casual fashion. Underneath the loose-fitting garments were designer clothes, and brand handbags were a popular accessory. One woman hobbled past in Louboutin heels, jeans and a Juicy Couture jacket – no abaya and make-up suitable for a party. Another student, who helped me arrange a taxi, wore very cute, sequinned sneakers that peeked out beneath her robe. I complimented her on them and she smiled. 'They're Gucci.'

The gossip issue was interesting, but not unique. At the American University of Beirut I spoke to a young Palestinian woman, the daughter of a split family of refugees. She lived on campus and relished it, away from the chatter and prying eyes of people in her small town. And another woman, a Jordanian from Irbid, was single and living in Amman, relieved to not have her life overseen at every turn by other people. It's partly what kept her there – in Amman no one interfered.

This is a common problem, but it's easy to forget just how punishing gossip and the collective eye – especially the female gaze – can be on a woman. Even in Australia, Arab women talked about the brutalising pressure they felt to follow rules.

When it comes to Arab women, so much stems from, or plugs into, one tiny word, one swollen concept: *ayb*. It has a meaning – rude/inappropriate – but it carries greater depth than that. *Ayb* is an energy. *Ayb* is an inhibitor, painted as a dark master of desires. If you're doing something *ayb*, you're going against the preferred – nay, only acceptable – archetype of the modest woman. And if we're to have an honest conversation about modesty, it's important to consider what a loaded word it is and how it's used liberally to dress down women for something as small as laughing out loud in public. It encompasses so many aspects of being a female – dress, behaviour, even the sound of a woman's voice.

There's no tiptoeing around this as a reality for women anywhere in the world. The shaming of females comes in many forms, and while levels of offence are influenced by external and internal cultures, largely it's a problem experienced by women.

Lina, an Egyptian journalist who was chief editor of website Mada Masr when we met, grew up in a family that was on the 'more conservative side of things'.

'They were always concerns about coming back home late, what kind of things I'm allowed to do.' It was common, and Lina said, 'nothing special' to her.

She is Christian, but noted that she grew up in 'a broader Muslim society'. Interestingly, this wasn't a source of struggle for Lina, who suggested that her relative privileges in class, education and the like protected her from sectarian strife. Yet she described similar issues to many Muslim women.

'It's interesting. I was never very focused on the outlying gender politics that were in my life, my private life, my life with my parents and then later on, my life now. But retroactively I always reflected on what language they used. For example, when they would make requests or orders or commands related to me being a young woman. And, for example, they always say that the issue is that we are worried about you, we don't want to restrict you but we are worried about you. As opposed to, you're not allowed because the sheer fact that you're a woman does not allow you to do certain things. So there was this protective language as opposed to commanding language of "Because you're a woman you're not allowed to do this and that." And I'm not saying it's any better. I think it's equally bad, if not worse.'

Lina said it was interesting to utilise that language in developing a response: 'My defence has always been, "Oh well, let me show you what I will become for you to sense how much you'd worry about me on the basis of me being a woman." And then I start a career in journalism and it takes me everywhere in the country, but also even outside of the country, at some points to cover conflict zones, Syrian war. At some point, coming back from all these assignments, even those in Egypt, covering the terrorism that was happening at the beginning of 2000 and so on, going to Sinai, the site of a major insurgency by the militants against the state.

'Coming back from all these experiments and after having written about them and published about them, I go back home and confuse them because there's this pride of having a byline in all these newspapers and this confusion of, "Yeah, but we were supposed to look after you and worry about you and you're not giving us a chance."'

Lina went on to raise a nuanced point about being brought up female in a conservative society: she debunked ideas about her needs. 'I do things men are afraid to do, so the language and the logic you're worried about has very little meaning. If it is an argument that you're using to mask a much more boring agreement related to what are the norms, what's accepted socially and so on, let's talk this language, let's talk debunking this language. Our confrontations and our fighting were centred around this kind of logic. I think I managed to change my mother a bit and because I think essentially women have more of an ability to be honest to revisit things and critically ... I don't mean to be a sexist and make generalisations, but I feel like in my experience in general women have been more able to revisit the positions in a more critical way than men, and my mother is the first testament to that.'

The role of women in shifting mindsets cannot be overstated. Another casualty of a small, close society is how it tries to cover up wrongdoing by men, something women are sometimes complicit in – understandable given the risk of reprisal. Domestic violence goes unreported, explained Nurah. 'Even if it comes out and people know, they blame the woman. She must have done something to annoy her husband. A husband wouldn't just react violently like that. Or even when it comes to rape, people will not say anything because of the victim-blaming that would go on. They won't report it.'

However, while Nurah identified issues she has experienced due to laws affecting women, she doesn't blame her government – societal change is needed.

'The government is progressing a lot. And you can see this with Education City – they know Muslim women are not allowed to study abroad so they brought the universities to us.' (Education City is part of Georgetown University, where we met.)

'There are a lot of women like me,' added Nurah. 'They're from across the board. The funny thing is that the *shaykha* who opened [Education City], she's privileged. And most of the feminists are privileged, but you also see regular Qataris fighting for their rights, which is amazing.'

Neither Haya or Nurah were reluctant to 'air dirty laundry'. They're active on social media, responding to the needs of women by raising their voices against injustice. Given one of the major issues confronting feminists in the West is online abuse, it was interesting to hear how men respond to their vocal feminism.

Nurah said, 'When I tweet about things that bother me, I've gotten tweets from men where they're like, "Type in Arabic."

I'm not going to type in Arabic. First of all I'm more comfortable with English. Second of all, why are you giving me these orders? I can do whatever I want.'

'Do you ever get threatened?'

'Not threatened, but I believe I don't get threatened because of my high status in society,' Nurah said, in reference to her family, who are well off and of relatively high status. 'I know women who tweet and their social class is less than mine and they get threatened. Most of the time what bothers me is that when I go on these rants I get messages from men and they flirt with me.'

'They're trying to belittle you.'

'Exactly.'

'Like, aren't you cute?'

'Exactly. Or they say, "This woman is powerful, we can take her on." "I want to make her mine, just because she's a challenge. She's a strong woman, I can handle her."'

Abrar*, a Kuwaiti working in Dubai, raised a similar attitude she has experienced in the real world in her work. When men want to challenge her or a decision she's made, they will try to sweet-talk her. It doesn't work.

Haya said, however, that there are exceptions. 'My brothers are feminists. They don't care what I do with my life. They know I know right from wrong and they support me. And even if they don't, they just stay quiet,' she said.

'Even my eldest brother, who is a very quiet guy, I don't get as much vocal support from him, but he lets me do what I do. He doesn't step in. But I've had women friends who have met him, they've worked with him and they say, '"If you hear how he talks about you, he's very supportive."'

But she acknowledged that there are men who feel threatened by the success of a woman. She's seen it in the way they respond to the attention she gets, for example doing an interview like this one. 'They won't say anything, but you feel the threat is there. They will leave you alone. They can't say anything. They're not in your family, they're not your husband, or whatever. It's not their place to state an opinion. They fear the success of a woman.'

Perhaps this is the case everywhere. Isn't that what we're really fighting when a woman misses out on something? When a girl is denied her education in place of a boy? When a woman is expected to stay at home rather than work and receive an income?

'Yeah, that's everywhere. That's the thing, it's everywhere. It's a global issue.'

And what of the critical Western eye? At a time of intense focus on the Arab world and particularly the lives of women there, how does she see the role of the outsider who doesn't have to live her life but seems to have a lot of ideas on how she should live it?

'I don't appreciate the West coming in and basically portraying us as women who need to be saved by them. I do not appreciate that. Because, first of all, when they do that, it shows me that they're acting more superior to us, but you have your own feminist issues as well in your own country, and some of them we don't. Like in Qatar, a woman gets equal pay to a man. But that doesn't happen in America. That's just one example. Yes, we have issues, and yes they are to a higher extent, but we don't need to be saved.'

Haya added, 'Leave us to fight for ourselves. I appreciate you highlighting our issues – yes, that needs to be highlighted.'

Her attitude was common. I didn't hear any Arab woman criticise Western feminism outright as such; they noted an intrusion on women's rights in the Middle East, a vastly different landscape.

Meanwhile, Haya said feminists work according to their region. 'Where women are taking control, it's definitely a regional thing.'

'Would you participate in women's rights campaigns for Saudi Arabia or for Jordan?'

'I have, online. We support each other. I've had messages from women in Kuwait and Saudi Arabia and the UAE. We all talk to each other.'

'What does Arab world feminism look like today then?'

'I think it's more powerful than Western feminism. I think it's more united. Because when you look at the West and their feminism, you find white feminists, white feminism. We don't have that here. I think the sisterhood is more united. And you rarely see a feminist competing with another feminist.'

'What do you see as white feminism?'

'It's basically the feminism we see in America where most of the issues they talk about are primarily for white women. I mean, they don't take into account Hispanics or black women's issues. It ignores the minorities. We don't have that here.'

Interestingly, I didn't get the same impression of a united front speaking to women in Jordan. Competition for funding could be fierce and potential allies sometimes split in order to secure their programs. Because funding is generally conditional – as Sabine pointed out, loaded with a 'curriculum' – this strengthens divides. Women focused on a sanctioned cause will not speak out on unrelated issues.

Haya talked about the social anxiety she experiences at times. When she feels surrounded she reminds herself that God is with her. 'When I'm faced by women who don't like me, and I know this woman is not my friend.'

Haya has great friends, but there's this one woman in particular who challenges her. 'I know one sees me as this threat because she's a feminist. And I don't get why. Because the way it is, when women fight women, only men benefit. Especially when it comes to Arab society.'

'But you said you're more united here? Is this an exception?'

'We are. [She's] an outlier.'

SISTERS UNITED

That Islam is not seen as the issue, but more often the source of liberation by many Muslim women, is a pertinent point. This is the great challenge for feminism in the Arab world – many don't want an Islamic set of laws governing their lives, no matter how liberating other women find them.

It's an interesting tension and one I discussed with Samah, an Australian woman of Lebanese descent. Her activism has led her to the Arab world. In her own words, Samah Hadid has always been a human rights campaigner and was drawn to Egypt during the revolution, an action that eventually left her feeling depleted. She is now based in Beirut. She was well known in Australia, a regular on the ABC's Q&A, which frequently features politicians. Samah's life had changed, though: the humanitarian in her had been exposed to issues beyond her community in Sydney, the Arab Spring becoming a seminal turning point in her life.

'I was living and working in Australia ... this is after many years of not affiliating with my Arab identity at all ... in senior, high-profile roles ... Then I was watching the news and I saw this uprising. I saw people taking to the streets, millions, and something just clicked in me. It sparked this curiosity as to what is going on. Through and through I'm a human rights activist. Something is just really pushing me towards the Middle East, and wanting to explore this part of the world, and myself a bit more,' she told me.

'What I witnessed was unparalleled in my lifetime. It was something that was so inspiring – to see young Arabs of all walks of life question and challenge authority and dictatorship for freedom and dignity. It was a really instrumental moment. It was a turning point in my life, because I became far more fascinated in the Middle East, and in my Arab identity.'

It's also where Samah encountered women's rights activists and a feminist group recommended to her. 'I decided to volunteer with this feminist group. Because I naturally gravitate towards women's rights issues and women's groups,' she said.

At the time, Samah was still wearing hijab. 'They're these really staunch Arab feminists, and that for me was so challenging, because the hijab in the Middle East is so different ... It's such a loaded concept. It's not as easy as freedom of choice in Australia, where a woman chooses to put on a hijab, which is the common experience there. In Egypt, it is loaded with classicism issues and pressure and patriarchy. That was so evident to me,' Samah recalled.

'Then also just working, and immersing myself with these women – for me they presented a form of feminism that really made sense to me. Growing up in a Western society, the feminism that was presented to me was not appealing. And to be honest with you, even though I saw myself as a Muslim feminist, and aligned with that strand of feminism, it also didn't go far enough for me.

This was the first time that I discovered a feminism that worked for me. It was a culturally relevant one, one that acknowledges culture and an Arab identity, and also politics of colonisation. But also one that doesn't let down women, basically.'

It was eye-opening for Samah, and inspiring. She had been questioning the hijab for a very long time before that. 'Questioning the value of it … what modesty means, and why … the onus is on women to be the champions of modesty in Islam. I felt that it was unfair. Do we need to be covered up in order to be pious and righteous in terms of our faith?'

Samah does not wear hijab now, but she hasn't ruled out embracing it again one day.

It was a different world Samah entered in Egypt. Sexual harassment of women in the Arab world is well documented, and was frequently raised with me. At the roundtable in Amman, the women guffawed over the more outlandish advances from men on the street (pretty much the equivalent of 'Show us your tits'). Women in Lebanon openly declared that taking a *serviis* taxi could be a nightmare due to harassment from the driver. I was surprised by this until I experienced it firsthand: a series of questions to determine if I was married; more questions to ascertain if I was the loose type. I shut him down by calling him 'uncle'. I thought he was trying to make a point about me being by myself in a taxi, but one of my new acquaintances in Beirut assured me he was not. 'He was having a crack at you!'

Lamisse from Brisbane, who had also spent time in Egypt, said you get used to the sexual harassment, 'which is a really sad thing'. It was mostly cat-calling, and she was followed a couple of times when she did her shopping.

'As much as I'm an aggressive person in some ways, I'm also quite timid, so those sort of situations really freaked me out,' Lamisse told me. 'I don't yell, I don't scream at them to go away. I'll just dodge and find a way to get out of the situation.'

She was also exposed to the policing of women. The 'bawab' – doorman – unofficial guards of an apartment building. They'll get groceries for you, they'll check who goes in and out.

'The bawab we had took it upon himself to be like my surrogate father, and police my movements and who got to come in and out of the apartment, and that sort of stuff. That public morality, to be exposed to that ...'

For Samah, being in Egypt was a jolt from her life in Sydney.

'It was difficult, because I'd never faced that in Australia. What I faced in Australia was something else. Being a Muslim woman in a Muslim community can be quite restrictive because of the traditions, the diaspora community, the diaspora Arab community ... That was different. I never experienced physical harassment. That was confronting,' she said.

'I was working then with the feminist campaigning organisation, and we were working on sexual violence taking place in Egypt, and sexual harassment, which had risen to significant levels during the revolution. We were constantly bombarded with cases of rape, mass rape. It was horrific to see, and I was sexually harassed as well, as were many women in Egypt. It just became such a daily existence for women there. That again emboldened my feminism, and it was so depressing to see.'

But then there were the reactions from women's groups, which Samah found inspiring. 'Really, feminism in the West can learn so much from what is happening on the ground in various Middle Eastern countries. That made me angry, constantly angry. I didn't feel free. I felt free as an Arab, really free to explore my Arab identity, and my politics, but not free as a woman living in Egypt at all. That's eventually why I left.'

This prompted a move towards humanitarian work; a lot of the countries that were part of the Arab Spring had fallen into civil war and Samah felt she could help. 'I started working in the humanitarian aid field, and moving around from countries to countries working on humanitarian responses.'

Samah raised a significant point about being 'a Western woman'. 'I was still a foreigner. I had that privilege, whereas women in more rural areas weren't exposed to support,' she said. 'Also, I was supported. There were services available, channels to vent and seek support, whereas women in rural areas would not have that.'

It's why Samah feels more at home in Lebanon. While women face numerous issues: discrimination generally, legal discrimination, particularly for vulnerable women like refugees, and a plethora of gender inequality. 'The physical harassment is not as bad here.'

And the Arab world's approach to feminism is strong. Samah doesn't necessarily feel that there needs to be a meeting point between Western feminism and Arab feminists. 'I think Arab women are identifying what needs to change and are going about changing that.'

She acknowledged that some do see a need for solidarity in the feminist movement.

'You're saying Arab women have got it. We're getting there,' I said.

'Absolutely. I'm also a Western Arab woman, so I have to recognise my privilege within the context I'm living in in the Arab world. The women that I've worked with, and friends of mine, and role models in my life, have carved out ways of changing things in their lives and in their societies, and it's just about recognising that, and perhaps instead of trying to find ways to have a common understanding, perhaps it's fine that there's a divergent approach to feminism and to women's rights.'

Perhaps, again, it's about feminist movements in the West learning a thing or two about what's happening in the Arab world, she added.

I queried Samah on whether feminism in the Middle East, given the influence of Islam in the region, is oriented away from religion.

'Absolutely. It really is, it really is. And that's just because of the way religion has been imposed on societies in the Middle East. Islam in the Middle East is so closely tied into patriarchy, far more than it is in Muslim communities in the West. That's what we need to understand, and that's not quite how people see it. So there's nuance there.'

Living in the US and UK as well has allowed Samah to find greater freedom among Muslim communities, 'particularly for women to forge their own identities, to continue fighting on behalf of Muslim rights, but there's also far more freedom for them to express themselves as individuals.'

She believes that's because Muslim communities there are more established and ethnically diverse. 'Whereas in Australia, if you like, communities are organised along the same ethnic and cultural identities. So [a community is] not as diverse in its thinking. And Australia as a society as a whole is also very slow and disconnected from world trends. What's happening in the US and Europe is far more progressive than what Australian society is [doing].'

Indeed, Australia is a very closed-off society. We have both been on the end of community insecurity, which leaves little room for individual thought. I suggested that religion can act as a safety blanket; that it keeps people in fear, which is, oddly, a form of security.

'It is a form of social control and I've seen it in the way that it's controlled, particularly women. But then I've also seen the way that it's liberated women,' said Samah. 'Like you see the way women organise themselves in South-East Asia, like the Musawah movement [a global Muslim movement for equality and justice], which is brilliant. They're leading the path, really, in terms of a feminism within Islam. If we're talking about Muslim feminism, it's definitely ... South-East Asia, like Malaysia and Indonesia, that we need to learn from.'

It wasn't uncommon for the women I met to talk about improving the lives of other women through their work, promoting a healthy outlook that celebrates womanhood without deferring to men. But they didn't surround their beliefs with deference to the West either. Nor did they wholly reject them. Women freely talked about their studies in foreign countries, including the US and the UK, full of praise for the space that travel afforded them, to grow into themselves, away from the glare of the society in which they were raised. They were honest in identifying the problems women experience in Arab society, but also well versed in the universality of such issues.

These women are provoking real, life-changing shifts in cultural mentality and disrupting expectations. They are willing to be supported but not over-ruled by a judgmental Western overlord. It's time critics show Arab women enough respect; that they can be trusted with their own lives; that they are the game-changers and activists of transformation we need.

THE FIGHTERS

They said, 'You are a savage and dangerous woman'.
I am speaking the truth. And the truth is savage and
dangerous.

Nawal El Saadawi, *Woman at Point Zero*

The Arab world is in a state of flux and the status quo is being challenged from many directions. The strength of active feminism is significant, but I believe it's important to consider how women are at the forefront of social change through their many different fights for justice.

In Jordan, there is a growing focus on justice for women in a society that favours the man – in its legal system and cultural mores. Much of the commentary around women in Jordan has been centred on so-called honour killings, yet there are women – and men – who are, in the truest sense of activism, fighters for a more just legal system, and a culture that is less focused on gender roles. The women's movement in Jordan is targeting the entire penal code, said Salma Nims of the Jordanian National Commission for Women (JNCW).

'We're really looking at it and saying ... the part related to violence against women is not based on protecting the woman from violence but on protecting the honour of the families, and that's why we are revising the whole penal code. We are submitting a position paper towards it. To us, we're not looking at one act, we're looking at the whole spirit of the code and saying we need to change it.'

For example, the penal code dictates that if a man sleeps with a woman and promises her marriage but doesn't marry her, he goes to prison. 'From a liberal point of view, even this we're against. You're a woman, you made the decision to sleep with someone. I can't use the law to force someone to marry you. Because if this man marries this woman, not because he believes that she's going to be his life partner, but because he is forced because he slept with her, do you know what they do? First of all, his family do not respect her. She's actually dealt with like a *khadami* (servant), because this is how the society sees her. He could actually use her for prostitution. Because to him she's already lost her honour.'

In February 2017, Rana Husseini reported in the *Jordan Times* that The Royal Committee for Developing the Judiciary and Enhancing the Rule of Law (RCDJERL), chaired by former prime minister Zeid Rifaia, recommended ditching controversial Article 308 of the Penal Code, through which sexual assault perpetrators can escape punishment if they marry their victims. Outlined in a report sent to His Majesty King Abdullah, other amendments related to so-called honour killings were also made.

JNCW was established by cabinet decree; and Salma follows a distinguished line of women who have previously led the national organisation, which has a mandate to propose amendments or legislation strategies, and contribute to national plans towards progressing women's rights in Jordan and ending discrimination against them.

'We are considered the umbrella for the civil society to build consensus over civil issues related to advancing women's rights,'

Salma explained. 'We don't work directly with the local community, we work through the civil society and the NGOs that have a presence in these local communities to work through them to reach the communities.'

A major challenge is the scale of it all: 'We [deal with] everything under the moon,' said Salma. 'That's the problem. If you are an NGO, sometimes you focus on a region or you focus on one of the issues related to women's rights when you start programming. But for us, because we are seen as the semi-governmental organisation, we have to work on all aspects. We work on rights, economic empowerment, political participation, social protection – we have to handle all issues.'

In 2016, when I met with Salma, it was an election year in Jordan. The streets of Amman were papered in posters of smiling politicians, mainly men, but there were a handful of women, including a candidate in full niqab. Salma said that this led to a particular effort on legislating for more access for women to the Parliament. 'But also supporting women candidates and campaigning for … social justice and equality agenda.'

Despite a background in architecture, Salma has long felt the pull of social justice and women's rights. A gender expert, she's also the founder of a movement called *Taqaddam* ('Moving forward'), a social–political movement that works towards building positive discourse around reform in Jordan. 'We're calling for a secular country, for complete equal rights between men and women based on citizenship.'

Salma acknowledged her feminist leanings, saying that university was a formative time; she made certain friends and read certain books, such as the writings of feminists such as Fatima Mernissi, who talked about how women can be liberated through Islam.

'This is the position I hold in JNCW. I think that because ninety-five per cent of the society has religious sentiment, even if they're not quite religious, but the concept of religion is centre.'

However, Salma believes in secularism – Jordan might have a Muslim majority and be, in practice, a very Muslim society, but it has its minorities. 'If we can't have a secular country, then we have to see and look into new interpretations of the religious text and see how we can liberate women through Islam, not by separating Islam ... Otherwise I'm fighting their system of thought, their culture, their beliefs that they grew up with.'

'If you look at our legislations,' she said, '[Sharia law] is only applied on issues related to women and family. It becomes *haram* and *halal* when it comes to women. But in other laws, we don't apply Islamic laws – in business, economy, taxation.'

The laws around women remain in place, Salma argued, because it's about power and control. 'It's about that there are benefits that men have been having for hundreds of years, and anything that would give women equal power in this relationship means that they will be losing their privileges. In the private sphere as well as the public sphere, because women, if they are in power, they will have better presence in the public sphere as well. They will have access to more positions. They will have more influence on policies, they will have more influence on business. So it's a power balance. It has been there for years.'

'HONOUR' AS A DEFENCE

In recent years, so-called honour killings have received widespread coverage from the outside world, thanks to the efforts of women who are working to criminalise them. Their exertions have been primarily directed towards shifting cultural attitudes around these murders, and for the legal system to acknowledge the severity of the crimes by doling out heavier sentences.

In Jordan, efforts were dampened by objectors who accused the movement of bowing to Western pressure. Well-intentioned domestic activism was branded as harbouring a Western agenda. An aversion to Westernising Arab society – beyond fast food and music – is the argument used to stifle progress.

The deception of Norma Khouri, a con woman who duped the world into believing her best friend was the victim of a so-called honour killing in Jordan in her best-selling book *Forbidden Lies* regressed the movement several years. A country already sensitive about a perceived Western influence found a reason to delay changes to laws that were enabling male relatives guilty of murder to get off with a light sentence if the apparent loss of a woman's 'honour' was alleged to be a key factor in her murder.

That crimes of so-called honour occur is not in dispute, but as noted by Rana Husseini, the journalist who has spent years documenting them in Jordan, Arab women agitating for change don't need Western intervention to tell them that these crimes are wrong. They have spent years trying to increase awareness and shift cultural opinion in order to influence laws. They have achieved a level of success, but this is the crux of it: community opinion will continue to justify such crimes if they continue to view women as precious creatures who can only feel sexual upon getting married.

Rana has been heavily criticised for her efforts. 'I was like, "I'm not going to listen to anyone, I'm just going to follow my passion, I'm just going to follow what I believe in." But it was a challenge for me in the beginning, because people were accusing me left, right and centre, and I was like, "I'm not doing anything wrong, I'm fighting for the right of life and this is something that everybody should be fighting for." That's what I thought.'

Did she feel she was threatening because she was challenging culture?

'Yeah, I learned that in time.'

Rana realised that repetition is crucial to creating awareness, a discovery she made while studying in the US. She was an avid viewer of sports on TV, and ads were repeated twenty, thirty times a day. This led Rana to make a decision about her position as a journalist in Jordan. 'I want to write each and every murder, and keep writing and keep writing and keep writing until someone reacts. And at that time there was no social media, there was no internet, and the newspaper [in Jordan] started receiving letters to the editor, and that was like, wow, I was flying. Yes! There are people who are reacting, there are people who are starting to notice.'

Rana, who attended the roundtable at the Australian Embassy in Jordan, has been an instrumental force in acknowledging so-called honour crimes in Jordan, campaigning for harsher laws, and for a shift in cultural attitudes. Everybody got involved at one point, Rana said: the government, the royal family, the person who collects the trash in the street. 'And that was an important era for Jordan.'

Since then, she has seen all kinds of issues being tackled. 'Violence against women, it became more open. So-called honour crimes, abortion, prostitution, virginity, molestation, rape – all these things that you would not dream of reading in the nineties, now it's there. It's in the open.'

Rana even undertook a monitoring project on the Arabic and local press for several years and noted a difference. You can see the shift later, she said – more awareness, more people opposing violence against women.

'Of course, there are still people who believe or think that women should be killed or it's okay. They don't believe in women's rights. And now I go and lecture a lot, and I feel the difference, I feel that people aren't as aggressive as they used to be, especially men.

'I've been to several places where men told me, "Okay, if we are put in the same situation, help us [with] what to do?" Before, in the nineties, I would have men who would say, "Eh, I would kill my sister, so what?"'

Salma pointed out that so-called honour killings are not Islamic. 'I'm worried that the influence of radical thinking is actually [seeing us go] backwards. It's like, now we want to protect women more. And this symbolic fight between the West and Islam is making us become [stricter] about it. Yet, there are debates. Because also, the radical thinking of radical groups like ISIS also makes the Muslims say, "Let's take a step back. We need to reconsider what is Islamic and what is not,"' she told me.

'So there are opportunities; however, now there is restrictiveness. Yet I think it's like going through a process now; we're in the transformative process, where we see the community going backwards behind its walls and saying we want to stick to our Islam and our identity. And at the same time there are those who are saying, "But we need to ask the right questions."'

Salma wasn't the only person to express worry that, for all the progress, society is regressing in relation to women's status and treatment. Hadeel Abdel Aziz, director of the Justice Center for Legal Aid (JCLA) in Amman, Jordan, believes this is due to double standards in dealing with men and women.

Hadeel said Islam is used as an argument when it suits a

man's agenda. 'We have women coming in and telling us, "My husband said that if I leave him, he will say that I'm doing it because I have a boyfriend." But if you're so crazy about honour, how can you even perceive of accusing your wife of something like this? Thirty or forty years ago, yes, it was a very patriarchal system, but if someone would even mention this, they would cut off his tongue. It was held with such a sacred position [in the community], it was not used just for bargaining … This hypocrisy is the worst thing that's happening. This is why I truly believe we're going backwards.'

The penalties have got harsher, Hadeel noted. 'The worst thing we can do now is to deny celebration of achievements. It's not solved, of course. But right now the probability of a man getting six months for murdering his sister is almost minimum. Now things have improved. Still, they're not getting life like if they killed a man,' Hadeel told me.

'We have to celebrate the small steps, because the only way we can move forward is to take small steps forward. Now in Jordan we're changing the mindset that it's okay to kill your sister or your female relative and, more importantly, people don't think they will get away with murder if they just say it's in the name of honour.'

Court decisions over the last few years have delivered harsh sentences. But – there is a *but* – a personal rights waiver can help perpetrators halve their sentences. 'So as a victim, suppose it's not my husband. Say you come and you beat me up and then I go to court,' began Hadeel. 'If I waive my personal rights then the court will decide to drop the punishment by half. And this is something that is happening for all types of cases.'

The court takes into consideration the victim's decision to forgive the perpetrator; even if the victim doesn't want to press charges, the case can still go ahead but this will be taken into account. And in so-called honour crimes, the victim and the killer are from the same family. 'So when the family of the victim waives their personal rights, really they're forgiving the killer because he's their son. And this is what's happening. Now families are waiving their personal rights. This is why he gets twenty years in prison, but then it becomes ten years in prison. But ten years is much better than six months. Like, even just by having ten years, people are more likely not to murder others.'

This is the average sentence for so-called honour killings now, a huge improvement on the measly or non-existent sentences men were dealt in the past.

Rana's report in the *Jordan Times* on the RCDJERL's recommendation also outlined proposed amendments to sentence reductions for defendants relying on 'family honour' as a motive.

'Is it also changing the way people talk about these killings?' I asked Hadeel.

'Yes.'

Rana similarly acknowledged a shift in attitude. 'I used to feel that people were more hostile,' she said. 'I always say that our activism in the late nineties really broke taboos about many topics. I mean, if you opened the newspapers in the mid-nineties, it was all lame.'

You weren't going to find genuine interest in violence against women.

'Now it's different. Now you see all kinds of topics being [discussed] in the Arabic press. And that was one of my goals when I started, because people were telling me, "You write in English, you're catering to a certain audience." But at that time nobody was writing anything, and I wanted to document that there were these women who were living on this earth and somebody robbed them of their lives. And I didn't know I was a human rights activist until I won the second award [in 1998], which was a human rights award. I didn't know, for me I was just a journalist documenting cases.'

Rana suggested that fear is at the core of social problems like so-called honour crimes. 'Fear of what others might think of me. We live for others, that's our problem in this part of the world. We live for others, not ourselves. In the West, they live for themselves, not for others. That is one of the reasons why they are advanced.

'Here we're always worried. Now, about women, first of all there's a lot of reasons. One reason is fear, and another reason is they fear they might be punished. They fear the retaliation from their family members specifically. They fear being exposed: "What would people think if I said that?" The upbringing is not right, because the upbringing is always, "Oh, you're a girl" ... This is how girls are treated; they are treated as less than their brothers, their male family members.'

Rana said she was not a typical girl, shy, with her head to the ground, but she has always been a passionate defender of her culture, so I was sad to hear that the 'shy girl' archetype is still such a common expectation among Arabs in Jordan.

'It's a combination of things. The education system is a disaster of all disasters.'

Yet there is no shortage of hopeful stories: the woman who opened a gym to teach women self-defence; the sisters who opened a cooking school to preserve their family's recipes; the professional women I met with who don't sit in their Arabness, they simply get on with the march towards greater progress for their society.

A WAVE OF BLACKNESS

Hadeel Abdel Aziz is responsible for something quite extraordinary: the JCLA was the first legal aid service in Jordan. She established it in 2008: working in the courts, she observed the gap in legal justice for people who lacked the funds to seek representation.

Eight years later, the centre is frequently under attack: from people who accuse its lawyers of running a service that seeks to destroy Muslim families in order to get funding; and now from the legal profession itself. Hadeel's organisation relies on funding from international donors (easier to obtain for women, refugees and migrant workers than for criminal cases).

Her experiences in developing a legal aid organisation are instructive of the cultural challenge that social and legal justice advocates face in Jordan. The establishment of legal aid picks at deep-rooted cultural beliefs and threatens power balances.

'When we started, it wasn't about helping women. Women were the most vulnerable, but it was not meant to help only women. Right now, though, seventy per cent of JCLA's beneficiaries are women, because they are the most vulnerable, they are the most likely not to be able to access the court system, they are most likely not to be able to afford to pay for a lawyer. But it was not intentional. We thought we would be helping everyone.'

The centre primarily deals with cases related to alimony, divorce, domestic violence and crime, as well as juvenile cases. The economic position of women is a huge issue in divorce matters.

'In Jordan, the percentage of women's participation in the labour force is only thirteen per cent. I think it's one of the lowest, if not the lowest in the world. That [means] independence is very limited. Usually they rely on the husband or the family. And once you get into conflict, you will probably be losing both. Like, she's suing her husband, but in most cases the family do not want her to be in court as well. They would rather she sucks it up, she handles it differently. Families don't encourage their girls to get divorced, for example. So if she's choosing to get a divorce, it's very likely that she does not have the support of either her husband or her family, therefore she has no source of income.'

Halima*, a lawyer with a dedication to women's rights, said class and wealth can influence a woman's divorce. A wealthy woman seeking divorce can more easily rent a home and take the custody of her children. If she has no money, she will need her family's support. What stops women from getting a divorce is not having the means to live. She said women will accept violence against them because they don't have any other options. Her family might take her back, but not her kids. She didn't elaborate on the reasons, but based on various conversations, it would seem that financial circumstances are a factor, as well as the law.

I asked Hadeel how much she considers culture to be the issue. Violence is a human behaviour, not an Arab one, after all, but there is no denying the entrenched patriarchy of the Arab world.

'Culture has its toll on women in a much harsher way in this part of the world. But at the same time, it's about agency. This is the real issue. It's how women are perceived as minors ... in everything. In marriage, in handling their affairs, in making independent decisions. It's about the lack of agency, and this perception is very dominant ... Sometimes it's done with the best of intentions, they want to protect women. But even in

241

the systems, in courts ... passports and civil documentation ... civil status – you feel this. In banks: you go, you want to open a bank account for your child and they tell you, "We need the signature of the father."'

But it's not guardianship as it exists in Saudi Arabia or even the version in Qatar, which Nurah described.

'Nowhere in the world is as bad as Saudi Arabia. I think maybe only Afghanistan is worse than Saudi Arabia,' said Hadeel.

Still, the popular belief is that the head of the house is a man, even as single mothers raise children all over the world.

'Jordan has taken several steps to improve women's independence,' continued Hadeel. 'So now we have the sense of right to movement. Women don't need permission from their families or their husbands to issue a passport or to leave the country. The [authorities] will not stop you from leaving the country. But you know what? If [a husband or father] threatens your life, if she wants to live on her own in a separate apartment, for example – if he says, "I'm going to kill her," you know what happens? They will consider that there is a threat to her life and she is put in prison.'

It's been well documented that women are often incarcerated if they are in danger from a relative in Jordan. It is devastating to their lives, with some being locked up for years by a system that justifies it as protection.

Hadeel said there's no improvement on this – it's getting worse. At a time when civil war rages in nearby Syria, when the Middle East is undergoing seismic changes, governors, considered the keepers of peace and security, are now enjoying greater power. 'People are dismissing human rights in favour of security,' she said. 'So if you raise women's rights, the response is: "What do you think is more important? Her right to movement or her right to life?" She should not be made to choose. It's the government's obligation to protect both rights.'

Hadeel said she has publicly challenged defences of imprisonment of women for their protection, pointing out that a man under threat would never go to jail.

'What you're taking for granted when it comes to women is unthinkable if the victim is a man. They are such hypocrites because they will use the rhetoric of Islam to say we're an Islamic country, we have to safeguard Islamic principles, but they don't when it comes to things like a woman being threatened to be killed. Islam won't allow any man to kill his wife or to beat her ... [Yet] when it comes to things like corruption, Islamic rhetoric is never used. When it comes to things like torture in [police stations], they never remember that it's anti-Islamic to torture someone.'

'Do these women who get imprisoned for their protection get lawyers?'

'Not automatically.'

The centre takes on cases like this. 'The number of cases is low, but when you're successful, it has such a big bang. There was a woman we helped – she was in prison for twenty years and we helped [get her out].'

Recently, the centre collaborated with the Jordanian Women's Union in a joint effort. In this case, a woman was imprisoned for her protection when she ran away from a husband who beat her. The abuser reported her to the police and they took her into custody.

'Later, [the husband] just took his kids and went back to Palestine. And they picked her up and they would not close the file because her family did not want her. So they said, "Let her stay in prison." And they kept her there even though there really was no threat on her life, it was just her family thought it would be better off if she stayed in prison. So when we took that case, it almost took us one month to navigate the system and prepare. Because she had nowhere to stay, the government insisted on having a letter on where she will go. So we asked the Women's Union to keep her in the shelter; they did, and then they helped her get a job.'

'That's amazing.'

Hadeel broke out into a grin. 'Yes, it's one of the stories I would say have an impact.'

And she is realistic about the fight. For her, changing even a few women's lives is worthy and valuable. 'The thing is that you do feel very frustrated because the system is so broken in some areas. But at the same time, I always say that we cannot afford to give up. I have two daughters and unless we change the world in small pieces, they will not be able to live in this country. And things are getting worse. It's not like we're just improving a bad thing and it's become better. No, actually, we're also fighting this wave of blackness that's just engulfing everything.'

In Hadeel's work, demand outweighs supply. 'We cannot help everyone, and things are getting even more complex by the day with the refugee crisis. Now we have to help also Syrians, and Syrian women, whose cases are usually triple-folded in complexity, because she's a woman, she's being abused by her husband, but at the same time she's a refugee, she has nobody.' She has no rights because she's not a citizen.

Hadeel's tone changed slightly at this point. 'Let me tell you what it's like to be in this position. When we started this organisation, we did not at all think that it would cause any political issues. We thought people would say "Thank you," like you're helping through a crisis. And the more we work, the more it was obvious that this was very much political because, first of all, the Bar Association, they hate us. They want to shut us down. They think that legal aid is taking away business from lawyers.'

Hadeel's logical response is that legal aid exists to cater to those who can't afford lawyers. 'Because we have such high unemployment rates among lawyers ... Some will say that the recipients of legal aid would get help from family if legal aid didn't exist. Or maybe she can take a loan. You actually hear this. In the beginning I was always shocked. I was like, "Do you understand what justice is about? Are you sure you're a lawyer?" But now it's so common that I hear these things that I just dismiss them.'

At the time we spoke, Hadeel was navigating the Bar Association's complaint to government, which included a request – successful – for JCLA funding to be suspended. It had left a funding gap that subsequently saw senior staff donate their salaries to junior lawyers.

'It was such difficult times, I can't even begin to tell you,' said Hadeel. 'For me, it was, "You don't get to monopolise justice and you don't get to monopolise a service you do not provide to begin with." So in reality, what the Bar Association was saying is, "Oh no, this is our role, we will do it only." You know how many cases they used to handle a long time ago? Twenty-five cases per year. Now, after all this fight, they announced their numbers, and last year they provided two hundred cases [of legal aid] – this is what they claim. We do annually around 2400.'

Hadeel said it's still not enough: minimum expected demand is 17,000 cases a year. 'The number of people who are being denied services is much bigger than the people who are granted services,' she said. 'The consequences are really grave. When people lose justice and lose faith in the justice system, you can only go downwards on a social level. This is the beginning of the end. This is where they'll be more susceptible to extremism, more susceptible to injustice, to losing faith in the system; they're more likely to take things into their own hands; this is where chaos actually starts. So it's a really huge need and we cannot afford not to fight for it. And this is why we're fighting.'

Halima saw another issue at play: a pick-and-mix approach to activism. Human rights apply to all, not just your preferred cause. Halima had a way of distilling issues into truth bombs. When we talked about the Western focus on women's rights in the Arab world, the obsession with the right to drive in Saudi Arabia, for example, did, we agreed, fly over the real problem.

'I always say about the women in Saudi Arabia, the issue isn't to sit in the car and take the wheel. It's to steer your life.'

On the status of women, I asked Halima how much of this related to a lack of trust of women, the pervasive idea that they can't be trusted with freedom.

'[Men] don't trust women and they don't trust themselves. This is the situation. And this is why [men] use the justification that all men are wolves, they are evil, you can't trust them and we want to protect women.'

'Why don't we work on changing the men?'

'No one wants to work on changing men. It's easier to control women in our society because in our society if you have a daughter and a son, you will control your daughter and not allow her to go out late, but you will not control your son. Although your son will go to others and he will abuse other women.'

Like other women in Jordan I spoke to, Halima was vocal in expressing her frustration with the gender imbalance and the unconscious, or conscious, bias against women. Men, celebrated as the breadwinners and supporters, are not the enemy, but they are part of the problem. It's time they started listening.

(IN)JUSTICE

In perhaps the most striking moment in *Scheherazade in Baabda,* a play performed by the inmates of a women's prison in Lebanon, the women repeatedly say 'shame' until it resounds through the cramped space like a dark mantra. It comes at the end of the play, in a 'commitment pledge' scene – the women make a promise to change their lives in a way that will have a societal impact.

The revelation that shame is the universal currency in these women's lives followed eleven months of 'drama therapy'. This not only produced a play, but also uncovered numerous histories that speak of human – and particularly female – suffering. Most of the prisoners were drug addicts, many spoke of abusive relationships. Often the abuse began at a young age.

Scheherazade in Baabda is the filmed version of the final play, and at the helm of this stunning production was Zeina Daccache, a well-known Lebanese actress, director and drama therapist. By using drama therapy as a rehabilitation tool, Zeina has effected substantial change in these women's lives, many of whom are now out of prison and disseminating their lessons around Lebanon, touring schools and giving talks. An award-winning documentary, *Scheherazade's Diary*, goes behind the scenes of the play's production, following the women as they undertook Zeina's drama therapy.

In *Baabda*, women spoke of domestic violence and sexual abuse they had experienced as children and mothers. Zeina said it was revealing why women had landed in prison, that women turn to crime for different reasons to men. Men talk about why they are in prison almost boastfully; women tend to be involved in dealing drugs, or '[There is a] big percentage of women who murdered their husbands due to domestic violence.' Prisons are a microcosm of a society, she pointed out.

Until 2014, Lebanon did not have laws in place to protect women from domestic violence. Following the work of organisations such as KAFA ('Enough') Violence and Exploitation, the government ushered in laws in 2014 that finally offered women a level of legal recourse, though criticism abounds for the use of a narrow definition of 'domestic violence'. Meanwhile, in 2016, Prime Minister Saad Hariri announced that a parliamentary committee was taking the first steps towards abolishing Article 522, a law similar to Article 308 in Jordan, which sees rapists protected from prosecution if they marry their victim. No clear date for its abolition had been set out as of late 2016. In February 2017, however, a draft law went to Parliament for ratification.

When we met, Zeina had just come off a major three-year project funded by the EU: working with prisoners who are mentally ill or have life sentences. 'Why both? Because both have kind of the same destiny. They are both forgotten inside these prisons. The law does not protect them, because the mentally ill in Lebanon are still under a law that was created in 1943, and it never changed.'

She handed me the DVD of *From the Bottom of My Brain*, which was performed by the residents of the Al-Fanar Hospital for Neuropsychiatric Disorders in Beirut.

In brief, the 1943 law says that if you're 'insane', 'crazy' or 'possessed' and commit a crime, you stay in a prison psychiatric unit until you're cured.

'How can we call them insane and so on when they are mentally ill? And what is cured? So it means a life sentence. The play advocates for their cause, and in parallel we worked on two draft laws – one for the mentally ill offenders – to amend [that] law, and one for the life sentences – to amend the 463 law, which doesn't give them the benefit of a reduced sentence for good behaviour because the conditions put in the law are unrealistic.'

Helping people emerge from struggle is Zeina's forte; she's deeply invested in assisting the marginalised, what she called 'disadvantaged populations', including prisoners. In fact, she's been invested since childhood, when she spent her summers helping children with disabilities rather than shopping and going to the beach.

Societal and cultural change is parcelled in with her work. For example, her efforts in Roumieh Prison, a notorious men's jail in Beirut, delivered the award-winning documentary *12 Angry Lebanese*; and the play was credited with the push to bring forward the legislation to reduce sentences for good behaviour in Lebanon.

In our conversation, Zeina made a pertinent point: 'Arab women issues are universal issues – women's issues, people's issues, human beings issues'. And at the end of it all, she said she doesn't think about the fact that she's Arab in a way that defines her. 'I'm a human being doing something.'

Nonetheless, she has no qualms detailing the issues plaguing Lebanese society. When I asked her what she perceives as some of the greatest challenges for women in the Arab world, she said, 'To break the whole cliché, because the whole cliché is much bigger than [the reality]. With the whole turmoil around the region, things just got more difficult.'

Zeina has worked with Syrian refugee women for three years, many of whom were later deported to Europe by the UN. She's stayed in touch with them. 'These women are amazing, resilient women. But one thing they would always repeat is, "We wish our parents sent us to school." And I'd say, "Why?" And they'd say, "There is a war, we are refugees. If I knew how to spell my name, I might work as a secretary, but I can't do anything." This touched me so much.'

'Are there any opportunities for them to learn now?' I asked.

'These women were so eager to learn. We were offering them the drama therapy and other people were teaching them how to write, and other NGOs were teaching them sewing, others were teaching them secretarial work. They were like sponges – "Please teach us, we want to learn more." And most of their men were sitting at home and they would send them to go to work. And I was like, what? And they said, "Yeah, actually, our men are so devastated from the war that they don't move from the house." So she's the holder of the family with no education, and this is what they kept on repeating. "We wish our parents did their calculations better. They never expected a war. Guess what? In war time, women have to work." It was lovely how they said it.'

Now these women are insisting on a full education for their kids – boys and girls. 'If one thing is good in this whole disaster, it's that it was maybe a good lesson for these women.'

The future of Syrian refugee children is a priority for at least one NGO in the region. Nora Jumblatt, founder of the education foundation Kayany (among many other things), is focused on providing Syrian refugees with an education.

Nora is Syrian, the daughter of a national political figure. Her family sought political asylum in Lebanon when she was a child. Nora studied in Lebanon and abroad, and now much of her community work efforts go towards educating Syrian refugee children.

'The plight of the Syrian refugees is very dear to my heart, and we wanted, with some friends and family members, to help alleviate the predicament of countless children who lacked the bare minimum in food, clothing, medication and most importantly schooling. The most important thing for us was the children, and giving them education.'

Nora is active in the art world, and has raised money through exhibitions and partnerships with NGOs around the globe. A partnership with the American University of Beirut, which was undertaking a housing project, led to progress. 'We were able to build schools directly in the informal tented settlements. These GHATA classrooms are made of material that is bought locally, the workforce stems from the local community as well as from the refugees,' said Nora.

'We wanted to target the most vulnerable. That was going into the [refugee] camps, into the informal tented settlements that are in the Bekaa [Valley, near the border of Syria], and we started building our schools.'

Kayany has seven schools: five schools for boys and girls aged six to fourteen, and two Malala Yousafzai vocational all-girls schools for ages fourteen to eighteen. These provide education for 3500 children.

'When it was first established, Kayany provided refugees with humanitarian aid and medicine in Lebanon and inside Syria. However, our line of expertise lies in providing children with free and secular quality education. Our main partners are the Ministry of Social Affairs and the American University of Beirut.'

'People talk about the next generation of children being the lost generation,' I said to Nora.

'Yes, definitely. We are in danger of losing a whole generation of children. With half a million refugee children in Lebanon, only 200,000 were integrated in the public school system, leaving some 300,000 children out of school.'

Working against Lebanon is a lack of formal refugee camps – many refugees live in informal tented settlements. 'I don't know if you've been, but it is terrible,' said Nora.

'Lebanon has shown great support to the refugees, but six years into the crisis has impoverished both the host and the refugee communities. The refugees are spread out among the population and they put pressure on local education services, health services, on agricultural land.'

In the meantime, Nora continues to promote education and women. Most of the schools have female teachers. 'I call the Bekaa the empire of the women,' she said, noting that the majority of refugees there are women and children.

'This is the only future we can have in the Arab world, is educate, educate, educate. Educating girls is extremely import-ant as it is a lifeline to development. An educated girl has the skills and self-confidence that she needs to be a better parent, worker and citizen. I believe in the saying, "If we educate a boy, we educate one person. If we educate a girl, we educate a family – and a whole nation."'

Before I left, Nora asked me if I had room in my suitcase. 'These are made by refugees,' she said, displaying a basket of hand-stitched dolls. 'Would you please choose which one you want?'

Each doll had a story behind it, she added. I selected one. Tucked inside a back pocket was a note in Arabic and English:

'I am Souad. I have two girls. We have moved houses three times to stay safe. My husband had a little shop but it got destroyed. I still have my job and hope to keep it. With my very little income I send Lena to nursery so that she can grow up a happy girl.'

PALESTINE

As a child of Palestinian migrants you will very likely care about – and have an attachment to – the homeland. My father comes from a town called Arrabeh and my mother from the city of Jenin, both in the West Bank, around 12 kilometres apart. Palestine is a deeply personal subject for me.

Palestine, romanticised for different reasons to Beirut and Cairo, is a place that inspires its own mythos of tragedy and hardship. While it's by no means an easy place to live, and certainly not to thrive, the reality of life under occupation is often simplified to 'injustice' or 'triumph against the odds'. The motifs are ubiquitous: the stone-thrower; the illegal wall that cuts off Palestinians from their own land; the wailing, grief-stricken mother beating her chest; young men being marshalled into army vans to an uncertain future.

None of these stirring images is false, but the reality is far more complex than a neat snapshot of heartbreak. The experience of being a person who lives under occupation is not pure misery with several parts hope and aliveness. It is *life* and all that it entails.

I have visited several times throughout my childhood and adolescence, and twice as an adult on my own. Palestine has always been a soundtrack to my life. My family attended dinners held by Palestinian clubs; we socialised with other Palestinian families; and our walls were adorned with images and reminders of home, including a painting of the Dome of the Rock, vibrant and framed in gold.

But I didn't grow up in a political household. My family has feelings and ideas about Palestine, but we didn't intellectualise it. I discovered Edward Said through my studies and the activists around me. Mahmoud Darwish, regarded as Palestine's national poet, came to me during late nights of writing a novel about the experience of displacement. My parents are extremely *human* when talking about Palestine, and while I think there is no separating us from being Palestinian, it doesn't define who we are.

There is a popular view that Muslims are obsessed with Palestine, more than Arabs are. I had to laugh when one of my interviewees in Beirut rolled her eyes and said people need to move on from the fixation with Palestine, her claim being that a pronounced focus on Israel and Palestine masks other, personal issues. I suspected her criticism was directed to the people who overlooked their own national issues in favour of pointing out the flaws of Israel.

Palestine is all-consuming for some people. But Palestinians themselves don't have the 'luxury' of the same sort of activism we undertake in Western nations. They don't enjoy the same ease of assembly or power to express themselves freely without consequence. They live with checkpoints and restrictions, and even curfews at various times. The threat of imprisonment is a genuine, persistent reality.

I can only sympathise with the experience of living under occupation, speak out against it, or agitate for what will help people in the West Bank and Gaza; it's not my experience to own. Nor is it the sole domain of the outsider to fix things. In Palestine, people are constantly addressing injustice.

So how does it feel to be a Palestinian living in Palestine?

It really depends on where you live.

The 1990 Gulf War saw mass migration of Palestinians from Kuwait to both Jordan and Palestine. Much of my family was uprooted from their homes and I saw firsthand how many of them mourned their lives in Kuwait. Perhaps it's a case of romanticising what you once took for granted. Your new home, no matter if it's safer and offers more opportunity, is symbolic of loss of a high order. Not everyone recovers from it.

Palestine, the place that has always brought to mind affectionate relatives, olive trees, plump figs and endless cups of sage tea. When I visited family there, the excitement in the air was palpable.

My relatives peppered me with questions about my book. I explained that it was about women and how they live.

'Put me on the cover,' said my aunt, with a wicked laugh.

As I laughed with her, I thought about what a fantastic ambassador for resilience she would make.

WOMEN UNDER OCCUPATION

A few years ago *Four Corners*, the ABC current affairs program, broadcast a heartbreaking story about life in the West Bank, in towns that are home to Orthodox Jewish settlers, who are often accused of violence against the remaining Palestinians. The documentary showed footage of Israeli soldiers deploying tear gas as children rushed by on their way to school. It also went on to detail the atrocities facing families in certain areas of the West Bank, whose children have been arrested in the middle of the night.

Featured in the segment was Salwa Duaibis, co-founder of an organisation called Military Court Watch, which monitors the treatment of children in Israeli detention. She also works with the Women's Centre for Legal Aid and Counselling (WCLAC), which is focused on women's rights.

Salwa is not a lawyer; in fact, she studied biochemistry at Palestine's Birzeit University and, later, completed a second degree at the London School of Economics. It struck me as a huge departure to be working in human rights activism.

'Things are connected in weird ways,' she responded. 'I spent many years working in an organisation that basically focused on economic rights for Palestinians.'

Salwa was involved in the first manufacturing operation exporting directly to Europe and the United States, called Mateen Group. 'We made fancy women's lingerie, made out of one hundred per cent silk. The most important aspect of the project wasn't the business itself, but it was to identify obstacles directly.'

Obstacles to trade, more specifically, Salwa explained, then to try to overcome them. 'And then to show that if Palestinians are given the opportunity, they can excel, especially the Palestinian women.'

The project began in the late seventies. 'It ran for a very long time, but it evolved. We were forced to close down by the [Israeli] authorities in 1991.'

Part of the project's objective was to ensure that Palestinians have separate customs codes for products coming out of the occupied territories. 'Because obviously we were not part of Israel, and we're not part of Jordan. We wanted to export legally, and to make legal and political statements through that. That was very important. It was a long, long process of talking to officials in different countries, in the United States and European countries.

'Finally, they came back and they said, "Okay, you can say on the label 'Made in the Israeli-Occupied West Bank'," which was legally correct. Legally, unfortunately, we were not Palestine at that time.'

Salwa indicated that they were happy to use the label – a long one on a G-string is noticeable. 'That was a big achievement, I think. It was really of high quality. We sold to places like Victoria's Secret in the US. To Harrods ...'

Palestinian women were making the lingerie, and the entire cycle of procurement, production, design and beyond was controlled by Palestinians, unlike most other factories at the time. 'They were mostly subcontractors to Israeli marketing companies, so we were able to break out of that very rigid structure which held many businesses captive,' Salwa said.

'The Israelis didn't like the fact that we said, "Made in the Israeli-Occupied West Bank", and they thought it was a political statement packaged in a [G-string] ... In the end the Israeli authorities put a lot of pressure on lots of businesses at the time, including us. They made it hard to operate. They withheld a lot of cash that was owed to us and they basically cash-stalled us and we had to shut down.'

Salwa, eloquent, mannered and quietly spoken, but full of passion for justice, was a checkpoint for me: she was a reminder that focusing on the positive outcome is more significant than swimming in the darkness of the problem. She was another confirmation of my deepest beliefs about women, and particularly Arab women who are working to change the status quo. That we're not silent, that we're not voiceless, that we have our minds, that we have our will, our own set of abilities to succeed in life.

'You've always had that activist streak or a very proactive approach?' I asked.

'Yeah. I liked this project because it was a very clever way of confronting occupation. It was obviously non-violent. It was a true production to providing jobs for women who were very well paid, relatively speaking. It was showcasing Palestinians as being able to produce high-quality products competitive in the outside market. This was a very important challenge to the stereotypical image of what Palestinians are,' she said.

'The media portrays us as violent, as terrorists, as irrational people, and it's very untrue. It's just the other, more important and more truthful story was never given the opportunity to surface. This was my way of revealing the true face of Palestinians, not only women, but also men and the community at large. This was also a very clever way ... it was legal. We never made any political statements; we said, "This is what the law says. This is occupied territories. Here we are. We have fantastic products. We have clients who want to buy, and we want to do it legally, so please give us a proper label." It was totally innovative.'

'How did it improve the lives of the women working for you? Did you find that it had a trickle-on effect to improve other people's lives?'

'I think so. There's no way for me to quantify, but the products we were making – for example, if a gown takes an hour to produce, the value of that hour was multiple times more valuable than the hour of making, say, a t-shirt or cheap garments. So women who were working on this project had more money for the time that they put in.

'Also, because we targeted wealthy markets, people could afford to buy one hundred per cent silk made out of very good fabrics ... The women used to tell me, proudly, that they made more money than their husbands.'

'Did that ever cause friction at home?'

'I don't think so. No one ever complained to me. It was the opposite. One woman proudly said to me, "Salwa, today I gave my husband his pocket money because he's out of work – he couldn't find a job and I'm the breadwinner of the family." It gave them pride. It gave them power. It gave them status. They were proud of what they were producing.'

'Would you ever try something like that again?'

'I don't think so.'

'Too hard?'

'It was hell. We had to produce and deliver on time during curfews, during power cuts. The garments and the raw materials were held at the airport in Israel, they would not release them. It was like the challenges of a normal challenging business, but added to that the challenges of occupation, and the challenges of a Third World country without the infrastructure needed: the electricity, the things that normal businesses would need.'

'I love that you involved women. I think one of the big criticisms in the West at the moment is that a lot of NGOs are going to countries that are poor or disadvantaged or at war, and they don't really teach them how to be self-sustainable. They don't actually empower women themselves to improve their lives.'

'Yeah, the NGOs – foreign NGOs and local NGOs – have become a business. It's just a way to influence, politically mostly. Many people, including myself, are very critical of the NGO world.'

However, she says, 'I try to do my work as best as I can within the constraints and the challenges and the things that I don't like.'

I asked Salwa if she feels like she *is* her work, like so many activists I know. She said this was the case more so when she was younger, but she appreciates how important it is to look after yourself in order to help others. 'It's very important to be very motivated and focused and hardworking to achieve an objective. I think I was this kind of person. I put all my energy, all myself into the work I was doing. But with age, you begin to see life differently. I don't have much time left. Hopefully I will, but ...' she laughed, though she's only in her mid-fifties.

'It's just important to keep a good balance,' she said.

Salwa told me she grew up in a household that was very much affected by the events that took place in Palestine in 1948 and 1967. 'My mother's family was basically dispossessed. They lost their property. They had to flee their home. My grandfather was a very successful person, professionally. Overnight, he lost his business, he lost his property, he lost his community, he lost his future.' But her family remained in Palestine in 1948.

'My mother [is] eighty-one; she was twelve in 1948. Until today, she has an obsession talking about the injustice, talking about the conflict, clinging to any sign of hope that [it] will one day soon, in her lifetime, be resolved ... and I guess ... it took me time to understand if you go through trauma ... your life is shaped by it.'

'You must have inherited some of that, I'm sure.'

'In a different way. My mother talks about how can the world tolerate such injustice for such a long time? Me, I don't think I expect much from the world ... until Palestinian interests align with superpowers' interests, we're not going to get much. So focus on the little things. "What can I as a person do? How can I change somebody's life? How can I influence somebody's perception about who Palestinians are, what we're all about?"'

'And in terms specifically about Palestinian women?'

'We're fighting battles on more than one front. So we have internal issues in the society, which exist everywhere. We have the unique aspects of being an Arab country with a Muslim majority affected by all of these things. So women fight these fronts internally. Look for equality. Look for recognition.'

'Does it take a back seat because of the conflict? In Jordan, for example, I heard that because security is a big issue, one of the things that the government could say is, "Women's rights aren't our priority right now. Their safety is." It's almost like women's rights just become a side issue.'

'This was a very important debate in Palestine. People said, "Let's not talk about what happens in the family – whether a woman is beaten up by her husband or whether she's discriminated against. Let's not hang our dirty laundry because we have a more important issue to fight for."'

This was in the early years of occupation – the seventies to the nineties.

'It was a debate, so some women believed this. Other women believed the opposite. They said, "Women cannot wait. Women's rights have to be pursued and addressed now. There's nothing preventing us from doing both at the same time, in parallel."'

That was when the WCLAC was established, when a group of leading, pioneering women said, 'We're going to help women achieve equality and protect them from violence within the family and within the society and from discrimination, while at the same time, we fight occupation.'

I put it to Salma that there's a huge focus on men being advanced ahead of women because men are traditionally seen as the breadwinners, but, when you look at any society where women are given the chance to be educated, they excel. They usually perform better than the boys.

'Yes, I have this experience from my work. Part of my work with the Women's Centre is to visit women, to interview them, give them a voice, give them a forum to speak about their experience under occupation. I noticed that the first time I go and visit a family, all the men want to sit in the living room, and just start giving their opinions about the bigger picture, about Fatah, about Hamas, about the one-state solution, "No. Two-state solution ..." They talk the big talk. Women try to disappear and sit quietly. And my role is to basically tell the men to shut up because I'm here to listen to what the women want to say.'

'Is that hard?'

'I do it very assertively. I'll say, "I'm here to listen to the women. You can stay. You can listen, and if you have something to add I will listen to you, too, but please let's first listen to the women." The women don't believe it, that somebody cares about them, that I'm interested in what they have to say. First of all, there's this resistance from the men, and shyness and timidness from the women, and then within a second, that flips upside-down.

'And the women just start talking about not only the bigger picture, they have very, very deep understanding of the bigger picture. But they also talk about themselves, about their families, about how they're struggling, what they have to cope with. And they combine a very moving, personal story with ... they make it fit nicely within the bigger picture.

'The men sit and watch and they are surprised ... The next time around, I go back to the same family, and the men understand what my position is and they actually don't like it but they respect it, and they light a cigarette, and I say, "Please don't. Don't smoke around me," and they say, "Oh, who is this woman who is telling me whether I can smoke or not in my own house?" Again, the women start talking.

'The third time around, the men start talking like the women without much ego.'

'They show vulnerability.'

'They show vulnerability, exactly. They don't give that big talk. This is feminism in my way. Give an opportunity to women. Give them a little space, and then that's all they need.'

Another woman I met, Faiha Abdulhadi, similarly gives women the space to share their experiences. For years, she has recorded the oral histories of Palestinian women, with a particular focus on chronicling their political role from the thirties onwards.

'All my life I have been concerned about women,' she told me when we met in Amman.

Faiha is an author, poet, academic and director-general of Al-Rowat for Studies and Research, the institution where Faiha and her team document Palestinian social history, collecting oral testimonies of cultural value from marginalised groups who have been excluded from history books. At our meeting, she handed me a copy of one such collection of oral histories: *The Political Role of Palestinian Women in the 1930s*, which contains women's narrations collected in an exhaustive process that saw trained field researchers visit interviewees up to four times. Faiha has published four such books about the political role of Palestinian women, and recorded stories of women suffering after the Second Intifada in 2002 – their social and psychological maladies. She publishes the narrations as told, and includes her own analysis.

Faiha's work in oral history feeds her passion for women's issues. 'I started to discover this world and it was really a fantastic world ... I was really enchanted by it,' she said. 'I felt that everything I like is in oral history. I love poetry, literature, criticism (because my thesis is on criticism). And oral history is a social history, so oral history is about people – their pain, their hopes, their love, everything. So I loved being between people and hearing from people and to record what I heard from people then to write about that.'

Faiha was very focused on women who are illiterate, who have been ignored. 'I feel that I gave them a voice. You can't guess how they feel after they see their stories in the book.'

Interestingly, her analysis uncovers how political the women have been, despite many believing that they have not offered political input. A re-telling of their lives since childhood suggests otherwise. 'I understand politics is an everyday practice,' said Faiha. 'It's not the politics they talk about. Politics is in our daily life. So I consider that [each of these women] has a role in politics.'

That women in Palestine are political is important; however, it's equally important to consider what this means in a broader sense. In Jerusalem, I met Omayma*, who recounted a life marked by trauma. Amid her personal stories and lamentations – Jerusalem used to have so many bookstores, she told me – was a woman dedicated to Palestine, to the issues plaguing young Palestinians: education, which is controlled by Israel; the provision of services at a nominal fee under the Geneva Convention; having a future and work; pressure to marry.

Jerusalem – *Al Quds* – is frequently highlighted as a hot spot for trouble, and a sorely contested area. Speaking to Omayma, it became a bustling, hopeful place. There was no sense of grandstanding in her declarations that she couldn't see herself living anywhere else.

Omayma has a family legacy rich in activism, but also loss. She lost a brother in a tragic accident many years earlier, a man from whom she had learned a great deal – about what it means to be Palestinian, about their history and their rights to land. His death sent her into a spiral of despair, but Omayma eventually channelled her grief into something useful: activism.

Omayma described her connection to her country – Palestine – as not being tied down to political factions. 'Always my first and last allegiance is to Palestine. And this is why sometimes I don't find myself connecting with even other Palestinians, because they want to be faithful to factions, which I think divided the society in deep ways.'

There was something about Omayma that couldn't be put into words. She was so *full* in my presence, gradually working up to being more conversational and open after a reserved start. She was the embodiment of grief and hope all at once, but I don't know if she realised it.

'Is it a bit lonely?'

'Lonely, yes. It's lonely.'

'How do you deal with that loneliness?'

'My inner life helps. I'm always thinking of something to do, how to strategise to get something done. So it takes a lot of my interest and I feel a sense of achievement because I follow my plans usually to completion.'

'Do you ever do anything that is just ...'

'For me?'

I felt sheepish asking her this. Was it a luxury to care about ordinary things amid such chaos and conflict? I knew it was possible. I had seen the resilience of Palestinians many times before, and this journey proved no different.

'It feels like you live and breathe this,' I continued. 'Isn't it exhausting?'

'It is,' she laughed.

Omayma said she's not afraid to do what she likes though; she's not afraid of society as her mother was. She'd pursue a relationship if she felt like it, for example. And she immersed herself in hobbies – reading and handiwork.

'The crafts I started because I wanted to take my mind off the problems here.'

Also important to Omayma is her volunteer work with children, helping them to use and develop their voices.

'I have a project for high school students – they adopt a monument in the Old City … they go back to the history … If they don't want to go to libraries, I refuse their depending on Google only. So they have to go to libraries, they have to hold books in their hands, and if they choose not to, they can take photographs with a teacher of the monument – different angles, inside and out. And if they don't like either, they go into sketching the monument. After they finish, we put all the historical research, pictures and drawings on beautiful panels, museum quality, and we make exhibits. For the kids, they know their history.'

Omayma described a varied career. But it was clear what really drove her: 'My heart is in culture and history.'

NUMB

It's important to reiterate that life plays out differently for Palestinians depending on where they live. In some ways, life can seem very 'normal' in certain parts of the West Bank. In Ramallah, life moves at a frenetic pace. While Ramallah shares similarities with Amman in pace and mood, the differences are notable. Mobile phone reception is poor, development is stifled, and, like other crowded West Bank cities such as Jenin, market stalls crowd the pavements. These areas pulse with life.

Yet Ramallah doesn't have the feel of occupation. 'Life is more or less normal,' said Salwa. 'There's prospering economic activity, there's nice restaurants, clubs and swimming pools, and life is not so bad. I'm not saying it's good, but this is part of what this occupation is all about. It's basically making the majority of people's lives bearable so that they are pacified. They don't talk about occupation. They don't resist it, while people who live in villages near settlements, their lives are miserable. They are the ones on the frontlines of fighting this occupation. That is where I work.'

Location-wise, this means in villages near settlements, at friction points near the bypass road where things are still 'happening'.

'I give voice to these women whose livelihoods and lives have been stolen from them because of the construction of settlements next door. Their land is lost. Their freedom of movement is lost. Their economic activities, opportunities are lost. They're subjected to all sorts of violence arising from occupation, like repeated night raids. On average, we estimate that the Israeli military conduct 1400 night raids a year on these tiny villages … to make their presence felt.'

That would be 1400 night raids each year since 1967. That's more than 65,000 night raids since the beginning of the occupation. Salwa said that women tell her it's not a matter of whether their house will be raided or not – it's just a question of when. 'These are the villages that are surrounded by settlements, so women don't sleep at night. They worry that their children will be arrested.'

Both children and adults are frequently arrested by Israeli authorities.

Salwa's organisation Military Court Watch advocates on behalf of children who have been imprisoned. 'There is a lot of abuse in the system. The abuse ranges from being slapped and kicked, sleep-deprived, tied and blindfolded, transferred on the floor of a military vehicle, to more of the serious things like physical abuse, more intensity, some threats. Some kids are threatened with all sorts of things: "We will bring your mother and sister, if you don't confess ..."'

'What do they have to confess to?'

'To throwing stones, basically – that's the most common offence. The quickest way out of the system is to plead guilty, so even if that boy didn't do anything wrong, he will be advised by his parents and by his lawyer to plead guilty because that's the quickest way to get out of prison.'

The organisation collects testimonies from boys who have been arrested, around 150 each year, and analyses the testimonies and monitors some issues, raising awareness about them. Salwa said very few girls are arrested – she thinks one in the last few years, for throwing stones, and she spent time in prison. 'It's mostly boys we do, who are sought after. Basically, we do advocacy work around this issue, and we try to influence the Israeli government to change its policies and practices.'

'Have you had any successes?'

'Yes. Very little, maybe. There's a lot more to be done ...'

While some children may experience repeat arrests, generally, the experience is traumatising to the point of not wanting to leave the house in case they encounter a soldier.

In all of this, there are the women, often young, who show signs of severe anxiety before their families are actually subjected to violence from occupation – before the house is raided, or a son is arrested.

'In their minds, they are imagining the worst nightmare ever, and they stress, and they show physical symptoms, actually, even before anything happens,' Salwa told me. 'They see it around. They've probably ... heard about it from neighbours or relatives. They've never experienced it themselves, so they're expecting the worst. They don't know how they will react or what will happen.'

Then there are the mothers who have experienced this multiple times and have grown numb. 'A sixteen-year-old boy was snatched out of the house without his parents.' Salwa asked this woman how she felt. '[His mother] looked at me as if I was an alien from a different planet and she said, "Salwa, I don't allow myself to think because if I think, I will go crazy. I'll just deal with what I have moment by moment. I cannot afford to think or process what I see and what I experience. That will be the end of me. I will lose my energy. I will lose my drive. I will just ..." They make themselves switch off in order to cope.

'In the other spectrum, the women who haven't yet experienced anything, they mentally shiver in fear.'

Salwa made a pertinent point: that these stories don't make it to the front pages of any newspaper or magazine. 'Media likes blood and they like violence, and they like ugly images, and they run to these extreme stories ... Hundreds and thousands of very silent women who have to cope with hell every single day of their lives, no one talks about them.'

It's something that was touched on in an interview I did with film director Suha Arraf when she was in Sydney in 2015 to screen her melodic film *Villa Touma* for the Sydney Film Festival.

'We feel as Palestinians that we're victims of the occupation, victims of Israel, victims of the situation and victims of the war and the checkpoint,' she said. 'And somehow we enjoy putting the responsibility on the others. Everything is the occupation. When you become a victim, you like to play a victim or you feel a victim.'

But, Suha said, Palestinians like the big 'hero stories', despite their crushing losses over the past century.

'In all the stories, we win. We never lose any war in the stories.'

The problem is that the victim and hero stereotypes are the characters the world thirsts after in Palestinian cinema. 'Especially the victimisation. We saw [ourselves as] heroes or victims, but they saw us as victims or terrorists. And they ask us to show how we're victims so that at least they can have feelings for us – "Ah, the poor Palestinians." And I'm talking now not about governments, I'm talking about the people [in the street]. This is the cinema that we do.'

Suha's insistence on dealing with life, with unmasking and unpacking experiences and how they shape us, was incredibly refreshing. 'It's a formula. And I felt that we are losing the people, we are losing ourselves somehow. We are losing our humanity, because between the victim and the hero there is a human being, and the human being is a lot of things – bad things, good things, conflicts, drama, funny – we are losing this.'

Her words resonated as I spoke with Salwa, who delved into the humanity of Palestinians. Victims of occupation, their experiences tear apart the social fabric in the community and in the family.

The trauma continues after a child is released from prison. 'This is exactly what one mother said to me. She said, "Salwa, when my son was released from prison, we thought it was the end of the nightmare, but it was actually the beginning of a different, more serious one." The household breaks down, basically.'

Salwa said that she often senses an imbalance in kids recently released – numbness, being switched off.

'I suggest that maybe they should seek professional help, and almost immediately, almost always, the father will jump and say, "No! My son is fine. He doesn't need help. He's a hero. I went to prison, look at me. There's nothing wrong with me." The mother would roll her eyes up and down. I can tell there's something wrong. This denial, either out of ignorance, or it's probably a way of coping with severe trauma. They're not going to accept themselves, or see themselves as victims needing help. They want to see themselves as heroes. Every emotion, every feeling ... has to be suppressed.'

The mothers are the ones who deal with the subtle dynamics inside the family, Salwa added. They're the ones who ask for help – for their children and husbands. 'Mothers, basically, take a lot of pressure. They cannot afford, again, to be angry or drop the ball. Men usually go and work, or go out to the café at night, and they distract themselves with drinking tea and coffee, smoking. The women don't have this luxury. They have to stay home, take care of the children, make sure everybody's taken care of, that food is provided, and they keep the psychology of the family intact as much as possible. Sometimes they cannot and it shows physically on them.'

'How do you do this work? Do you have to switch off a part of yourself?' I asked Salwa.

'It's not switching off. It's channelling. I dealt with and still deal with a lot of frustration and anger and fear.'

I wondered how Salwa coped; so many activists I've spoken to seemed jaded, worn down. Compassion fatigue overload.

'It's very easy to get mad,' said Salwa. 'But I think ... the challenge is to direct your madness and anger in a way that will produce results, even if they are small results. Every drop counts because none of us have enough power or ability to change things in the bigger picture. I can be responsible for what I do and what I say and how I act and most importantly, to how I react to what I see.'

'Do you need counselling? All the women who do this kind of work tell me that they need counselling.'

Zeina Daccache had even said that it's unethical not to get therapy when you do this sort of work: 'Things move inside you, so you have to share it with someone.'

For Salma, one of her fears is not to be moved by the stories or realise the need for counselling. 'My fear is that I become immune to them because I see and hear them over and over again.'

I thought of Hadeel, whom I'd only met once. I couldn't know if her manner that day was typical, but there was a softness, almost sadness, to her as she spoke. She seemed drenched in compassion fatigue, a side effect of her work. 'I think the moment I feel hollow is the moment I will resign ... It still hurts, it still angers me,' she said.

Salwa said she would be devastated if she lost her sensitivity to the people with whom she works. 'As long as I still have tears in my eyes, I'm okay.'

FORCED

In Australia, I met a woman who had begun the public conversation about women's issues, including domestic violence, on an

Arabic-language radio program decades ago, long before it was considered acceptable to do so.

Years later, in 2008, with a small coalition of local Arab Muslim women, Salam and Susan in Brisbane decided to establish a shelter for Muslim victims of domestic violence because they were seeing Muslim women experience discrimination at shelters elsewhere. It is called Sakina because, Salam said, it means 'tranquillity', and the shelter is intended to be a safe space for women and their children.

The board of Sakina is composed of Muslim women with a vested interest in social work, wellbeing and fairness. 'We realised that we have seen more women from culturally and linguistic diverse backgrounds who have been getting into domestic violence disputes and there weren't a lot of culturally aware organisations out there to support them properly,' said Salam.

'As a social worker I started coming into contact with more women who were being put in shelters, who were being force-fed ham, for example, not being provided with halal food, being physically abused, being verbally abused. These [were] actually my clients who were in these shelters ... And then the media not helping out, always putting Muslims in a negative outlook. So you had women being more exposed to this racism than previously.

'I also came across a lot of women who were not Muslim but came from different cultures who were also going through the same thing.'

Salam and Susan are but two of the amazing women building Sakina, which also takes in girls who may be experiencing abuse by parents. Like many domestic violence services, the property isn't large enough to cater to the demand and suffers from a lack of funding, but it has undoubtedly made a fundamental difference to many women escaping domestic violence.

Joumanah El Matrah, CEO of the Australian Muslim Women's Centre for Human Rights, extended a crucial point, an idea that I hope this book supports: there is no point saying that we see empowered Arab women – of course we do, in the women who have absolute authority over their lives. 'That is an uncomplicated reality,' said Joumanah. 'But what you also see, which really helped me define [the Australian Muslim Women's Centre] and give it its framework, is an enormous number of Arab women working for their rights, and trying to generate legal reform and undertaking street activism, trying to improve the status of other women. All over the Arab world, women are working for the improvement in women's status, trying to change sexual reproductive health laws, citizenship laws, domestic violence laws.'

A focus for Joumanah and the organisation has been domestic violence and early and forced marriages. Laws in Australia were introduced in 2013 that allow the federal police to alert an airport if they become aware that a girl under the age of sixteen is being taken overseas for the purposes of marriage.

Joumanah said that a problem in addressing domestic violence or early and forced marriages is that most societies can tolerate a great deal of violence against women and children. This, she says, is evidenced by the very long struggle the women's movement across the world, including Australia, has experienced to ensure that violence against women is treated seriously, and that laws and protections have been instituted to safeguard women.

For minorities such as Arabs and Muslims, serious consideration and care for their plight is even more difficult to secure.

In Australia, a Muslim girl who leaves home because of early and forced marriage goes under the control of authorities and generic welfare services. Arab women in the community and activists often can't get access to these girls.

'We have tried repeatedly to get access to women experiencing early and forced marriage. This means that non-community members control how that problem is resolved. The only thing the young women have to go by is the experience of their families. They're only young women. They have no way of knowing that actually there are Muslim women who are profoundly concerned with this issue, who would arduously advocate for their rights and the eradication of early and forced marriage, and this would be really important for young women to know, and good for their wellbeing.'

Joumanah said authorities do not trust Islamic organisations to assist and she considers the lack of co-operation a symptom of racism. 'So, again, it comes back to the question of, does white society know how to contend with violence against minority women, including Arab and Muslim women? Unless it can be the rescuer, it appears not. Communities, and women specifically, have a fundamental right to address issues of violence and inequality within their confines, but this is a right increasingly being denied to communities in Australia.'

The casework goes to the Australian Federal Police (AFP), then the Red Cross will work with them, and only the Red Cross. The AFP Trafficking Unit will only refer a case to the Red Cross, which also has a trafficking unit. But early and forced marriage isn't a trafficking offence.

At the time we met, no prosecutions had been made as a result of the laws passed in 2013, prompting Joumanah to query what role the police have to play. But then an imam in

Melbourne was charged with 'conduct that caused a minor to enter into a forced marriage' at a Bosnian mosque. The man the minor was forced to marry was thirty-four years old.

Speaking to Shakira Hussein for *Crikey*, Joumanah said the extent to which early and forced marriage is a problem in Australia is not known. 'There is no evidence from which one can really generalise ... It is useful to note that the number of cases our centre responds to annually has not significantly increased – that's roughly seven to twelve cases per annum.'

For Joumanah, the issue is not confined to early and forced marriage. 'It's around the ways in which Arab and Muslim women are not allowed to attend to their own issues in this country, and the fact that if they were able to do that, [with] violence against Muslim and Arab women ... we'd be in an entirely different situation now. And awareness by young women growing up would also be entirely different.'

Christine*, a Lebanese migrant who came to Australia from the civil war, has a background in community development, working primarily in local government – in social policy, diversity development, training and customer service. She has similarly done work in the area of early and forced marriages.

'We know that it's always happened to a certain extent, that among Arabic families, when a girl, or sometimes even when a boy reaches a certain age, they might take them to Lebanon and introduce them to cousins or whatever, and marry them off. Sometimes there is a fine line between arranged and forced. The issue about being forced is very contested because there is pressure. They may not really force you by putting the gun to your head, but there is all this emotional and psychological pressure,' she explained.

'There may be a whole lot of circumstances associated with the benefits of doing what the family wants. You kind of feel you want to retain your family, you love your family but you may not really want to go down that path. You feel conflicted, and you feel torn.'

A girl might have more confidence and articulate her wishes to her family that she wants to delay her marriage, and they might listen, but there are other families who won't, who do not want their children becoming adults outside of marriage.

'It happens with boys as well, but more so with girls,' said Christine. 'I did an interview with a group of men who are older now ... in their fifties; two of them were forced to get married to their wives.'

'Arab men?'

'Yes. One, his marriage ended up well, the other one, after thirty-five years of marriage, they divorced.'

'So it happens to men too, and we don't know.'

'Again, it's pressure, pressure and conforming.'

Like Joumanah, Christine showed signs of fatigue. 'I wish I was [someone] who just accepted reality as it is. Not fight it. It would have made my life more smooth running, but I was always someone who challenged things, even when I was at school. Anything to do with injustice, if something is unjust, I fought it.'

In her experience, she found that it was difficult to create change beyond the neat boundaries laid out for her – as the Arab employee hired to implement elements of diversity. And some women, she said, were their own worst enemies. 'I've had amazing men in my life who were more empowering towards me than the women.'

Christine has a granddaughter, and it was lovely to hear the hope in her voice as she spoke of her. Christine wishes to encourage, even at a micro-level, a strong sense of self in her. To offer her different teachings to the ones so many females are taught growing up.

'I do think of her from my perspective about being a woman, being in the jobs I've had, having lived the life I did and the struggles I went through, and seeing the struggles of the women in my life,' Christine told me. 'I look at her and I say, "What should I instil in her as her grandmother now? What can I do to contribute to her life so that she's prepared for a future where she needs to be strong, in charge of her life, assertive, empowered, and being able to achieve what she wants to achieve in life, and you know, her best?"

'Being able to achieve her best. I feel that very strongly ... I didn't have anyone, really, in my life to do that for me.'

THE TRUTH ABOUT ARAB WOMEN

One day, after I'd returned from the Middle East, my mother and I were talking about life choices and the path I've taken. It became clear quickly that for my mother it's never been a question of love when she hasn't agreed with my choices – it was more that I challenged what she believed to be a better way forward for me.

It was that simple and that complex. A parent mapping out their ideal life for you, and, like a snow globe, you shake it up, obscuring the reality before the snow descends.

While I had long ago understood, and truly accepted, that my parents only wanted good outcomes for me – I felt a release. My trip to the Arab world had thrown up a lot of things in my mind that needed to be cleared. For so long I had felt like a huge disappointment to my parents, given, as it has been pointed out to me, that I didn't make things easy for them.

A bigger moment of truth followed.

'You're rebellious,' said mum, her tone matter-of-fact. She almost scoffed.

Me, rebellious? I laughed. 'Hardly.'

I suppose I went through that phase at thirty. But I grew out of it eventually.

'You don't like tradition.'

And it was then that it clarified for me, what has haunted me for so long: that I was supposed to accept the life I was born into, what I inherited – through ancestry, culture and religion – even when I felt pulled in other directions. My desires sat in me not as the antithesis of what I knew; they were just other ways of being, of living, of seeing.

I have slowly but surely challenged them all, motivated not by a desire to change the world, only to begin with changing myself. When I brought my Anglo (now) husband to my parents, their initial calm reception brewed into a state of turmoil. I believe it was my mother who felt it the most – I perceived her resistance as feeling a betrayal of sorts. I had brought home a man who, yes, could easily convert to Islam, but he would never be Arab.

Now, if we talk about it, my mother puts it more plainly: 'I just didn't want you to suffer.' Because many immigrant women have suffered, leaving behind their families, their language and cultures. They try to instil in their children the best parts of those things, but fear can overtake good intentions. And women everywhere in the world pay for bad decisions, or the ones made on their behalf.

'There is some kind of censorship from the male society towards the female society. Let's be realistic about this,' said Lebanese cinematographer Muriel Aboulrouss. 'Of course, not all of us are equally free. Some of us have chosen freedom and we are responsible for it, some of us are maybe lucky to be born in a certain environment that allows us to be more free than others, but you have to admit that a lot of Arab women, especially who are living in very conventional religious societies, are limited to what they can or cannot do or can or cannot say. This is a reality, we have to accept it.'

Muriel introduced herself as 'a citizen of the world' who happened to be 'born in one of the most amazing cities in the world' – Beirut. She also said that she is one of the lucky ones. 'I was brought up to be who I am and to embrace who I am, and to believe in who I am and always state what I have to state with love and care. And, you know, I never was censored to do anything or say anything. I am lucky. I chose to take it to an extreme where I really am who I am, with no compromises whatsoever.'

With Denise Jabbour, Muriel has produced a stunning video series called *Zyara* (Journey), a sort of 'Humans of New York' for Lebanon, featuring five-minute video portraits that peer into the diversity of human experiences. She has since rolled out the second series, which features people with disabilities.

Muriel spoke of people as human first, not as interested in labels as personal journeys. '*Zyara* is a representation of who I am entirely. It represents everything I believe in ... They say I directed *Zyara*, but for me I was a free-flying cinematographer, just shooting what I feel, bringing it together to actually paint a tiny bit of your soul into the screen.'

I lost track of time with Muriel; we had a lot in common, her passion and viewpoints similar to mine. 'I have something to do here. I have something to change, there is a lot of issue in this society, it's chaotic, but it's magically chaotic. I live in magic constantly. I see people hitting each other, and two minutes later they're playing chess together, or they're playing a tower together, or they're having coffee together, talking about the fight they had five minutes ago.'

I end with Muriel because in many ways she encapsulates my purpose with this book: to tell stories, not judge them. To show the beauty and tragedy of life through the eyes of people who are so often diminished to a series of overworked stereotypes, devoid of normality.

Frequently, the women I met commented that they were pleased I was writing the book. Some wished they had the opportunity to do something similar, to unpack the experiences of being a person who happens to be a woman of Arab heritage.

Rana Husseini told me that books like these are needed to counter the perceptions that all women in the Arab world are powerless, an important statement from someone who has spent years fighting for those whose power has been compromised. 'The image is not very clear to people. It's amazing to see somebody like yourself coming here. I think it's very important, because we are the people who can convey the real message.'

This book is testament to the fact that Arab women are capable of addressing the difficulties in their life, and that their lives amount to more than their problems, that there is much to celebrate. This book is about women, by women. I don't see it as an investigation into other women's lives. I consider it a co-creation. Or as Rula Quawas put it: midwifing.

'Part of it is undoing the sense of "we're not as free as other people",' said Lamisse from Brisbane. 'And what I've seen is, across the world, regardless of which society you're in ... there are violations of women's rights. There's high domestic violence in Australia, regardless of the fact that it's secular, or whatever it wants to think it is. And that was a huge thing for me, where I thought that the oppressions I faced as a Muslim woman were because of my culture and my heritage and my faith. And leaving it, I saw that it just was the same shit manifested in a different form, basically. The oppression took on a different face, you know?'

It's simply about being a woman.

'In structures of patriarchy, it doesn't matter what your culture or faith is, it just changes the way in which your oppression is manifested. Once we get on to that equilibrium of understanding, where it's like, you're not really more oppressed than the other, it's just different forms of oppression. And solidarity across – being Arab women and having a very particular experience of oppression – but then that wider solidarity of ... women have it tough across the board in so many ways, right?'

Lamisse believes Arab women leading together and on their own is the way forward. Women in the West can support in solidarity, but they shouldn't define what the change should look like nor steer it. I have to say that I agree with her. And, like me, she was critical of the books written by Anglo women in search of the truth about Arab women.

'That's our battle. And we're the only ones who understand the problem as a lived experience. Anybody can go and intellectualise it, but ultimately it'll always be hollow because you haven't lived it, you haven't understood it, you haven't felt its impact on your wellbeing, on your soul. You'll never really grasp it. And that's why these books are so hollow. We're not characters or curiosities. It's just so uncomfortable and offensive.'

And that encapsulates my deep frustration with perceptions about the Arab world and women: like the Hollywood blockbusters with paint-by-number Arab villains and Western heroes, there is a pervading us-versus-them mentality that requires someone to emerge superior. But no one has ownership over the ideal way to live.

In their explorations of the reality of life for so many Arab women, these stories will, I hope, throw in the air our received beliefs about these women. I trust real experiences and authentic voices will disrupt assumptions. Arab women, like people everywhere, are full of hopes and ideals. They are moved by personal experiences and beliefs. They are drawn to purposes and opportunities that can be more challenging because of their circumstances, yet they pursue them anyway, all the time.

There is no simple way to define us, nor is it possible to truly capture the sheer diversity of experience. But these stories demonstrate that women are forging careers and lives based on personal choices and passions, shaping a new way forward.

There is so much I wanted to include in this book. Women who are paving unthought-of pathways – ground-shapers, in my mind, because to call them ground-breakers would be to diminish the valuable efforts of those who have come before us. I know I have barely scratched the surface.

Women have many labels: mother, daughter, sister, wife. But clichés about Arab women abound. That we are oppressed, limited, powerless, conservative, burdened, veiled, religious, shapeless in mind but exotic in body. The ideas about us are plentiful; non-exotic storytelling is not.

These stories, full of truth and emotion, are evidence that Arab women are so much more than that: conflicted by life's duties, pulled towards life's joys like so many people.

Seekers, change-makers, ground-shapers.

The future is in our hands.

ACKNOWLEDGEMENTS

This book would not have been possible without the support of several people. Firstly, thank you to my agent, Tara Wynne of Curtis Brown, who didn't skip a beat in taking the book on. I am so grateful for my publisher, Meredith Curnow, who, from our first meeting, understood my purpose and allowed me to meander my way through the many experiences researching and writing that it involved. My brilliant editor, Catherine Hill, had no small task in taking on such a wide-ranging work and I am eternally grateful for her efforts in marshalling the content into its final form, and for her sensitivity and passion for it.

My family and friends have been nothing short of incredibly supportive and encouraging. Writing this book meant a great deal of reflection and soul-digging, which helped me to see and understand my experiences and relationships in new ways. I love you all.

I must thank my husband, Chris Larsen, for accompanying me on such an intense journey, and for being such an understanding partner as I wrote the book (often at odd hours). I'm so happy you got to see the Middle East.

I would like to thank the Council for Australian–Arab Relations (CAAR), in particular Genevieve Richards and Rachelle Wood – you have been so helpful to me in writing this book and I am very grateful. Thank you also to Richie Merzian for that initial contact, which set the ball rolling.

For their invaluable endorsements of my project: Helen Szoke, Fadia Abboud, Helen Razer, Waleed Aly and Tom Switzer.

My deepest gratitude to the Australian Embassy staff in Jordan – Deputy Head of Mission Kate Luxford and Manal Saroufim – the roundtable you hosted for me was a highlight in the Middle East. Thanks to Nathan Goldstein and the Australian Ambassador to Qatar, Axel Wabenhorst, and Marcia Pius at the Australian Representative Office in Ramallah. In the UAE, Australian Ambassador to the UAE Arthur Spyrou, the Deputy Head of Mission Kim Debenham, and Lia Svilans. In Canberra, thank you to His Excellency Dr Obaid Alketbi of the Embassy of the UAE in Canberra and Matar Ali Al Mansoori.

Thanks to Oxfam staff in Australia and Jordan for their assistance in arranging a visit to Zaatari refugee camp in Jordan, in particular Louise Perry, Alice Plate, Max Baldwin, Joelle Bassoul and Aisha Shtiwi. And thank you to the wonderful Oxfam staffers at Zaatari who were so welcoming.

For various offerings of guidance and support, many thanks to Nora Amath, Lara Ayoub, Rula Quawas, Suheir Kassis, Chadia Hajjar, Shakira Hussein, Joumanah El Matrah, Rachael Turk, Laurie King, Kerstin Fehn, Patty Kikos and Melanie Pitkin. Gratitude to Jedediah Underwood and Jessica Lahoud at Mineralism in Sydney for their kind gift when I began writing the book.

To my editors at SBS Life – Belinda So, Caitlin Chang and Yasmin Noone – you have been amazing supporters from the start and I feel very blessed to be working with you. To Steven Turner at ABC, thanks for your unrelenting commitment to the stories I brought you. To the team at Al Jazeera who offered their support to my project – Imad Musa, Omayma Abdellatif and Mohammed Zaoud – it was a great experience to visit HQ in Qatar.

Finally, to every woman who sat down with me and talked about her life, her fears, her joys, her loves, her work, her purpose – this book is yours.

Amal Awad is a Sydney-based journalist, author and screen-writer. She abandoned her career as a lawyer early in her practice, becoming an editor then eventually pursuing her writing passion as a journalist and writer.

Amal is a screenwriting graduate of AFTRS, and a regular contributor to SBS Life. She has written for such publications as *Elle* and *Frankie*, and online portals Daily Life, The Vine, Sheilas and Junkee. Amal has also worked as a producer for ABC Radio National, which included producing and presenting segments that explored experiences of multiculturalism and religion.

Amal's debut novel, *Courting Samira* (2010), was a semi-finalist in the Amazon Breakthrough Novel Award. She is also the author of the novel, *This Is How You Get Better* (2015) and a collection of columns and essays, *The Incidental Muslim* (2014). Amal also contributed to the anthology *Coming of Age: Growing up Muslim in Australia* (2014).